THE GUITAR PLAYERS

THE GUITAR PLAYERS

ONE INSTRUMENT AND ITS MASTERS IN AMERICAN MUSIC

James Sallis

University of Nebraska Press
Lincoln and London

Acknowledgment is made for material quoted herein:
From Bruce Cook, *Listen to the Blues.* Copyright © 1973 Bruce Cook. Reprinted
with the permission of Charles Scribner's Sons.
From *John Hammond on Record.* Copyright © 1977 John Hammond. Reprinted
with the permission of Feinman & Krasilovsky.
From "Riley Puckett: 'King of the Hillbillies' " by Norm Cohen, *JEMFQ* (Winter
1976). Copyright © 1976 Norm Cohen. Reprinted with the permission of
the John Edwards Memorial Foundation.
From Al Kooper, *Backstage Passes.* Copyright © 1977 Al Kooper. Reprinted
with the permission of Stein and Day Publishers.
From Anthony Scaduto, *Bob Dylan.* Copyright © 1971 Anthony Scaduto.
Reprinted with the permission of Grosset & Dunlap, Inc.

Special acknowledgment is due Guitar Player Publications for permission to quote
from several articles appearing in both *Guitar Player* and *Frets,* chief among these
the following:
On Sam Chatmon: *GP* February 1981, article by Jas Obrecht.
On Roy Smeck: *GP* December 1972, *Frets* September 1979, both by Bob Yellin.
On Charlie Christian: *GP* January-February-July 1977, columns by Barney
Kessel; also material from August 1979 and November 1979 issues.
On T-Bone Walker: *GP* March 1977, article by Kevin and Peter Sheridan.
On George Barnes: *GP* February 1975, interview by Bob Yellin.
On Hank Garland: *GP* January 1981, article by Rich Kienzle.
On Wes Montgomery: *GP* July/August 1973, interview by Ralph Gleason.
On Michael Bloomfield: *GP* June 1971, interview by Michael Brooks;
          GP Apr 1979, interview by Tom Wheeler;
          GP May 1979, column by George Gruhn.

Acknowledgment is also extended to the magazine *Living Blues,* whose two-part
interview with T-Bone Walker (September-October 1972) was extremely helpful;
and to Paul Oliver whose book, *Conversations with the Blues,* was similarly useful
in many regards, especially in relation to Lonnie Johnson.

First Bison Book printing: 1994
Most recent printing indicated by the last digit below:
10 9 8 7 6 5 4 3 2 1

Library of Congress Cataloging-in-Publication Data
Sallis, James, 1944–
The guitar players: one instrument and its masters in American music / James Sallis.
p. cm.
Includes index.
Reprint. Originally published: New York: W. Morrow, 1982.
ISBN 0-8032-9225-2
1. Guitarists—United States. 2. Guitar music—History and criticism. 3. Popular mu-
sic—United States—History and criticism. I. Title.
ML399.S24 1994
787.87'092'273—dc20
93-41234 CIP
MN

Reprinted by arrangement with James Sallis

∞

To Carol and Judy

CONTENTS

Preface to the Bison Book Edition   1

Introduction   9

Mississippi Sheiks: THE BLUESMEN   13

Mr. Johnson's Blues: LONNIE JOHNSON   29

The Genius of Sal Massaro: EDDIE LANG   53

The Wizard of the Strings: ROY SMECK   77

Charlie's Guitar: CHARLIE CHRISTIAN   97

King of the Hillbillies: RILEY PUCKETT   121

Daddy of the Blues: T-BONE WALKER   155

Further Adventures of Captain Guitar: GEORGE BARNES   173

Jazz Winds from a New Direction: HANK GARLAND   195

Apostasy: WES MONTGOMERY   213

Carryin' It On: MICHAEL BLOOMFIELD   231

Currents: RY COODER,
            RALPH TOWNER,
            LENNY BREAU   265

PREFACE

The Guitar Players was written fourteen years ago, in a room
cluttered with stringed instruments of every sort: ukuleles, a
1924 Martin tiple, various Hawaiian lap guitars, old Gibson
and Guild electrics, banjos, mandolins. There were stacks of
Guitar Player, Frets, Living Blues and jazz magazines, and shelves
of books mostly salvaged from second-hand bookstores. From
time to time I'd break off work on the book as students arrived
for lessons: thirteen-year-olds wanting to copy *Purple Haze* or
the latest Van Halen, adults in cowboy shirts, boots and belt
buckles you could use as dinner plates who wanted to jam mandolin like Ricky Scaggs but couldn't be bothered learning
scales, would-be Dobro and banjo players who couldn't find
the beat with a dowsing rod. And, yes, a few who actually became good players.

I was living then in Texas, a true musical crossroads for reasons elaborated herein, but a place at the same time strangely
devoid of history, where one forever lives in a kind of perpet-
ual present. Now I have returned to New Orleans, a city saturated in its past and saturated, too, with music. In an old uptown house, with a framed poster of Robert Johnson on the
wall, I'm writing a series of novels about a Southern black
man's struggle toward redemption. And so I must think often
of blues, of music's place in African society, of early jazz and
other American musics.

From the first, *The Guitar Players* was intended as much as social history as musicology, and like most social history may say as much about the time in which it was written as about its subject.

Musically, the time in which I wrote was in many ways an extension of the sixties, when, with the popularization of folk music, retrieval of indigenous American musics began. With bluesmen old, black, young and white, with groups such as The Newgrass Revival, R. Crumb and His Cheap Suit Serenaders, with electrics like David Bromberg, that retrieval was ongoing. But the new guitarists had grown up hearing Jimi Hendrix, George Benson, and Ry Cooder alongside John Lee Hooker, Lonnie Johnson, and Doc Watson: the stew was growing richer all the time.

I began *The Guitar Players* because I wanted to know more about players who were important to me, guitarist's guitarists like Lonnie Johnson and Eddie Lang, whom everyone talked about but about whom so little was known. Admiring cultural historians such as Edmund Wilson, I also wanted to apply their tools to American musics and see what sort of house might get built.

Information was difficult to gather. Much of what is here was cobbled together from brief references in books long out of print, liner notes from albums, old interviews. Only one magazine devoted to the guitar existed when I began; another was just tottering into life. Yesterday in Bookstar on North Peters in the Quarter I counted nine.

Recordings were still more difficult to find. Things had improved since college days, when we'd hunch down over a handful of Folkways recordings for hours at the time, but treasures like a Riley Puckett album or Charlie Christian's jams at Minton's were still rare birds, tough to snare. A passage from Peter Guralnick's *Searching for Robert Johnson* recalls the heady anticipation and delight of early discoveries.

> Sometimes I can evoke the breathless rush of feeling that I experienced the first time that I ever really heard Robert Johnson's music. Sometimes a note will suggest just a hint of the

realms of emotion that opened up to me in that moment, the sense of utter wonder, the shattering revelation. I don't know if it's possible to recreate this kind of feeling today—not because music of similar excitement doesn't exist, but because the discovery can no longer take place in such a void.

Because we've *found* Robert Johnson now, you see. I have his poster on my wall, all his recordings, including alternate takes, on CD in Columbia's Roots N' Blues series. (You want to know where rock came from? Listen to Johnson's alternate take of "Come on in My Kitchen.")

As I write this, in fact, I'm listening for the first time to some incredible cuts by Oscar Aleman. I knew this guitarist only by word of mouth, had heard of him for years. Now a French company has reissued thirteen cuts (along with seven by Django Reinhardt and six by Jean Ferret) in its Jazz Time series. There's interest here in the States in this sort of thing, but the primary thrust is still European. England's Travelin' Man label has produced a number of fine retrievals such as Bukka White's complete sessions and Son Houses's Library of Congress sessions. Document Records in Austria appears to be intent upon releasing every historical blues ever recorded in multi-volume, single-artist CDs; their three-volume Willie McTell collection has a favored place on my shelf.

When I first began playing, the guitar was an uncommon, still somewhat suspect, instrument. Folk music and rock would change that, and some days now it seems that every third person strolling through the Quarter carries a guitar case. Much of the playing's still bad, but the general level of it these days, both among serious amateurs and professionals, is incredibly high—exponentially above what it was even when I began writing this book. And all about, there's a variety of guitar music I could only have dreamed of. On any given day here I might easily catch Snooks Eaglin doing his trademark traditional New Orleans music, sit in on classical guitar and mainstream jazz at numerous venues, head uptown for a John Mooney set of bottleneck blues and oddball R&B at Carrollton Station, or hit the weekend jam by Jackson Square, where there will be at least a couple of old National resonator guitars, generally a fine washboard player, and always some great blues.

You'll find in this book discussions of many of the ways recording has worked to change the music itself, sometimes to the music's good, sometimes to its detriment. This symbiosis continues. As technology increases—not only with new techniques such as digital recording and DAT but also with the ability to clean up and thereby give new life to older recordings—the influence of recording on music now being written and performed can only grow. When I began *The Guitar Players*, musicians might reasonably aspire to a four-channel recorder in their home, with its possibilities of overdubs. Not too many years before, Mike Seeger's old-timey album on which he played all the instruments himself had been a revelation. Now one man can sit at his bank of MIDIs and interfacers and in a day or so compose, arrange, play all parts of, finally record and deliver an entire movie score.

There's a wonderful scene in Jack Womack's alternate-history novel *Terraplane*. Doc is leading Luther and bodyguard Jake (who listens to nothing but Robert Johnson recordings) through a nightclub to safety.

"He's let the lights burn out again," Doc mumbled. Light eking from an open door midway downhall helped us guide our steps. Inside the lit room I vizzed Vernon confronting a tall, lean man standing in a corner as if for punishment, his face turned from view. Upon the dressing table lay a battered wooden guitar.

"It's copacetic," Vernon said to him. "Ever'body's shy sometimes. You're gonna do fine—"

"Not in front of these people," the man said, scratching his face with long, slender fingers.

"Once you get goin' it won't matter. Come on, Bob—"

We continued on; I had to pull Jake along. "Luther," he said, "that was *him*—"

"He'll be playing again, Jake."

But he won't, of course. And one of Womack's tragic points in an altogether tragic book—the crowd, as Johnson sings "Hellhound on My Trail," shouts out for "Darktown Strutter's Ball"—is that Robert Johnson's unique, ultimately fragile music so easily might be lost for all time.

Sometimes I fantasize a world in which great artists might somehow, by cloning, by some intrinsically DNA-like pattern in the work they've left behind, by magic or magical science, be recreated. We would then hear Mozart play the C-major concerto, O'Carolan his own works for harp. Or, yes: Robert Johnson doing "Hellhound" on (the mind boggles) a Stratocaster.

So much is gone forever. And yet so much remains.

Over the years, all over this country, I've given dozens of talks on American music. Often I take along six- and twelve-string guitars to play examples of Piedmont, Delta, Memphis and Chicago blues styles. Or haul along banjos, mandolins, harmonicas, and fiddles to talk about British ballads, Appalachian derivatives, and the country music I grew up with.

Every time, whatever my specific subject, I tell audiences that much of all that is finest in American music comes, directly or indirectly, from the blues, which in turn derives from African call-and-response patterns, from pancultural techniques like whooping and hocketing, from the replication of African instruments and rhythm.

And every time, I also read them this, from the original introduction to *The Guitar Players,* maybe the closest thing to a credo I have:

> One of the great sadnesses of American culture is certainly that it contrives to destroy its own past. The richness and variety of our music are lost in endless variations on predictable pop forms. Where now (except of course in his home) can a young person gain exposure, even introduction, to string-band music, to early jazz, Hawaiian music or Delta blues? These are treasures to be found only by those who seek them out—and their existence goes largely unsuspected.

Perhaps the sadness is even greater now than when I first wrote those words. For while reissues such as those from Columbia, Travelin' Man, and Document have gone a long way toward restoring richness and variety, their existence seems suspected by fewer and fewer.

In one early story about an aging poet I wrote, "I suppose when I was a young man I cared nothing for history of any sort." Now I can only hope that my interests in *The Guitar Players* were not so delimited; that, aging myself, I hadn't elevated history to *all*, hadn't simply cast my eye back to things that *were:* to the swank, Republican pastures of yesteryear.

I'm pretty sure I hadn't, mind you.

I've just listened again to Robert Johnson's "Terraplane" and Willie McTell's "Broke Down Engine Blues."

New Orleans
September 1993

THE GUITAR PLAYERS

INTRODUCTION

As a child I lay in bed at night and listened to torrents of Ernest Tubb, Jimmy Reed and Buddy Holly from the jukebox of a nearby drive-in restaurant. The music I selected for myself at that time was devoutly classical, a lot of Mozart but also Beethoven, Mahler and Tchaikovsky which seemed to echo my own roiling emotions. About my junior year of high school I finally discovered rock and roll, waking at 3:00 a.m. most nights to find the radio still on and tuned to WLS-Chicago.

The town was Helena, Arkansas. It had been a center of blues activity in the thirties and forties. Robert Johnson lived there for a time. Roosevelt Sykes, Robert Lockwood and Robert Nighthawk were all from Helena and many others passed in and out, attracted by radio station KFFA, at the time I grew up still broadcasting Sonny Boy Williamson's daily *King Biscuit Hour*. My brother, now a philosopher, had gone to school with Harold Jenkins, now Conway Twitty.

The folk revival came along about this time too, and I joined in. I wasn't able to find a guitar for a while, though I remember my father and I drove to Memphis one Saturday afternoon in a vain attempt to trade my nineteenth-century German violin (I also played French horn) for one.

I learned to play during my first two years of college at Tulane. The Gibson I had found in a New Orleans pawnshop was bought out from under me before I could get the money together, so I wound up with a Sears Silvertone, never realizing how squarely within the blues tradition that put me.

For by the time I actually got the guitar my tastes had moved on from commercial folk music to people like Pete and Mike Seeger, Bob Dylan, Doc Watson, then (after hearing John Hammond's first album) blues. Somewhere along here I learned to play blues harmonica and a little bottleneck guitar, both rarities then, and was usually welcome at folk clubs or parties. I later got a Gibson, but was forced to abandon it in London, not having money for its fare, in the late sixties. I found it a good home.

I was making my living (more or less) as a writer, and music subsided gradually from the foreground of my attention. I listened to a lot of popular music for a while, Simon and Garfunkel, the Beatles, Leonard Cohen and Joni Mitchell, then picked up on country music and stayed with that for several years. I even started (but never finished) a book on it back in 1970. I lived variously in New York, Boston, rural Pennsylvania, London, New Orleans.

In 1975 I moved to Dallas and took root. I bought a phonograph for the first time in many years (I'd been moving around too much) and started listening to the local National Public Radio affiliate and to another listener-supported station, KCHU, which is now defunct but then had a great four-hour blues show every Saturday afternoon as well as regular programming of old-time, ethnic and other alternative musics. My wife bought a guitar for me at Montgomery Ward. I began reviewing records for *Texas Jazz*, doing pieces on music and musical instruments for a number of magazines, and soon was spending as much time listening to music and writing about it as I was writing the poetry and fiction I still consider my primary work. I also learned to play other instruments: mandolin, banjo, fiddle, Hawaiian guitar, ukulele, even sitar. Not with the intention of playing them professionally (though I have upon occasion, and have also taught them) but simply to learn more about the music these instruments brought about—to find out what American music of every sort *felt* like, and the ways of thinking it required.

This book grew slowly, as most books do, over those same years. Many of the guitarists referred to most often by players and writers were poorly represented in print, and I really knew very little about them. There was a brief essay on Lonnie Johnson in one of Sam Charters's books; a single piece on Eddie Lang in Macmillan's line of jazz books; one or two pieces on Charlie Christian. Such information as did exist was widely scattered, often contradictory and generally obtainable only with difficulty. These guys were like a floor: you didn't have to talk about it or look at it, you just walked on it; it supported you. So the original motive was toward a simple synthesis, and I began gathering material on some of these players from jazz books, guitar publications, autobiographies, histories of country music, wherever I found a relevant line or two. But a far deeper synthesis occurred as well, and I came to recognize that my true intention was to write a history of American music: that the guitar and American music were inexorably intertwined.

Thus, *The Guitar Players.* The selections were difficult and of course finally rather arbitrary. I did try to stay away from players I felt already well documented. So you'll not find Chet Atkins here, or Doc Watson (written about at length during his sixties "discovery"), or many others (George Van Eps, Johnny Smith, Billy Byrd, Hubert Sumlin, Eldon Shamblin) who should be. There is, alas, just so much space and time. Another consideration was the manner in which a player reflected currents flowing about him. Roy Smeck I chose as much for his pioneer work in instruction methods, his early emphasis on Hawaiian guitar and tenor banjo, and his ground-breaking exposure in vaudeville, early moving pictures, TV and recordings, as for his exceptional guitar playing. Similarly, Mike Bloomfield's early involvement with the blues revival, his star status in the rock world and later rededication to acoustic music and guitar styles of every historical sort, seem to touch directly on many vital strains in recent American music.

One of the great sadnesses of American culture is certainly that it contrives to destroy its own past. The richness and variety of our music are lost in endless variations on predictable pop forms. Where now (except of course in his home) can a young person gain exposure, even introduction, to string-band music, to early jazz, Hawaiian music or Delta blues? These are treasures to be found only by those who seek them out—and their existence goes largely unsuspected.

Just so, one of my own great joys is that so many young people today have dedicated themselves to preserving our musical heritage. All about America as I write, musicians are playing Delta blues on National guitars from the thirties, groups are doing old-time swing and string-band music, players are restoring instruments like the mandolin, hammered dulcimer and zither to use.

One cannot speak of the guitar in isolation, outside its historical and musical contexts. Neither I think can one make jazz, country music, pop and blues antithetical or discriminatory: they are not separate destinations but different roads taken. Here are a few of the starting places and landmarks.

MISSISSIPPI SHEIKS:

The Bluesmen

"THE HISTORY of a specifically American music," Frederic V. Grunfeld writes in *The Art and Times of the Guitar*, "begins precisely at the point where the European-trained musician first becomes aware of the African-trained musician and makes an attempt to imitate him." This commingling of traditions began in the early days of slavery, and by the late nineteenth century, black rhythms, figures and harmonies had permeated nearly all American music. In the final decade of that century Antonín Dvořák, teaching composition in the New World, recognized that "the future of music in this country must be founded on what are called the Negro melodies," and few researchers would dispute blues as the fundamental American music, manifesting variously through country, rock and jazz avatars. Like the nation itself, American music was built on the backs of black slaves; these are the giants whose shoulders we all stand on.

At the time Dvořák made his statement, 80 percent of black Americans lived in the rural South. With the withdrawal of supportive Northern troops in 1887, the failure of Reconstruction was freely acknowledged and the black American's imminent disenfranchisement clear, further emphasized by "Jim Crow laws" then springing up at a furious rate. The first significant absorption of black music had come with mid-century minstrel shows and persisted in "coon songs" popularly written and sung by white musicians. In New Orleans Buddy Bolden's band was boss of the streets, as direct a precursor to jazz as we have, and American music everywhere was awash with the sound and pulse of ragtime, a music derived directly from America's only native instrument, the banjo.

In the seventeenth and eighteenth centuries Senegambia, a stretch of West African coast running from present-day Senegal down to the northern coastline of Guinea, became a favorite source for slavers. The entire Senegambia region hosted a wealth of stringed instruments, from single-string gourd fiddles to small lutes with as many as four strings and harplike lutes with up to twenty strings. The Wolof *halam,* a five-string instrument with one drone string played in a down-picked, "clawhammer" style, seems to be the direct ancestor of the American banjo, and the name is apparently a corruption of *bania,* a generic name for similar instruments found in Senegal. The Wolof were choice guides and interpreters for the slavers, chiefly because their own language retained wide currency in the wake of a huge sixteenth century empire. The *halam,* or the idea of it, thus may have passed from them to America-bound slaves, whose attempts to copy the instrument in the New World resulted in the banjo.

Banjos were reported in Maryland as early as 1774, always in the hands of black plantation musicians, and until 1830 or so were associated exclusively with them, Thomas Jefferson writing in 1781 that "the instrument proper to them is the Banjar, which they brought hither from Africa." An 1832 novel depicts a banjo-playing slave equally at home playing for slave dances or serenading the young ladies of his master's household, and by 1847 there are accounts of Negro dances where banjos and fiddles were played together.

Slaves of course readily adopted the instruments and the music of the masters. Drums and horns were denied them by law, but Senegambians who had played gourd fiddles could adapt easily enough to the European version, and their banjos were acceptable to the white man's ear and his music. Since a slave's value was greatly increased by musical ability and he was often given lighter duties as well, many learned to play, and slave orchestras consisting of banjos, fiddles, small percussion instruments such as bone clappers and triangles, occasionally flutes or fifes, were an early fixture of plantation life; it was these slave orchestras that the blackface minstrel troops dominating American entertainment from about 1840 until well past the Civil War parodied.

Many of the plantation musicians, however, learned elements of European music, which they combined with African playing habits, and a few actually became adept performers of classical music. The two strains at this point become hopelessly entwined, and we begin to perceive the earliest truly American music. "Over the nearly three centuries between the first accounts of slave music in North America and the earliest recordings of black folk music in the South," Robert Palmer observes in *Deep Blues*, "blendings of innumerable kinds and degrees took place. By the period of the Civil War, almost every conceivable hue of the musical spectrum must have been present to some degree in black folk culture, from the almost purely African to the almost purely white American." Palmer notes in this regard the Mississippi band led by Sid Hemphill which Alan Lomax recorded in 1942, its repertoire running from panpipes played in the African whooping style to imitations of white fife-and-drum bands, brass-band marching music and country string-band numbers. This mutability was far more rule than exception, gradually declining with later commercial emphasis on blues to the exclusion of other black music; still, old-time reels and popular songs were an important part of the repertoire of songsters such as Mance Lipscomb and Mississippi John Hurt when they were "rediscovered" during the sixties' folk revival.

"My pa was a fiddler," Lipscomb said. "He was an old perfessional fiddler. All my people can play some kind of music. Well, my daddy he was a perfessional fiddler and he played way back in olden days. You know, he played at breakdowns, waltzes, shottishes and all like that and music just come from him to me, that's why I learned it from him. Papa were playing for dances out, for white folks and colored. He played 'Missouri Waltz,' 'Casey Jones,' just anything you name he played it like I'm playin'."

Few distinctions were made then between white and black music; fiddle tunes, ragtime dance music and pre-blues ballads like "Frankie and Johnny" or "Betty and Dupree" were thrown together indiscriminately.

In the first decades of the 1800's portions of the black folk tradition began passing into white folk tradition. Whites in the southern Appalachians learned clawhammer banjo from itinerant blacks; they would preserve the instrument after its passing from mainstream American music until it finally filtered back in, via bluegrass, in the early 1950's. (They provided similar refuge for Hawaiian guitar and mandolin.) About the same time a commercial tradition of banjo music emerged. A Boston musician by the name of Graupner, encountering blacks singing to banjo accompaniment while on a visit to Charleston, bought and learned to play the instrument, going on in 1799 to write what is probably the first minstrel song. Billed as "The Banjo King," Virginian Joe Sweeney (whose name is often mentioned as "inventor" of the banjo) toured widely through the South, impressing listeners and musicians alike with the banjo's potential. By 1850 the instrument was well established in white America, and banjos were being manufactured and merchandised in quantity. From 1890 to about 1910 a tradition of "classical" banjo flourished with players such as Ves Ossman and Fred Van Eps, and many communities supported banjo orchestras comprising everything from ukulele-size "piccolo" banjos to huge bass instruments.

Not only were these the first inroads of black music, they also represented the first challenge to the fiddle's supremacy in American folk music. But with the emergence of jazz, the five-string banjo gradually yielded to its four-string cousin; by 1930 fingerstyle banjo had vanished completely, and within a few years the tenor instrument was gone as well, supplanted by guitar.

Blacks in fact had changed to guitar much earlier, and by the 1920's, when the first recordings of black music were made, there were few remnants of the black banjo tradition. A far more adaptable instrument, easier also to secure and maintain, the guitar was actually better suited to their music, particularly with the emergence of blues as a dominant form. "As one would expect," Robert Palmer points out, "the African instruments with the most highly developed solo traditions tend to be instruments like the widely distributed hand piano or the harplike lutes of Senegambia that can simultaneously produce driving ostinatos (repeating patterns) and chording or melody lines that answer or comment on the player's singing. The persistence of this principle in America helps explain the alacrity with which black musicians in the rural South took up the guitar once white musicians and mail order catalogues introduced it to them." Sometime after the turn of the century the instrument was introduced into the hills by traveling blacks, as the banjo had been before it, and found a ready home there, joining banjo and fiddle as a regular member of country string bands. For some time it was used only as a rhythm instrument; not until Riley Puckett (who himself began as a banjoist) would the first intimations of a virtuoso country guitar style emerge.

It was not only the guitar's existence that rural southerners learned of from blacks. Translating ragtime rhythms and banjo technique to the new instrument, black musicians had devised a distinctive finger-picking style that often relied on a steady alternating or walking bass and a treble melody, picked simultaneously. Through players like Sam McGee, Ike Everly, Merle Travis and Chet Atkins, this fingerstyle guitar has passed into the mainstream of American music and, merging with classical, into the jazz guitar of Duck Baker, Lenny Breau and many others. Sam McGee said,

> Well, where we learned the most about the style was from the black people. My daddy ran a little store, and these section hands would come over from the railroad at noon, and they bought pork and beans, sardines and all that kind of stuff. Well, after they finished their lunch, they would play guitars. Two of them—great big black men, their name was the Steward brothers—they played real good, and that's where I learned to love the blues tunes. Black people were about the only people that played guitars then.

The guitar actually entered society from three points, eastern cities emulating London trends in drawing-room music, the Spanish Southwest and the Negro South, but of these the last influence proved far the most vigorous and enduring. "The Negro blues guitar," Grunfeld writes, "fascinated hillbilly ears for precisely the same reasons that the subsequent American jazz and pop styles have taken the whole world by storm: its rhythmic ingenuity ('two centuries ahead of Europe,' as W. E. Ward once wrote of African music) and its marvelously flexible harmony."

Many homes among cultured upper-class families in the North harbored guitars, which were played in the parlor tradition then current in London homes, but from about

1890 that parlor tradition gradually devolved to the lower middle classes. The music remained light and semiclassical, and until at least the turn of the century the many guitar and mandolin societies that sprang up remained the province of the middle class. C. F. Martin began producing the first American guitars in 1833, and by 1902 the Gibson company was turning out a small battery of mandolins, banjos and guitars. Though challenged by interest in other stringed instruments, beginning with the banjo craze during the final years of the century, the fiddle retained its secure position as leading American folk instrument. Guitar as a folk instrument had already gained acceptance in the Southwest from the example of Spanish and Mexican players, and was teamed with fiddle for country dances there as early as 1900. Nationwide interest in guitar-based Hawaiian music following the 1898 assumption of control of the islands, and exposure of American troops to guitar during the Spanish-American War and World War I, doubtless added to its popularity.

It was left to Sears to democratize the guitar. By 1894 seven models were available by catalogue, priced from about four dollars (the cheapest Gibson then was around one hundred dollars), and the impact of this ready access was crucial to the guitar's dissemination as a folk instrument. Rural counterparts of northeastern guitar and mandolin societies sprang up all about the country as string bands, playing a melange of popular songs, transformed Celtic fiddle tunes and old minstrel or square-dance music. Blues continued to gather authority, rolling toward the great classical blues period of the 1920's, and somehow, probably in New Orleans brothels, crossed with ragtime to become jazz. Lonnie Johnson and Charlie Christian, from New Orleans and the Southwest respectively, both areas with strong guitar traditions, were laying the groundwork for that instrument's imminent disclosure.

Nor did the mainspring of black motive abate. World War

I offered the rural black his first real chance to escape the South, when the demand for cheap labor created by severe reduction of European immigration triggered an explosive diaspora. By 1920 the number of black Americans living in the rural South was down to 65 percent and by 1950 had declined to 20 percent; in the single decade 1910–20 the black population of Detroit increased 611 percent, that of Chicago 148 percent. In the cities downhome blues acquired a heavy beat and volume to become rhythm and blues; with a growing audience among white teenagers and their subsequent adoption of its styles in the early 1950's, rock and roll eventuated. New Orleans jazz developed in tandem among black and white performers in the Southwest and in Chicago to a high degree of musicianship, then with bebop to a near-awesome virtuosity and sophistication. Both blues and country recording activity were centered in Chicago for some time, and country recordings regularly rode on the contributions of guitarists like Chet Atkins, with his black-derived, jazz-inflected fingerstyle playing; jazz- and blues-based prodigy George Barnes; and another prodigy, country guitarist-cum-jazzman Hank Garland. It is difficult to overlook the debt of Jimmie Rodgers to bluesmen, or of early performers such as Riley Puckett and Sam McGee to ragtime, at the birth of commercial country music.

The trip from Mississippi plantations to Maxwell Street or Minton's was a remarkably brief, and remains an inexhaustible, one.

Probably no single group of musicians better demonstrates the transformations of black music through the years than the Chatmon family of Bolton, Mississippi. The patriarch, Henderson Chatmon, had been a fiddler in slavery days, playing breakdowns and dance music for white get-togethers, numbers like "Turkey in the Straw" (originally published in 1834 as "Zip Coon"), "Liza Jane" and "Old Gray Mule." The entire family played professionally, and at least three of them gained some fame as recording artists; Charley Patton, the first professional bluesman and a man of staggering importance in the development of blues, is often claimed as a half brother.

From about 1910 until 1928 most of the family worked together as the Chatmon Brothers, playing mainly ragtime pieces, waltzes and two-steps and becoming one of the most popular groups in the area among both black and white audiences. As their popularity increased they traveled north to Memphis, even to Chicago, occasionally picking up jazz trumpet players or drummers along the way. (Louis Armstrong was one early acquaintance, and Sam Chatmon played banjo with him briefly.) "We didn't play no blues until later 'cause we was playin' for white folks," Sam Chatmon has said. But with the rapid growth of commercial interest in the music following publication of W. C. Handy's "Memphis Blues" and others in 1912, the Chatmon Brothers added tunes like "St. Louis Blues" and "Beale Street Blues" to their repertoire.

Beginning about 1930, Lonnie Chatmon, Walter Vinson and often Bo or Sam Chatmon recorded regularly as the Mississippi Sheiks, their first records for Okeh bringing them considerable acclaim among both blues ("race") and country ("hillbilly") listeners. "Sitting on Top of the World," recorded in Shreveport that year, became a Delta and Chicago blues standard and even twenty-seven years later, a hit for Howlin' Wolf. Robert Johnson's classic "Come in My Kitchen" was a fairly straightforward cover of the Sheiks's tune, and Muddy Waters remembers that "Sitting" was, with Leroy Carr's "How Long, How Long Blues," one of the first songs he learned on guitar. It was absorbed into country music quite early as well and remains today a bluegrass favorite. As Bo Carter, Bo Chatmon went on to become one of the most-recorded early bluesmen, his instrumental skill and facility for inventing double-entendre blues making the recording studio in fact his primary performance outlet; of other Mississippi bluesmen, only Memphis Minnie cut more records.

Lonnie seems to have been the central figure, not only in the Sheiks, but in the Chatmon family as a whole. However, as Sam lived on into the sixties' folk revival and indeed still plays today, "one of the last survivors of the central Mississippi blues tradition" in Stephen Calt's words, much of our documentation concerning the Chatmons and the Sheiks necessarily derives from him. It is interesting to note that recordings made under Walter Vinson's name in 1929, with accompaniment by Bo and Charlie McCoy, bear much the same sound as that generally associated with the Sheiks. Still, both the Sheiks' sound and success unquestionably stem in part from Lonnie Chatmon's affinity for white music and his thoroughgoing professionalism. He appears to have been a rather unpleasant individual—his blustering manner earned him the family nickname "Big Guff," and he always had trouble remembering to give other players their portion of the band's earnings—but he had learned to read music from a relative named Neil Winston, affording him great prestige with other, unschooled musicians, and he could play virtually anything by ear, specializing for a time in requests. His fiddling, consistently tasteful and polished, is probably our best example of the once-thriving Negro blues fiddle tradition in which Lonnie Johnson began his career.

Singer-guitarist Walter Vinson, who also used his mother's maiden name, Jacobs, taught himself guitar at age six, and by the time he reached his teens was playing widely in the Bolton area, working the Crystal Springs juke joints with Tommy Johnson and Ishman Bracey, or with Jackson bluesmen like Rubin Lacy and Charlie McCoy. Jackson, fifteen miles from Bolton, was the major stopover for musicians on their way to Memphis and a favorite of performers like Memphis Minnie, the Memphis Jug Band and the Chatmon Brothers. Vinson may have joined the Chatmons as early as 1922; by 1928, when Sam, Lonnie and Bo moved to Hollandale, he was playing regularly with Lonnie and went along. Vinson always valued Lonnie's fiddle for its distinctive blues lead and, though an accomplished guitar stylist, confined his playing behind Lonnie to basic rhythm; he felt his own singing made him similarly indispensable to the fiddler.

"When Sam Chatmon began learning guitar," Jas Obrecht wrote in a recent piece for *Guitar Player*, "Teddy Roosevelt was president of the United States and most of the people in rural Mississippi were listening to rags and reels dating back to slavery days. Seventy-seven years later, Sam is still proud of his remarkable facility with 'the old-fashioned music that first was handed down.' "

Sam Chatmon was born January 10, 1899, in Bolton. Both Bo and Lonnie were a few years older, and Sam, about age four, started climbing up on a chair to get their guitars down while they were away from the house: "When they come in, says, 'Oh, my string broke off my guitar,' I say, 'I ain't had it. I ain't *had* it.' " As he got older his father would help him learn the tunes, the two of them sitting together playing for hours at a time. He started right off fingerpicking, learning "the old, old-fashioned blues" like "Make Me a Pallet on the Floor." About age seven he began playing bass (he had to carry around a box to stand on) with his brothers. From the first, the Chatmon Brothers preferred playing for whites, and their repertoire comprised country dance tunes, waltzes, popular ragtime and what was then called hillbilly music. Sam remembers that one man in Hollandale would pay sixty cents a day for plowing but would give you as much as five dollars for playing three or four songs up at his house. You'd also get fed when you played a party for whites, Sam says, and the hours were always a lot shorter than for black get-togethers.

> We started out with music from our parents—it's just a gift that we had in the family. Our mother and our father, they both could play. See, my father played in slavery time. When the white folks wanted it, he had to play. It was ragtime music—square dances, breakdowns. So music was handed down to us. There were nine whole brothers; I can't tell you how many halves I had. . . .
>
> All of us was about a year apart. My brothers Lonnie and Edgar would play the violins; Harry would play guitar, piano or second violin; Willie and Bert played guitar; my brother Laurie beat the drums; and Bo would play guitar and tenor banjo. We had guitar, tenor banjo, mandolin, violin, piano, saxophone, clarinet—anything we could borrow, hire or pick up. Daddy didn't try to teach no one how to play. All of us just learned ourselves.

Apparently each member of the family could pretty much play whatever he wished. Though Sam retained guitar as his primary instrument, he could also handle violin and mandolin, banjo, bass, piano and harmonica. On some cuts with Walter Vinson, Bo added fiddle parts not far removed in style or competence from Lonnie's own; with his brothers he often filled in on tenor banjo or bass (which he may have tuned like guitar) and in his solo work played guitar in at least five discrete tunings.

Though Bo first organized the brothers as a band, Lonnie was the central figure. "Didn't but one of us read music," Sam told the authors of *Beale Street Black & Blue*, "that was my brother Lonnie. A man there in Bolton—he was a good violinist—he taught him notes. Lonnie knowed how to play, but he just wanted to learn by the notes. See, that's the way we learned all our pieces. He'd learn 'em and we'd play 'em behind him."

Their versatility and diversity of repertoire partially explain the Chatmons' celebrity; other factors include the variety of keys and rhythms routinely employed (at a time when many string bands had one beat and maybe a couple of keys), the overall high standards of their musicianship and a clearly articulated, decidedly swinging style. Together these served not only to catch, but to hold, their audiences' interests.

"We played all different kinds of music—'Sheik of Arabee' and 'Sittin' on Top of the World'—oh, man, we played so many different pieces, I could be here two hours tellin' you about it. . . ." Sam told Paul Oliver. "Now when we moved to the Delta in Hollandale here, in twenty-eight, we got to playin' up at Leroy Percy Park for the white folks all the week. 'Eyes of Blue,' that's what we played for white folks. 'Dinah,' that's another for white folks. But we played blues for colored. I just couldn't tell you when I first heard blues, but when I was big enough to hold up a git-tar I went to playin' 'em."

The Chatmons' recording career dates from about the same time as the move to Hollandale, and during the next eight years they recorded over one hundred sides for numerous companies (Okeh, Paramount, Bluebird, Brunswick, Decca) in various permutations and under various names (the Chatmon Brothers, the Mississippi Blacksnakes, the Mississippi Mudsteppers, the Jackson Blue Boys, the Mississippi Sheiks) in widespread locations (Atlanta, San Antonio, Chicago, New Orleans, Memphis, Jackson, New York, Shreveport and Grafton, Wisconsin). During the same period they continued to work country dances, parties, suppers, picnics and fish fries throughout Mississippi, Tennessee, Georgia, Louisiana, Illinois and New York.

The last recording session was in 1936. "Some of my brothers, two of my sisters and my mother died, and I didn't feel like playing no more," Sam says. More to the point, blues tastes had shifted radically away from easy-going, country-based blues to the more aggressive, driving sound of urban bluesmen like Sonny Boy Williamson, and by the time of the Sheiks' final session (only eight years after the first that produced "Sitting on Top of the World," "Stop and Listen" and "Corrine") blues had developed as a genre so rapidly that the Chatmons were ancient history. Bo made a few more sessions on his own, but by 1938 or so he too was dropped. He turned to farming work around Glenallen, Mississippi, then in the early forties moved into Memphis, dying there in 1964. ("By 1960, Bo Carter was prematurely aged and blind," Paul Oliver wrote in *The Story of the Blues.* "His guitar was almost unplayable because the frets were worn through.") Walter Vinson moved to Chicago, also working largely outside music, but recorded for the Riverside label, then with Sam Chatmon in 1972 for Rounder's *The New Mississippi Sheiks,* before his death in 1975.

Sam Chatmon continued working as a farmer and plantation supervisor around Hollandale; later as a night watchman. In 1960 blues historian Paul Oliver and Arhoolie Records producer Chris Strachwitz found Sam while in search of Bo Carter; thereafter he resumed recording and performing on a fairly regular basis. He has worked at the New Orleans Jazz and Heritage Festival, the Smithsonian Festival of American Folklife, the American Folk Music Festival and many others in recent years, also appearing in three TV specials: *Land Where the Blues Began, The Devil's Music* and *Good Morning Blues.* Aside from *The New Mississippi Sheiks* and an album called *San Diego Blues Jam* on Advent, Sam has cut one album on Blue Goose (*The Mississippi Sheik*) and another on Rounder (*Sam Chatmon's Advice*). Meanwhile, vintage Mississippi Sheik/Chatmon/Carter sides are available on reissue albums from the Mamlish, Agram, Yazoo and other labels.

Many performers pulled from obscurity by the sixties'

folk revival were surprised at the reception their old music received—surprised even more, perhaps, to find themselves playing before exclusively white, middle-class audiences. Sam Chatmon, however, took it in stride. "It didn't surprise me that my music became popular again, because everywhere I went when I was five or six years old, the first thing they would do when I walked in the door was the folks would start pantin' and hollerin' to the other man pickin' the guitar, 'Let Sam have it! Let Sam have it!' And I'd get that, man, and wooh! I'd put life all in there. And it's the same thing right now."

It's "the same thing" in many ways, in fact. Any performance or album by Sam Chatmon (or by others, largely departed in recent years, such as John Hurt, Skip James and Son House) recreates for us traditions now lost, ways of making music—ways of *thinking*—subsumed like a body in the forest by falling leaves and new growth, strange to us and yet so much a part of our everyday lives as to be instantly recognizable. It takes no great imagination to hear in these sparse songs the sound of banjos with their pulsing rhythms, echoes of the tonal languages of Africa, the dissembling complaints and lamentations of slaves. When Sam Chatmon picks up his 1910 Gibson guitar, we return to the beginnings of American music.

"You know the blues partly come out of New Orleans and jazz, too," Chatmon says. "And they brought the blues down from church songs. And I'll tell you why the blues come about. It's a expression that a person have—he want to tell you something, and he can't tell you in his words, he'll sing it to you. . . . All them things come out of slavery time."

MR. JOHNSON'S BLUES:

Lonnie Johnson

In 1944 Bruce Cook went with his father to a concert sponsored by the Hot Club of Chicago, a program of traditional jazz in the old New Orleans style. The father was a serious jazzman who never made much money at it but played occasionally and practiced over an hour each day, running scales and jamming with records by Bix Beiderbecke, Red Nichols and Louis Armstrong. Ten-year-old Bruce had already found, at the bottom of the drawer, a small stack of records quite different from the ones his father listened to, ruder and more primitive, tunes from people like Tampa Red, Bessie Smith, Cow Cow Davenport. But this was Bruce's first encounter with a bluesman live.

Almost thirty years later, in *Listen to the Blues,* Cook described it.

> His name was Lonnie Johnson and he was the real thing.
> . . . I remember my own impression in listening to him was that it would be hard to imagine anybody playing better. There is a quality that the real virtuoso communicates, an added dimension to his playing, that makes it immediately and recognizably distinct from that of one who is merely proficient. Lonnie Johnson had it that day, and he may always have had it, for Pops Foster, though then hardly more

than a boy, remembered him as "the only guy we had around New Orleans who could play jazz guitar. He was great on guitar. Django Reinhardt was a great jazz player like Johnson." And here he was, at fifty, playing deep rolls and treble runs that he extended with amazing subtlety, torturing out the last nuance of melody from those simple blues chords.

But the blues is essentially a vocal art, and Lonnie Johnson was preeminently a blues singer. I remember his voice as hushed and rather insinuating in tone; he was a singer with a style that managed to say more than words alone might allow. He was a dapper man, light-complexioned, with a pencil mustache, and dressed in a careful and precise way that reminded me a little of my father. (I remember he kept his hat on as he played and sang, and that struck me as odd.) He was the very picture of the urban bluesman, and that was the image he projected as he sang—knowing, world-wise, a man who had no illusions left but who still had pride in himself. . . .

My father's attitude about all this was interesting. I remember asking him on the way home what he thought of Lonnie Johnson. He said he was a good guitar player, one of the best he had heard—and that's all he would say. I tried to draw him out on the blues we had heard, the odd, hushed style in which they'd been sung: I asked him what he thought of the blues and how come he didn't play them more himself. He just smiled, and shrugged, and changed the subject.

It was some time before Cook divined his father's attitude: that he, like many second-generation jazzmen, was more than a little ashamed of the vulgar origins of the music he played and loved, and had to distance himself emotionally from it.

Cook's memoir is a fine introduction to Lonnie Johnson. Like Bessie Smith, Victoria Spivey, Tampa Red and others, Johnson was of the first generation of bluesmen to conceive a music rooted in, but distinct from, older country styles. Forfeiting the ponderous rhythm and jagged emotionalism of the older styles, this earliest urban blues was built around smooth, easy delivery. Bessie Smith, for instance, used only "high class musicians" (jazz instrumentalists) for her shows and identified little at all with the boogie-woogie pianists and jugband music prevalent in the late twenties. "I sing city blues," Johnson told Valerie Wilmer in a 1963 interview for *Jazz Monthly,* and he regarded himself with considerable pride as an accomplished, all-round musician able to perform ballads, blues or jazz with equal facility. Yet he recorded extensively in formats much closer to the Delta than that of most other city bluesmen, and though far too talented to be *merely* a blues guitarist, as Joel Vance notes in *Stereo Review,* Johnson "never quite made the commitment to a broader view of jazz, electing to think mainly in blues terms."

The truth is, Lonnie Johnson sat comfortably on many fences—comfortably for him, if not for critics, historians and fans who like things neatly labeled. He had one of the longest recording careers in blues history, from 1925 through the mid-1960's, during which he produced a barrage of basic blues, hokum, haunting vocals, jazz guitar instrumentals and rhythm and blues—by his own count, 572 songs. He accompanied blues shouter Texas Alexander, contributed solo parts to recordings by Duke Ellington and Louis Armstrong, cut the first jazz guitar duets with Eddie Lang. "His whole musical style and manner," Giles Oakley writes in *The Devil's Music,* "spoke of urbane sophistication, from the clarity of his bittersweet voice to the clean-cut precision of his highly original guitar-playing. Yet when he accompanied the hollering Texas Alexander, while never abandoning his technical proficiency, he showed a sensitive empathy for the rough, emotional directness of the country blues."

Lonnie Johnson is the major transitional figure in American guitar. Everything that came before—the complex patterns of Papa Charlie Jackson on six-string banjo, the rag-time blues of Blind Blake, the idiosyncratic runs and me-lodic flexibility of Blind Lemon Jefferson—comes together in his playing; and much that follows, issues from it, right up to the jazz lines of Kenny Burrell or B. B. King's whiplike call-and-response guitar accompaniment.

Another important point is that Lonnie Johnson was from the first not an entertainer like Charley Patton, not a barroom singer or street musician like Blind Lemon and so many other bluesmen, but a professional musician. As Sam Charters points out in *Sweet As the Showers of Rain,* there was a proliferation of such artists in the thirties: "The blues, in their terms, was becoming another aspect of the profes-sional music world, and it was that that drew them to the music." Lonnie was a serious musician before he was a popular bluesman, playing violin with dance orchestras and doubling as well on piano, harmonium, tenor banjo and guitar. In the blues he recorded, his refined guitar and vocals transcended regional styles and, in many cases, the blues idiom itself. He remains to this day one of the origi-nals, uniquely both a first-generation bluesman and jazz-man—an innovator and model musician whose authorship of modern blues guitar alone would guarantee his position in the history of American music.

A template for Lonnie Johnson's career:

1923—Advent of field recordings, breaking deadlock of northern studios and opening up market to folk and tradi-tional music. First recordings of Bessie Smith.

1924—Papa Charlie Jackson, earliest male blues record-ing star, begins putting to wax first documented versions of standards like "Spoonful," "Salty Dog," "Shake That Thing."

1925—Lonnie wins blues contest at Booker T. Washing-ton Theater, St. Louis; is recorded by Ralph Peer for Okeh Records; marries Mary Williams.

1926—First Blind Lemon Jefferson records. Big Bill Broonzy hired by Paramount as accompanist for various blues singers.

1927—Carter Family and Jimmie Rodgers recorded by Ralph Peer; Lonnie records with Louis Armstrong; first Blind Willie McTell records; duets with Eddie Lang.

1928—Tampa Red's first recording, "It's Tight Like That," a huge hit (covered the following year by Lonnie and Spencer Williams as "It Feels So Good"). Leroy Carr and Scrapper Blackwell's superbly uptown and influential "How Long, How Long Blues" comes out.

1930—Mississippi Sheiks's first sessions bring together the string band and blues traditions on record.

1936–37—Robert Johnson sessions in Dallas and San Antonio.

1947—Lonnie debuts with electric guitar on record; begins association with King Records.

1948—Fats Domino's first record, "The Fat Man."

1953—First Jimmie Reed record.

1954—Lonnie works as janitor in Philadelphia hotel.

1960—Begins recording again, plays coffeehouses, folk clubs.

1970—Last public appearance.

Lonnie Johnson was born February 8, 1894, at Rampart and Franklin in New Orleans. The years 1889 and 1900 have also been given, but 1894 seems the likeliest and was the one given on his passport. Big Bill Broonzy remembered that "Lonnie told me he was born in New Orleans in 1894, but he looked to be, in 1952, about forty-seven years old." The entire family appears to have been musically gifted, and after a brief stint in a lumberyard, Lonnie began working with them, more or less professionally. "We all played music—five sisters and six brothers, mother and father," Lonnie recalled years later in conversation with

Paul Oliver. "We played for banquets and weddings and things like that all around."

Bassist George "Pops" Foster remembered Lonnie in his autobiography. "Lonnie Johnson and his daddy and brother used to go all over New Orleans playing on street corners. Lonnie played guitar and his daddy and brother played violin." One assumes that, like other string bands of the period, they mixed popular tunes, old-time fiddle music and blues.

During World War I an influenza epidemic killed all of his family save one older brother. Working with a theatrical company touring overseas to entertain troops at that time, Lonnie returned to find himself alone in New Orleans. "So I started playing music for a living," he told Oliver. "And the blues was all the go then and from then on I loved blues and I just continued to playing them." He worked at the Iroquois Theater for a time, then at Frank Pineri's on Iberville and Burgundy. "Strictly blues all the way—on the violin. And I made several numbers on the piano—I used to play piano for a while, but only blues, no popular songs. Then I bought my guitar. I bought it in 1917. It's a beautiful instrument."

Soon though Lonnie took to the road, inevitably heading north. "I got to ramblin'—usually people get that way. I couldn't keep my feet still so I just started traveling." He stopped over in Texas, then made his way to St. Louis, playing on the excursion boats there and eventually joining Charlie Creath's band on the steamer *St. Paul.* He was with Creath seven years, recording with him as vocalist and violinist for Creath's 1925 Okeh session. "I played violin then, but I never went back to violin any more after that. My brother, he played piano, *and* violin, *and* guitar. He was better than me."

Lonnie and his brother James played together frequently in St. Louis. Big Bill Broonzy said, "I remember I came to

St. Louis, Missouri, in 1921 and I met Lonnie Johnson and his brother. They called him Buddy Johnson. Then Buddy was playing the piano and Lonnie was playing the violin, guitar, bass, mandolin, banjo and all of the things that you could make music on, and he was good on either one he picked up and he could sing too, just as good." There's some evidence that Lonnie left Creath for a time about 1922 following a disagreement, and this may have been the period in which he worked extensively with his brother. A piano player named DeLoise Searcy eventually joined them. James played violin, Lonnie the guitar, though occasionally they'd "switch it around" just for fun.

The same year Lonnie recorded with Creath's band, 1925, a blues contest was sponsored by talent scouts from Okeh Records at the Booker T. Washington Theater in St. Louis. Lonnie entered and won, receiving a recording contract with Okeh. His first record was cut a few days after the Creath session, his appeal to black audiences proving so strong that for a couple of years Okeh issued a new Lonnie Johnson record every six weeks.

"I win first prize for eighteen weeks," Lonnie told Paul Oliver in 1962. "I win every week for eighteen weeks and I got an eleven-year contract with Okeh and that started me in the business. Made some fine recordings for Okeh. . . . And that's the way it started, and from then on I've been singing blues and I've wrote a whole lot of numbers in my life. . . . I recorded so many numbers . . . it takes a lifetime to figure them all, but yes, I know how many. Five hundred seventy-two. I know, I got copies."

During the first year or so of recording, Lonnie played violin, piano, harmonium and guitar; from about 1927 on he abandoned all other instruments in favor of the guitar. He also worked as accompanist on records by Spencer Williams, Clara Smith, Victoria Spivey and Texas Alexander. He'd met Alexander in Dallas after departing New Orleans, and when Lonnie went north, Alexander followed and began his own recording career, a modest but successful one. Big Bill Broonzy years later wrote that "Texas Alexander plays something like Lonnie Johnson"—apparently not realizing that Alexander in fact played no instrument at all, and that the guitarist on his records *was* Lonnie Johnson.

Also in 1925 Lonnie married a woman from Yazoo City, Mississippi, named Mary Williams.

A word about the black fiddle tradition.

The instrument was as popular with blacks as with whites at the turn of the century, and blacks used it to play not only the breakdowns and dance music required of them by whites, but also their own. The fiddle's expressiveness and flexibility, along with its wide range of tone color, make it a natural for blues; it is, after all, the instrument closest to the human voice, capable of tones and effects achievable by no other.

In 1920 Leroy Parker became the first blues fiddler to record, accompanying Mamie Smith on her second session. Bessie Smith recorded with fiddler Robert Robbins in 1924, and Clara Smith with Leon Abbey in 1925, the year of Lonnie Johnson's first records. Jelly Roll Morton recorded with a pair of fiddlers the following year. Henry Sims accompanied Charley Patton on several records; Peg Leg Howell recorded frequently with Eddie Anthony on fiddle. In 1930 the Mississippi Sheiks featured Lonnie Chatmon's lead fiddle on all their records.

"The black fiddling tradition lingers," Nick Tosches wrote in *Country: The Biggest Music in America*. "In 1972 fiddler Claude Williams, who was born in 1908 in Oklahoma, cut a beautiful and not at all archaic album with pianist Jay McShann for Sackville Records. . . . Williams was the fiddler with Andy Kirk and His Twelve Clouds of Joy in the 1920's and 1930's."

Fiddlers who continued the black tradition into jazz were Eddie South, a conservatory violinist equally at home with classical pieces, gypsy music or jazz who recorded with Django Reinhardt in 1937 and himself led a number of combos, and Stuff Smith, who played raucous "barrelhouse jazz" on an amplified instrument. Fiddlers such as Papa John Creach, Don "Sugar Cane" Harris and Clarence "Gatemouth" Brown today carry on this tradition.

Bill Simon, reviewing the evolution of modern guitar in his piece on Charlie Christian for *The Jazz Makers,* wrote:

> Johnson came first. He began to record around 1925, mainly backing blues singers, and musicians began to notice that, more than just voice with accompaniment, he was beginning to make each side a partnership. Single-string obbligato figures, interesting chord changes and voicings, and occasional solo passages by Johnson took the guitar a giant step from the primitive rolling rhythm backings of the cotton-field pluckers, and introduced the first virtuoso elements.

Lonnie soon became, in fact, the model for most contemporary bluesmen.

"I began to listen to Lonnie Johnson's records in the late 1920's," Brownie McGhee recalls. "I had never thought that kind of music could be made with voice and guitar, and I just kept listening. . . . His musical works may and should be the first book of the blues bible."

By 1930 Lonnie's influence was sweeping, and it continued to deepen. Memphis Minnie's single-string lead guitar often sounded remarkably like his; some of Blind Blake's instrumental choruses were similar in conception to Johnson's own; and Blind Willie McTell put out several numbers such as "Death Cell Blues" and "Bell Street Blues" which both in vocal inflection and accompaniment style could almost have *been* Lonnie's.

Another big fan was Robert Johnson. "He often talked

about Lonnie Johnson," fellow bluesman Johnny Shines remembers. "He admired his music so much that he would tell people that . . . he was related to Lonnie Johnson." Like McTell, Robert Johnson put out several sides, among them "Malted Milk" and "Drunken Hearted Man," that sound eerily like Lonnie himself. Even after the Depression drove him from music for a time in the mid-thirties, Lonnie's influence continued not only in the cities but also (and perhaps particularly) in the South, where the next generation of bluesmen avidly studied his distinctive guitar style, restrained vocals and the subtle interplay of the two.

That guitar style clearly paved the way for the first electric guitarists, Eddie Durham and Charlie Christian, and closely prefigured the postwar evolution of blues guitar. Lowell Fulson credits Johnson as a prominent influence in the development of his own style; T-Bone Walker stated that Lonnie and Scrapper Blackwell were far and away his favorite guitarists. And B. B. King says, "There's only been a few guys that if I could play just like them I would. T-Bone Walker was one, Lonnie Johnson was another." In this respect, the title given an Australian album, *Lonnie Johnson: The Originator of Modern Guitar Blues* (Blues Boy 300), is not at all hyperbolic.

Lonnie's marriage lasted seven years and is sketched by Giles Oakley in *The Devil's Music,* chiefly through references to songs recorded by Lonnie and Mary—for she became a popular blues singer in her own right. We do know that she and Lonnie separated with considerable bitterness on both sides in 1932, and that Mary moved back in with her mother, eventually turning away from blues and singing only for the church.

It is never easy, of course, when man and wife follow the same profession, especially in the arts; and the life of a working musician, with late nights and irregular hours, drink, all-too-accessible partners and a basic insecurity, has domestic difficulty built firmly into it. Then, too, one assumes financial problems (for Lonnie was having increasing difficulty finding steady work as a soloist because of the Depression) played a part.

Mary had begun by helping Lonnie with some of his songs, then began writing her own. "I got some of my ideas from my husband, Lonnie Johnson," she told Paul Oliver in 1962; impoverished, she was living with her mother in a small apartment above a fish wholesaler in St. Louis. "He didn't give me the ideas exactly; I think you know you just have a talent for some things. I used to help him a bit. We were sittin' there and I give him a few ideas on the 'Tornado Blues,' that's when the tornado hit St. Louis. And he says, 'Sweetheart, why don't you compose your own numbers and we'll play 'em for you and you make good yourself.' And so we did." Mary worked the St. Louis clubs, often with pianists Roosevelt Sykes or Henry Brown, and had a large following.

The year she and Lonnie separated, Mary recorded both "Rattlesnake Blues" ("Ah, that's all right, daddy, that's all right for you / Some day you'll want for Mary and she'll be so far from you") and "Mary Johnson Blues" ("I once was a married woman, sorry the day I ever was / I was a young girl at home and I did not know the world").

Lonnie himself would not record from about 1932 to 1937, but a 1939 session yielded these titles among others: "Why Women Go Wrong," "She's Only a Woman," "Trust Your Husband" and "She's My Mary." It would be impudent, naturally, to insist on parallels between private life and commercial recording. But it is inconceivable that Johnson, an artist deeply involved with the mutability of human emotions and relationships, who stressed that his blues came from "the heartaches and the things that have happened to me in my life," did not use the raw material of his own life for transmutation to art.

In May 1927, Lonnie and Mary moved for several months to New York City. Lonnie recorded with Victoria Spivey and Texas Alexander in this period, then in November cut his first guitar duets with Eddie Lang. These proved so successful that two more dates were set for May and October the following year. Also in 1927, on December 10 and 13, Lonnie joined Louis Armstrong and His Hot Five for their last recording sessions, helping produce four titles that are, according to critic Richard Hadlock, "good examples of Louis near the apex of his musical career." The titles were "Savoy Blues," "Hotter Than That," "I'm Not Rough" and "Mahogany Hall Blues Stomp." Sam Charters describes these cuts in *The Country Blues:*

> He and Louis seemed to inspire each other, and two of the blues they recorded, "I'm Not Rough," on Okeh 8551, and "Savoy Blues," on Okeh 8535, are among the Hot Five's classic performances. For "I'm Not Rough," Lonnie played an insistent doubled rhythm, playing almost a drumming chord, and continued the rhythmic idea in his solo while Johnny St. Cyr, the group's banjo player, played the chords softly behind him. During Louis's vocal, Lonnie, with St. Cyr very much in the background, was the only accompaniment, and he played a rhythmic variation that emphasized the rough, shouted quality of Louis's hoarse singing. The group finally seemed to give way to Lonnie's rhythmic intensity, and as the record ended, they broke into a fierce double rhythm. As if to demonstrate his versatility, for the recording of "Savoy Blues" Lonnie didn't play until after a beautifully lyric solo by Armstrong and a gentle ensemble strain by the group. With St. Cyr playing a second guitar behind him, Lonnie answered Armstrong's lyricism with an almost song-like solo. His reputation as a jazz guitarist was secure.

In early 1928 Lonnie was on the road. He recorded in San Antonio and played the Ella B. Moore Theater in Dallas, coming in second to local favorite Lillian Glinn in a blues contest there. He was on the TOBA and RKO cir-

cuits, playing in "everything that was playable. Every theater there was and every place they could make into a theater
or call a theater," from New York and Philadelphia down
to Texas and New Orleans. He made the repeat dates with
Eddie Lang that year and joined the Duke Ellington band
in January and again in October to record "The Mooche,"
"Hot and Bothered," "Misty Mornin' " and "Blues with a
Feelin'."

Lonnie also toured southern theaters with Bessie Smith
about this time. "Nobody I knew could sing better than
Bessie," Lonnie said. "She didn't mind shouting over a
crowd to wake them up and make them listen to her sing.
She didn't need a microphone, either. Bessie was lively and
full of fun, but nobody pushed her around." She once stood
up to a group of Klansmen who started pulling down the
tent she was performing in, leveling so much abuse at them
while threatening to bring the whole audience out there
that they turned and left.

Lonnie and Bessie got pretty friendly, and Bessie's niece
Ruby Walker recalls, "It was a constant thing to see Lonnie
coming in and out of Bessie's stateroom, and he kept her
company on the whole tour. I thought it was strange seeing
her messin' around with someone her own age, but they
really carried on together." In a 1959 interview Lonnie
said, "She was sweet on me, but we never got real serious
—Bessie had too many things going for her."

Lonnie's duets with Eddie Lang are certainly among the
best produced in their decade and the most influential guitar music ever. Various sources report that for these sessions Lonnie used a twelve-string guitar, a guitar with
additional treble string or one with single bass (E-A-D) and
doubled treble (G-B-E) strings. We do know that Lonnie
once favored the twelve-string: "He played the first twelve-
string guitar I ever heard," George Barnes said. And Lawrence Cohn writes, "Most of Johnson's jazz solos were
taken on the twelve-string guitar," but he believes Lonnie

had discarded the instrument by the mid-thirties. It is impossible to tell from the records what Lonnie is actually playing, and no other documentation exists.

The liner notes to Yazoo Records's *Pioneers of the Jazz Guitar* beautifully describe one of the duets:

> "Handful of Riffs" follows their usual presentation, with Johnson . . . playing lead and Lang supplying bass. Although it takes a conventional twelve-bar blues progression in D, its spontaneity and supple rhythms (qualities virtually absent in early jazz guitar-playing) give it a true jazz character. Spinning an improvisatory melody line, Johnson toys with the beat in a different fashion on each verse, changing the tempo after the seventh verse and launching a perfect series of pulled-off triplets. His creativity is further evident in his distinctive guitar tone, touch and texture, all of which made Johnson Lang's most formidable twenties' rival.

The primary difference in the two guitarists seems finally one of tone: Lang's archtop has a cumbrous, rather dense tone, while Lonnie's flattop is somewhat brighter and more labile. The duets remain today fresh and exciting. When recorded, they were revolutionary.

Two contemporaries.

Teddy Bunn had much in common with Lonnie. Both were singers with sophisticated urban blues guitar styles, and both early on in their careers worked extensively as accompanists for other bluesmen. However, where Lonnie elected to work primarily in the blues idiom after his early contacts with jazz, Bunn's later career was exclusively jazz oriented.

Bunn started off playing banjo-guitar. He recorded with Spencer Williams and with the Washboard Serenaders, playing fluent single-string solos, then in 1929 with Duke Ellington, also touring with him briefly as a substitute for the ill Freddy Guy. Bunn worked regularly as part of the Spirits of Rhythm for many years, recorded with Sidney Bechet, Johnny Dodds and others, and was among the first to champion the amplified instrument, playing electric guitar at least as early as 1938 in an organ/drums/guitar trio. Another interesting point is that Bunn played with his thumb, something for which Wes Montgomery became famous many years later.

"When seen in perspective," Norman Mongan noted in an article for *The Oak Report,* "it becomes clear that Bunn continued Lonnie Johnson's pioneering efforts. He took the guitar out of the blues context and into the harmonically more advanced musical horizons of the swing era."

Another neglected and now-obscure guitarist of the period is Snoozer Quinn. Based in New Orleans, he was a favorite of Bix Beiderbecke and Frank Trumbauer and worked for a year with the Paul Whiteman Orchestra but eventually returned to New Orleans, working club jobs and at one point backing up hillbilly singer (later governor) Jimmie Davis. There are few existing recordings—none in print at this time—and Quinn even in his own time was unknown to the general public. He seems to have been something of a missing link between country blues guitarists and early soloists like Lonnie and Lang. He retained the steady bass roll (alternating thumb) of "ragtime" blues, adding partial chords on middle strings and melody line on top, rather the way later guitarists like George Van Eps and Lenny Breau have come to play. Quinn was, writes Mongan, "an artist whose style represents an important evolutionary step in jazz guitar history. Unfortunately for the twenties' public, Snoozer's intimate, swinging guitar sounds were lost in the clamor of the Whiteman organization.

"Contrary to the common belief, jazz guitarists didn't lack talent in the early days; they just lacked volume."

* * *

By 1929 Lonnie had serious difficulty supporting himself as a soloist. The record companies themselves were feeling the crunch of the Depression; Okeh, a subsidiary of Columbia since 1926, was drifting into bankruptcy. Lonnie cut his last record for the label in September 1932.

Sometime in 1929 Lonnie teamed with Putney Dandridge. "I was with Putney Dandridge for a long time," he told Paul Oliver, "and we had thirty-three dollars between us and we were makin' for Chicago but we couldn't make it so that's what run us into Cleveland, Ohio, round on the Lake there." They played at a club called the Heatwave in the Majestic Hotel and began doing two fifteen-minute radio shows each week over WATM. They were there only four months before Dandridge ran off in pursuit of a woman he'd corresponded with. "So I was back on my own again. . . . I tried to make it in Chicago but I had to quit the music business."

For several years Lonnie worked outside music, first for a railroad tie manufacturer in Galesburg, Illinois, then at a steel foundry in Peoria. He played his blues at night and may have worked sporadically on other radio stations such as WJAY and WHM.

By 1937 or so things were improving generally, and Lonnie's career took a dramatic upswing. He received an offer from the Club Three Deuces on North State Street in Chicago and worked there until the club burned down in 1940. He was playing with New Orleans drummer Baby Dodd, a veteran of the King Oliver Band and a cornerstone of modern jazz percussion.

"I would have to play along and try to do as much as I could to fill in the different parts," Dodds said. "Then, too, I had to play very softly and soothing, so as to let the guitar's sound protrude over the drum. I had to think all the time what to put in, and what not to put in. But it was a great experience and helped make me both versatile and light-handed."

About the same time Lonnie recorded an excellent guitar solo on Jimmie Noone's *Keystone Blues.* Noone was the first of the great jazz clarinet players, a profound influence not only on other clarinetists such as Joe Marsala, Frank Teschemacher and Benny Goodman, but on young guitarist George Barnes and the entire evolving "Chicago sound" as well.

After the Three Deuces, Lonnie went into the Boulevard Lounge on East Fifty-first Street, probably with another guitarist and a bass. He eventually moved on to Square's on West Fifty-first Street and remained there several years. By 1948 he was working with Roosevelt Sykes at the Flame Club on South Indiana. Pioneer blues harpist Sonny Boy Williamson was playing just around the corner. Lonnie described that time in his career.

> So we would alternate on our intermission time and go 'round to the Plantation Club and keep him company and play with him, and on his intermission time he'd come 'round to the club where I was workin' at, place called the Flame. So he just come 'round, and then he went back, went 'round the corner. He said, "Well, I'll see you after a while, when you get off. Come on 'round to the club." I say, "OK." And about five minutes later a feller came round and says he's dead. And we thought he was kiddin' you know? He had seventeen holes in his head with an ice pick. They ganged him. He was 'bout one of the finest fellers I know. They never did find out who killed him.

Lonnie eventually moved to Ruby Gatewood's Tavern on West Lake and North Artesian Avenue, called the Gate by bluesmen such as Kokomo Arnold, Big Bill and Memphis Minnie who played there. "Ruby Gatewood was a hard person to work for," Lonnie told Paul Oliver. "That's right. You work all right—but try and get your money! Memphis Slim was the only one could get it; he'd go behind the bar and get it. Go to the cash register and just take it. He was the only one would do that. The union got behind her—and *still* didn't make no difference. She still wouldn't pay, that's all." Lonnie wound up working for a Mr. Gaston on West Lake: "I worked a year for him at a hundred five dollars a week! And he paid every week, he was a great guy. He's still in business. He don't have music but he still has the same crowd he had on Lake—they follered him out there to Seventy-ninth and Wentworth. Great crowd."

Lonnie Johnson also resumed his recording career in 1937, with Decca Records, and one of his first releases must have expressed what most blacks and other impoverished people were feeling:

> People ravin' 'bout hard times,
> I don't know why they should.
> If some people was like me they didn't
> have no money when times was good.

In 1939 Lonnie moved to Bluebird Records for five years and his new recordings, often featuring fine piano accompaniment by Joshua Altheimer, Lil Armstrong or Blind John Davis, were soon even more popular than the older ones. Several of these cuts are available on *Lonnie Johnson: The Originator of Modern Guitar Blues* (Blues Boy 300). Some of the earlier, 1937–38 recordings (with Roosevelt Sykes on piano and Ransom Knowling on bass) are on *The Blues of Lonnie Johnson* (Swaggie Records 1225). *Mr. Johnson's Blues* (Mamlish 3807) contains work from 1926 to 1932, five of the fourteen cuts as accompanist to other vocalists. Both *Lonnie Johnson* (Collector's Classics 30) and *Lonnie Johnson* (Origin Jazz Library 23) are devoted to the early recordings. *Eddie Lang and Lonnie Johnson* (Swaggie Records 1229), subtitled *Volume One*, contains four solo cuts from each of the guitarists, six of their duets and one cut apiece with Louis Armstrong.

Soon Lonnie was back on the road promoting his new

records and was in considerable demand once again. He played Detroit and down through the Midwest, across to St. Louis and Kansas City, and swung out to the West Coast. From the beginning of his career to 1945, about two hundred titles came out under Lonnie's name; postwar, at least one hundred seventy-five others were issued. As earlier mentioned, Lonnie himself set the total number, including his work as accompanist to others, at five hundred seventy-two.

In 1946 Lonnie cut six sides for Disc Records and in June the following year debuted on electric guitar with Aladdin Records. Ironically, the player who set the course for modern blues guitar was never as convincing with the electric as with an acoustic, nonamplified instrument; just as with Django Reinhardt, some vital sensitivity or response was lost in the translation. Primarily, I think, this is a matter of tone.

By late 1947 Lonnie had affiliated with King Records, an emerging independent label from Cincinnati. Henry Glover, vice-president for Starday/King, reported,

> When I came with King Records, as a recording director in the late 1940's, Lonnie Johnson was a blues singer-guitarist. I had known him for many years because he had been in Detroit, singing in different clubs . . . Lonnie was what you would call a table troubadour and he would go from table to table singing and playing . . . Lonnie had moved to Cincinnati and he lived over in Rockdale where he had purchased a house.

During his five-year tenure with King, Lonnie had four big hits in the rhythm and blues market: "Tomorrow Night," "Pleasing You," "So Tired" and "Confused." Rhythm and blues was then the catchall term for black music, in much the same way as companies in the thirties and forties had spoken of "race" records, and Lonnie's own sides were ballads often as not, smooth crooners with lush backgrounds in which his guitar was lost or wholly absent. A two-volume reissue of the King recordings entitled *Tomorrow Night* periodically surfaces in cutout bins or on clearance lists.

"With the mass impersonality of the city and its problems of acute economic distress and social instability," Giles Oakley writes, "the language of communication needed a wider currency than the metaphorical allusiveness of the country blues could provide." By 1952 when Lonnie toured England, his popularity at home was subsiding rapidly. Commercial music hurtled toward the heavy beat of Chicago-style blues and rock and roll. Artistry and subtlety of Lonnie's sort were superfluous. His association with King Records ended that year as well, and a handful of scattered sides on various labels throughout the rest of the decade sold poorly or not at all.

Resulting from the reissue of his older records and a growing reputation there, Lonnie's eleven-month tour of England met with a mixed reception. Many fans were disappointed, expecting the early singer and guitarist they knew from the records and not responding too enthusiastically to the new, slicker music. A subsequent, more relaxed series of concerts, however, helped reestablish his standing.

Returning from England, Lonnie settled in Philadelphia and began working as a janitor at the Benjamin Franklin Hotel. He was located there by jazz writer Chris Albertson in 1960, during the peak years of the folk-music revival, and urged back into the studio. Lonnie cut seven LPs, five of them for Prestige/Bluesville, as well as miscellaneous anthology tracks. His new audience must have been something of a surprise to him: young, predominantly white, middle class. But he played the coffeehouse and folk-club circuits, just as he'd much earlier played vaudeville's, and in 1963 toured Europe with the American Folk Blues Festival. He was the oldest member, Paul Oliver wrote, but "still able to demonstrate his remarkable command of the guitar."

As the rediscovery craze of the sixties continued, however, Lonnie's name began appearing less frequently in blues publications and on concert posters. "It became apparent," Per Notini suggests in the notes to *Lonnie Johnson: The Originator of Modern Guitar Blues,* "that the white middle class were not appreciating black artistry (as represented by Lonnie) as much as black primitiveness (as executed by Mance Lipscomb, Robert Pete Williams, Fred McDowell, etc.)." Once again, Lonnie Johnson was caught in the middle ground. His pop ballads, sentimentality and polish (professionalism) offended the seekers of "pure" blues. Paul Garon, in an obituary for *Living Blues,* complained bitterly of Lonnie's relative obscurity and the inclination of blues researchers to involve themselves exclusively with prewar rural singers and postwar urban ones. Lonnie did not fit any convenient category; he never had.

He did find admirers in Canada, and spent most of his last five years there. For the notes to *The Blues of Lonnie Johnson* in 1969, Bill Haesler observed, "At the moment Lonnie Johnson is enjoying his 'rediscovery' in Toronto, but to a man who forty years ago was the number one 'race' artist for the Okeh record company the present popularity must seem insignificant indeed." Not long after this was written, Lonnie was hit by a runaway car on a Toronto sidewalk and hospitalized for several months. Just as he began to recuperate he suffered a stroke to his left side.

Lonnie Johnson made his final public appearance at a Toronto blues show in February 1970, accompanied by guitarist Buddy Guy. Four months later, June 6, he was dead.

"He was a serious man, much concerned with the complexity of human relationships and the stresses put upon them, and over the years of his recording career he continually returned to the subject, worrying away at it, sometimes with a melting sentimentality, sometimes with anger and bitterness and sometimes facing the anguish of failure with attempts to understand," wrote Giles Oakley about Lonnie's pervasive theme and its several manifestations.

Recognition of this complexity is an essential key to Lonnie Johnson. His work was never one-dimensional in the manner of Son House or Bukka White, nor obsessive like Robert Johnson's; he came at his subjects from many directions, seemingly aware that there could be no simple truth, no unmixed emotion. From published interviews, his speech seems also to have reflected this, his mind moving back and forth easily in time, making uncommon connections, trying to grab in a single handful as much of the shifting world as he could. And one suspects his own awareness of such complexity prompted the subtlety of his guitar playing and sinuous, reserved vocals.

Lonnie Johnson probably should be as well known as Bessie Smith or Louis Armstrong: his artistry is at that level. But when I began planning this book, I could find in none of the books in my jazz library more than brief comments about Lonnie, and books on blues offered little more. What I did find was often contradictory and misleading. Of the albums I owned then, one had been rescued from a cutout bin for $1.99 and the others were imports from Sweden, Denmark, Australia, England.

It is as a guitarist that Lonnie Johnson is best remembered now, though this may well change as the instrument passes from current idolatry and general musical directions change. Certainly his graceful lines, delicate embellishments, use of combined duple and triple meters over ninth and diminished chords are major cornerstones in modern guitar. His touch, the expressiveness he achieved on the instrument, was a revelation in his time and still affords a rich and rare harvest to guitarists. And his were the first solos to be actually *built*—constructed around subtle changes, gathering momentum directly from the music itself, climaxing in a way that also followed from the music and made perfect sense.

Duck Baker described for *Frets* what happened when three young guitar wizards got together one time in London to listen to Lonnie's records:

> Lonnie Johnson was an absolutely terrifying guitar player. There's no explanation for the way he played! Stefan [Grossman] was recently trying to figure out how Lonnie Johnson was playing his solos, and Stefan had gotten the tape and was playing it at half speed. Ton Van Bergyk and I were in there trying to figure it out with him. What eventually happened was that Stefan made a very nice instrumental, playing at half speed! Nobody could really figure out what Johnson was doing. All right, Reverend Gary Davis was a great guitar player, and Blind Blake was a great guitar player, but I can understand what those guys were doing. When it comes to Lonnie Johnson, he was so quick; and even the records where I know what he's doing, well to make his fingers move like that, he was a little along the lines of Django Reinhardt. Those duets Johnson did with Eddie Lang are some of the best things ever. Eddie Lang as a rhythm guitar player—I don't think anyone's ever topped that.

It seems likely that Lonnie, whose recording career in the twenties was profoundly successful, who came back and built another career in the late thirties and again in the forties and yet again in the sixties, has still another, posthumous career ahead—perhaps the greatest of all—as increasing numbers of guitarists and blues and jazz enthusiasts rediscover his inimitable music.

THE GENIUS OF
SAL MASSARO:

Eddie Lang

IN THE EARLY TWENTIES forces were gathering that
would transform the entire nation's musical habits and attitudes.

It began with the dissemination of the phonograph during the early years of the century. With this small machine,
music became for the first time instantly accessible. Previ-
ously, families, friends and entire communities would join
together to make their own music: string bands for dances,
group singing of sentimental ballads, marching bands, light
classical ensembles of various kinds. But the piano now
became less and less the center of the parlor, the phonograph increasingly so; and music began to be perceived not
as something one participated in, or did oneself, but as
passive entertainment. The songs reflected this and, written for performance by professionals, grew rather more
sophisticated and demanding. Since the record's time was
set pretty much around three minutes, composers and arrangers found that the narrative songs and ballads so popular in the previous decade didn't fit the new format; lyrics
now must be terse, efficient. And since early recording
equipment was rather insensitive, loud, rhythmic music was
best. For these reasons ragtime and jazz recorded extremely well, and the record companies' reliance on them

greatly reinforced the general acceptance of jazz. Benefiting as well from a dance craze that began about 1900 and ran through the twenties, these recordings radically modified popular music styles.

Introduced in the early twenties and organized as an industry by the early thirties, radio completed the transformation begun by the phonograph. Radio made music still more accessible, and it was free. It required many hours of programming, and for years to exclusion of all else, music filled that role. Further, the concept of sponsorship, for someone of course had to meet broadcasting costs, subtly identified music as a willing, profitable handmaiden to commerce.

Radio and phonograph, with assistance from motion-picture musicals starting about 1927, took music away from the people and turned it into an industry, one of the biggest of businesses. In a sense they did not change what we know as popular music: they created it.

Joel Vance in *Fats Waller: His Life and Times* observes,

> The decades of the 1920's and 1930's were, arguably, the most productive period of distinguished and persuasive urban, literate popular music. The 1930's were a beneficiary of the adventurous and experimental music of the preceding decade, when pop music began to absorb and adapt jazz, classical and futuristic elements. . . . the latter decade kept the essence of the new elements but eliminated the silliness of the "jazz age" and "flaming youth" . . . although tunes continued to be romantic and frisky, their descriptions of love or pleasure were definitions of adult behavior instead of candycane sentiments. In the Depression era, there wasn't time to be cute or silly, and the fact of youth had no social premium or mystique, as it does today.

1925: *"I'm Sitting on Top of the World," "Yes, Sir, That's My Baby"*
1927: *"My Blue Heaven," "Ain't She Sweet"*

1928: *"Makin' Whoopee," "I Can't Give You Anything But Love"*
1930: *"Am I Blue," "Moanin' Low," "Stardust"*

The mandolin enjoyed tremendous popularity from about 1900 into the early twenties, and most communities supported mandolin orchestras playing a mix of popular and semiclassical music on various-sized mandolins and other stringed instruments. Before that time the banjo had been the popular instrument among amateurs and hobbyists, and the mandolin orchestras had their counterpart in banjo orchestras with instruments ranging from tiny piccolo banjos to huge bass ones. From 1925 to 1930 the ukulele was ubiquitous in American popular music. Sheet music came with ukulele chords; almost everyone strummed the little instrument that came home with returning soldiers and sailors, and many popular singers of the day (Cliff Edwards, Gene Austin) recorded with ukulele accompaniment.

The mandolin orchestras declined sharply with the trend toward vicarious music, and the instrument itself was not at all appropriate to the newer, more raucous music. Its fifth string dropped and neck shortened, the banjo returned to favor. This "tenor banjo" was tuned in fifths, and a mandolin or violin player could make the transition rather easily. It quickly became the standard rhythm instrument for early jazz and dance bands: Bud Scott and Will Johnson with King Oliver, Freddy Guy with Duke Ellington, Johnny St. Cyr with Louis Armstrong's Hot Five.

Nick Lucas, later a popular singer, was one of the first to use guitar with the new music. For an article in *Frets,* Lucas told Mark Humphrey,

> The banjo has a metallic tone, and it penetrates. Instead of a string bass, we had a tuba in those days, and the tuba player and I would sit at the end of the room in the recording

55

sessions. They recorded on a thick wax cylinder, and they had to keep the cylinder warm so the needle would make a groove in it. I had to be very cautious with my right hand and the tuba player had to be careful not to blow too hard, because one note too loud would cause the needle to jump out of the groove.

Lucas eventually suggested that Sam Lanin, the bandleader, let him try using guitar instead. "It will never record," Lanin insisted, but the next day Lucas sat down with his guitar almost directly before the recording horn and played rhythm.

"It was amazing! Sam had a smile on his face; he said, 'You know, Nick, it's there and it's not there. But my headaches are over, and I'm not going to have any more troubles with the wax. From now on play the guitar.' I think I was the first one to inject the guitar into a recording orchestra." Lucas continued carrying both instruments along for live jobs, playing guitar on waltzes and other slow songs, but Lanin finally told him to forget the banjo and play guitar all the way through. That first recording with the guitar and orchestra was about 1921; the following year Lucas went into the studio and cut what are probably the first recorded guitar solos, "Pickin' the Guitar" and "Teasin' the Frets," for Pathé.

Studio and stage veteran Hy White in 1978 recalled the gradual change to guitar as he saw it. He'd begun his career playing violin and would become an outstanding guitarist.

> Little by little the guitar overtook the banjo. It was decided by our band that I should have a banjo—since every other group had one, and I bought mine for somewhere around eight or ten bucks; the chord book was thirty-five cents. I must say that although I couldn't play well, I looked good! But then all of a sudden every banjo player started doubling on guitar. When a band played a waltz or a soft ballad, the banjo player typically switched to guitar.

Some players, such as Carl Kress, retained the banjo tuning when they made the switch to guitar. (Interestingly, many studio players today, called upon for a banjo part, tune their banjos like the top four strings of their guitars.) Still, one by one, the banjo players became guitarists. Duke Ellington's Freddy Guy was one of the last holdouts, finally making the change in 1933.

There are many explanations for this change: the far superior adaptability of the guitar to changing styles and trends; the advent of electronic recording and microphones which eliminated volume difficulties; the increasing popularity of the string bass, with which the guitar blended better, over the tuba, with which the banjo fit well. But more than anything else the change resulted from the playing of Eddie Lang.

Roy Smeck, a contemporary of Lang's, says, "He was in a class by himself. He was so far ahead of everybody. He was playing Rachmaninoff's 'Prelude' when everyone else was trying to pick out melodies." Critic Leonard Feather agrees: "Eddie Lang was the first to elevate the guitar to the stature of horns and piano as an adult jazz voice."

And not only were his success and prestige chiefly responsible for the guitar's replacing banjo in jazz bands of the late twenties, but also, according to guitar historian Rich Kienzle, "Lang's use of the original Gibson L-5, the first modern archtop acoustic with f-holes, was so copied by other players that aside from his considerable musical contributions, Lang was probably more responsible than anyone else for connecting the jazz guitarist with that type of instrument. The image has sustained for over half a century."

Eddie Lang was born Salvatore Massaro in South Philadelphia either in 1902 (the year after Queen Victoria died) or in 1904 (the year after the Wright Brothers made their first, twelve-second flight). Fats Waller was born in 1904, and Bix Beiderbecke by comparison lived from 1903 to 1931. Lang died at about age thirty in 1933, the year Prohibition was repealed, Franklin Roosevelt came into office and Bob Wills left the Light Crust Doughboys to form his own western swing band.

Lang's stage name apparently was taken from a boyhood baseball hero. His father was a banjo and guitar maker with a taste for classical music, and Eddie's own first instrument was the violin, which he began studying at age seven. "In Italian families," Joe Venuti said, "everybody played a couple of instruments." Eddie seems to have inherited from his father a love of classical forms; he later transcribed Rachmaninoff's Prelude in C# minor for solo guitar, and several musicians recall his playing other pieces such as Debussy's "Maiden with the Flaxen Hair" (never recorded). Lang also had a profound admiration for Segovia. There are many echoes not only of classical guitar but of flamenco as well, in his playing over the years.

Eddie's early training almost certainly began with traditional Italian *solfeggio,* or sight singing. Venuti, a lifelong friend and musical partner to Lang whose own training began at age four, explained *solfeggio* to a *Down Beat* interviewer many years later as "the Italian system under which you don't bother much about any special instrument until you know all the fundamentals of music. It's the only way to learn music right." Anyone who has tried to teach a beginning musician to find his way about an instrument, keep the count and cope with shifting golf clubs on a musical staff, all at the same time, cannot fail to appreciate the logic of that.

We can't say with any authority when Lang made the change to guitar; possibly, exposed to banjos and guitars at home, he'd been playing them since childhood. When he and Venuti got their first paying job with Bert Estlow's quintet at Atlantic City's L'Aiglon restaurant in 1921, he was still playing violin but may have been experimenting seriously with fretted instruments too. The following season found him playing banjo with Charlie Kerr's orchestra. He also played and worked casually with Red Nichols, the Dorsey brothers and Russ Morgan during this time. Lang played a regular four-string tenor banjo for a while, then a six-string "banjo-guitar." This hybrid instrument, essentially a banjo with a guitar neck and tuned like the guitar, was popular with several of the older jazz players. Johnny St. Cyr played one for a time, and New Orleans's Danny Barker made it his regular instrument. In later years both bluesman Reverend Gary Davis and country finger-picker Sam McGee recorded on the banjo-guitar.

By 1923 Lang appears to have settled on the guitar, though presumably he was still required to play banjo on some jobs. A photo of Adrian Rollini's band at the Club New Yorker in 1927 shows Lang holding a tenor banjo, his guitar resting on the floor before the band.

He was playing guitar behind Venuti in 1923 when Red Nichols first heard the duo playing "concert music" at the Knickerbocker Hotel in Atlantic City. Nichols, the Dorseys and Morgan were all with the Scranton Sirens, a group with which Lang also worked for a time the following year. He and Venuti had been working out duets since childhood, first playing standard mazurkas and polkas, eventually starting to improvise. "I'd slip something in, Eddie would pick it up with a variation. Then I'd come back with a variation. We'd just sit there and knock each other out."

Lang's first professional break came in the summer of 1924 when the Mound City Blue Blowers were booked into Atlantic City's Beaux Arts Café.

The group—Dick Slevin on kazoo, Jack Bland on banjo and Bill McKenzie who sang jazz choruses with a comb and tissue paper—had teamed in 1922 as the Novelty Jazz Trio, but for their debut recording on Brunswick, they had become the Mound City Blue Blowers in celebration of St. Louis, where they (and, incidentally, ragtime) originated. That initial session produced "Arkansas Blues," a hit for them. Frankie Trumbauer, soon Bix Beiderbecke's musical confrere, also recorded a number called "San" with the group that year, and his solo on the record became a set piece imitated almost universally by jazz saxophonists. McKenzie went on to become an influential talent scout for the Okeh company, where he was instrumental in getting recording contracts for a number of jazz artists, Bix among them.

The Mound City Blue Blowers were an uptown version of the Negro jug bands being recorded sporadically at about the same time by Ralph Peer and others. Two major traditions existed, the Louisville-based minstrel/novelty groups (Phillips's Louisville Jug Band, Dixieland Jug Blowers) and the blues bands of Memphis (Jed Davenport and His Beale Street Jug Band, Cannon's Jug Stompers, Memphis Jug Band). Using various stringed instruments, a hodgepodge of harmonicas and kazoos and usually the jug for bass lines, these groups offered straight blues, stringband music, nonsense songs and covers of popular tunes. The traveling medicine shows, with which many of the musicians worked off and on, and the novelty instrumentals common to latter-day vaudevillians like Sam Moore and Roy Smeck, certainly had their influence as well. Later city musicians such as Tampa Red and Georgia Tom mimicked the sound of these bands by adding kazoos and the like to their own music; this came to be known as hokum and in Paul Oliver's description, "imitated country bands but with urban sophistication."

As Lang jammed with the Blue Blowers in casual sessions, McKenzie was not only impressed with his playing, he quickly recognized the substantial contributions Lang's guitar made to the Blowers' rather tenuous sound. By August Eddie was a regular member, remaining in Atlantic City but going up to New York whenever he was needed for theater or record dates. The band played the Piccadilly Hotel in London that fall and another engagement in Limehouse, apparently without great success, and was back in New York by year's end.

As Richard Hadlock points out in his fine essay on Lang in *Jazz Masters of the Twenties,* recordings with the Blue Blowers contain in germ many of Lang's characteristics. His tone is full; he tends to vary his rhythm playing far more than customary by using a different chord position, inversion or substitution on each beat; he employs vibrato and artificial harmonics uncommonly associated with popular guitar at the time. "In contrast to the monotonous chopping of most banjoists of the day," Hadlock writes, "Eddie's ensemble guitar sparkled with passing tones, chromatic sequences and single-string fills."

Lang continued to appear with the Mound City Blue Blowers through most of 1925, also playing or sitting in with Venuti at various Atlantic City clubs, but it was obvious to all that the group's popularity was declining while Lang's was steadily rising. "From late 1925 on," Hadlock notes, "the guitarist was more in demand than perhaps any other jazz musician in the country."

Lang became in effect the first ace studio guitarist. Electronic recording microphones easily allayed volume problems, and in some sessions with Ross Gorman's studio band (drawn largely from Paul Whiteman's orchestra) his guitar was removed totally from the rhythm section and utilized as a solo instrument while a banjo played conventional rhythm behind the group. Singers found Lang's mutable chords, single-string fills and rippling arpeggios valuable to their performances, and during this period the guitarist worked as studio accompanist to a number of singers, including Cliff Edwards ("Ukulele Ike") and Al Jolson. He also worked as a pickup member with various New York jazz groups. He and Venuti drifted individually and rather randomly through various bands but generally wound up, one way or another, playing together.

Working with the Gorman band, which also included Red Nichols, Miff Mole and Jimmy Dorsey, seems to have given Eddie just the opportunity he needed to mature along his own lines. His harmonic sensibilities deepened; his solos and command of the instrument grew ever more sure. One Gorman number, "Sleepy Time Gal," featured Lang's guitar in a duet with baritone sax, a startling combination that prefigures Charlie Christian's ensemble playing years later. On other numbers, he and Venuti would contribute "hot" duet parts.

The musical partners developed a considerable reputation. In October 1926 producer Eddie King brought them in for a session with the Jean Goldkette Orchestra because "People know who they are, and they'll help sell the records." The session did not go well. The songs (chosen by King) were inappropriate to the group; King, disliking hot jazz, had little in common with the orchestra musically, and there was bitterness between the producer and Bix Beiderbecke. King's refusal to allow Bix to play on a Goldkette side two years earlier had led indirectly to Bix's dismissal from the band he'd just rejoined.

The session did initiate a lengthy if somewhat loose association of Lang and Venuti with the fourteen-piece Goldkette group, and they may even have given Bill Challis a hand with some of the Goldkette arrangements. This association also led to a working partnership with Beiderbecke, and the duo recorded frequently with the group centering around Bix and Frank Trumbauer's orchestra. Lang's utility on these recordings has been recalled emphatically, though peripherally, by jazzman Max Kaminsky. "When I think of those twenties bands with that dreadful twenties beat that Bix was usually trapped in (except when Eddie Lang was on guitar), it's no mystery to me that he drank himself to death."

Many of the Goldkette sides are memorable. "Singin' the Blues" from a February 1927 session quickly became a jazz classic, chiefly due to Bix's solo. Directly supporting the cornetist, Lang used the arpeggio style usually reserved for singers; his rich chords and inversions in other passages were no doubt picked up by Bix's unfailing ear and transformed into fresh lines. For "I'm Coming, Virginia," another hit from a May 13 session, arranger Irving Riskin voiced Lang's guitar lead over supporting horns, an extremely novel approach.

The same session that produced "I'm Coming, Virginia" also found Bix on piano playing in trio with Trumbauer and Lang. Lang's solo here is among his best, supported and no doubt fueled by the modern chords for which Bix had a decided taste. A reworked version of "I'd Climb the Highest Mountain," the tune was issued as "For No Reason at All in C." On the final chorus Bix picked up his cornet.

The Goldkette Orchestra disbanded for financial reasons on September 18, 1927, three days after a final recording session had produced "Clementine." Resulting from a carefully worked-up head arrangement and separate section rehearsals, this tune contained the longest Bix solo on any Goldkette record (a full chorus over sustained chords) and was, according to trombonist Bill Rank, "undoubtedly the best record we ever made." It was quite unlike other Goldkette performances, as though the band wanted to leave one final piece of hard evidence that it not only existed, but truly flourished. "By any standard," the authors of *Bix: Man and Legend* observe, " 'Clementine' is an extraordinary record. . . . The band, lifted by Lang's guitar, sings along with a freshness and rich tonal balance rare on any recording of the 1920's and a rhythmic relaxation looking a good decade into the future."

Two days after the "Clementine" session Trumbauer, Bix and Lang returned to the studio as a trio and cut "Wringin' and Twistin', " written by Trumbauer and Fats Waller, probably at one of the daily Harlem jam sessions hosted by Fletcher Henderson. Again Bix played out the last chorus on cornet; Lang echoed his final flourish and ended on a harmonic.

In the same 1926–27 period Lang was recording with Red Nichols and the Five Pennies, a popular group that carried Lang's name to an ever greater audience. Experimental and often uneven, this group produced some highly original music and provided the setting for several excellent solos from Lang on pieces such as "Washboard Blues" and "That's No Bargain." Eddie's solo on "Get a Load of This" is reminiscent of Bix and was later developed by Lang into a specialty he called "Eddie's Twister." It became his first recorded solo piece.

Also in 1926 Lang and Venuti began cutting the duets that are certainly among their most influential work. The first, from the fall of that year, was a thinly disguised "Tiger Rag" issued as "Stringin' the Blues," backed with "Black and Blue Bottom." Venuti's skittering violin is clearly the feature of these recordings; still, Lang's command of dynamics and accompaniment modes is everywhere evident.

In his autobiography, *Jazz Band: My Life in Jazz,* Max Kaminsky writes about those duets.

> The records Venuti made in the late twenties with the marvelously gifted Eddie Lang were uniquely beautiful, and they were way ahead of their time. These two men were so attuned to each other musically that they composed as they went along as if they were one mind. . . . Eddie Lang's death in 1933, at the age of twenty-seven or twenty-eight, was a

great loss to jazz. He was one of the rare two or three musicians with whom Beiderbecke recorded who was equal in musicianship to Bix. For instance, on the Okeh record of "Singin' the Blues," made in 1925, Lang not only plays magnificent ensemble and counterpoint to Bix's cornet; he is the only one in the band who is keeping time. I have never understood how Django Reinhardt could have been so highly praised—except, of course, that he lived some twenty-five years longer than Lang—and Eddie Lang's genius so neglected. And though the Django Reinhardt-Stephane Grappelly records did have a good flavor and a good sound to them, they were regarded by many musicians as merely hillbilly versions of Venuti and Lang.

Following dissolution of the Goldkette Orchestra, in which Venuti and Lang had really been but occasional members, the duo lodged for a while with a new band just coming together under Roger Wolfe Kahn. Kahn had bought out the Arthur Lange Orchestra and was restocking it with some of the best New York talent. He had little trouble getting that talent because the band spent the majority of its time in town, paid very well and worked only from 11:00 P.M. to 1:00 A.M., thus permitting lots of outside recording, radio and theater work. Arthur Schutt, pianist with the band, remembers everybody averaging $400 to $500 a week, and says in one seven-day period he made $1,250.

We have memoirs from two jazz giants who heard Lang and Venuti with the Kahn Band. The first is from George Van Eps, the son of virtuoso banjoist Fred Van Eps, who would himself become a titan of jazz guitar, approaching the instrument as a "lap piano" on which he simultaneously played bass line, chords and melody.

"As a very young fellow," Van Eps told Ted Greene for a *Guitar Player* article, "I was in the habit of building crystal radios, and one day I happened to get the cat's whisker in the right place and I picked up WEAF in New York. There was a live broadcast from the Pennsylvania Hotel of the Roger Kahn Big Band featuring the wonderful Eddie Lang on guitar. When I heard him, I said, 'That's it—that's what I want!' But I couldn't afford a guitar then—it wasn't until a year and a half later, while playing banjo in a little group with my brothers, that I was able to scrape up the money. . . . And that was the end of the banjo for me."

In his autobiography, *The Kingdom of Swing* (written with Irving Kolodin), Benny Goodman tells of his first trip to Harlem in 1927, accompanied by Glenn Miller and Harry Greenberg.

> Then, too, before we opened we went around to the Perroquet, where Roger Wolfe Kahn had his band at the time, with Lang, Venuti, Miff, Tommy Gott, Leo McConvell and several other good men. I liked this band a lot, because the kind of guitar that Eddie Lang played was absolutely new at the time, and his use of the instrument was pretty much responsible for its taking the place of the old banjo. In all the kid bands I had played with, and for a while after that, the banjo was always the thing. Then Lang came along on those old records of the Mound City Blue Blowers (around 1924–1925) and it was something so different that musicians took notice of it right away. The tone is so much better for blending, and the stringing is so much more flexible for harmony that it soon came into general use. Though musicians never cared much for fiddle in a dance orchestra, Venuti was the first fiddle player to make sense in a jazz band. Folks who didn't know much about music used to laugh at Kahn in those days (because his father was rich and interested in things like opera, while his son was going in for jazz) but he knew who the good musicians were, and had one of the best bands of the time.

In 1934 George Van Eps was guitarist with the Benny Goodman Band, though he remained but a single year. And of course it was Goodman who from 1939 to 1942, as a vessel for Charlie Christian, introduced modern jazz guitar to the world.

While continuing their heavy commercial recording schedules in 1927–28, Lang and Venuti also began paying more attention to their own music, putting out an array of duet, trio and quartet recordings. Lang made his first solo records at this time too, beginning with "Eddie's Twister" and going on to "April Kisses," "A Little Love, A Little Kiss," "Melody Man's Dream," "Church Street Sobbin' Blues" and others. On several of the earlier cuts he is supported by pianist Arthur Schutt from the Kahn Band; on later cuts, Frank Signorelli replaces Schutt. Altogether there are about fifteen sides on which Lang is solo or primary performer. Some are readily available on Yazoo Records' *Eddie Lang: Guitar Virtuoso* (Yazoo 1059).

Steve Calt contributed excellent notes for the Yazoo album:

> His most memorable ensemble recordings of the late twenties were the seventy-odd sides he produced as part of Venuti's Blue Four and Blue Five groups; together they pioneered a medium that has been termed "chamber music jazz" for its emphasis on pure sound, rather than dance music or extra-musical effects. The same phrase could describe Lang's own featured recordings, most of which were made with the backing of pianist Frank Signorelli, a member of the Trumbauer Orchestra who coauthored such works as "I'll Never Be the Same" [a solo recorded by Eddie in 1928 with Rube Bloom on piano]. By composing many of his own pieces (such as "Rainbow Dreams," which was written for his wife Kitty), Lang parted company with other top-notch guitarists of the decade, like Roy Smeck.

Every signature of Lang's style is manifest in the solo pieces: the strong attack and fluent, bluesy lines with intriguing use of smears, glissandi and harplike artificial harmonics; unusual intervals, particularly the pianistic tenth and Bix-like parallel ninth; sequences of augmented chords and whole-tone passages; the relaxed, hornlike phrasing. Although primarily a plectrum player, Lang would periodically tuck the pick away in his palm and perform fingerstyle, especially when playing arpeggios and fills behind a vocalist. In fact, it seems that toward the end of his career he may have been using fingers as often as pick.

Guitarist and Lang student Marty Grosz has described one of the Lang solos, "There'll Be Some Changes Made," recorded in 1928, as "a journey from Naples to Lonnie Johnsonville (New Orleans, Natchez, South Side Chicago) in two and a half minutes. After a cadenza right out of the bagnios of old Italy and a few F. Scott Fitzgerald chords from pianist Signorelli, Lang proceeds to play a slower than expected 'Changes' in the simplest and yet most eloquent manner . . . blue and melancholy as hell. It is a very difficult matter to play a lead as simply and directly as that and to make it come to life, especially on guitar. Here is the real genius of Sal Massaro. This is the honest bread stick. How Eddie Lang found out I don't know."

Lang in fact had become, in addition to his regular work with jazz bands and vocalists, something of a blues specialist, recording with singers such as Bessie Smith, Victoria Spivey and Texas Alexander, also doing instrumental sessions with older jazzmen like Joe "King" Oliver and Clarence Williams. He recorded more than two dozen sides with black blues artists, certainly more than any other white musician of his time. For these interracial recordings—"mixed bands" were uncommon well into the forties—he generally used the pseudonym Blind Willie Dunn.

One session with Lang, Hoagy Carmichael, Lonnie Johnson, King Oliver and Clarence Williams was released by Okeh as from "Blind Willie Dunn's Gin Bottle Four." Another, a 1929 jam among Oliver's protégé Louis Armstrong, Jack Teagarden, Joe Sullivan and Lang, a simple, straightforward blues, came out as "Knockin' a Jug."

But Lang's finest essays into the blues idiom were his ten instrumental duets with Lonnie Johnson. Johnson, like Lang an ex-violinist, had much the same reputation and influence in black music circles as did Lang in his. Just as jazz guitarists find their roots in Lang, so contemporary blues guitarists like B. B. King bridge directly back to Lonnie Johnson. The man's technique was astonishing, his taste and originality constant. A highly developed guitar stylist, he linked modern blues to the older forms, in his lengthy career recording everything from Delta-style acoustic blues to Chicago rhythm and blues, working also as a sideman on records by Louis Armstrong, Duke Ellington and others. Johnson sat in as a casual accompanist to some of the same singers as did Lang, among them Texas Alexander and Bessie Smith, which is presumably how the guitarists met. Considering Lang's taste for blues and inclination to jam pretty much at the drop of a guitar case, it couldn't have been long before they were trading licks. Unfortunately, no details of their association survive.

"Eddie could lay down rhythm and bass parts just like a piano," Johnson is reported as saying. "He was the finest guitarist I had ever heard in 1928 and 1929. I think he could play anything he felt like." Johnson later referred to the duets with Lang as his "greatest musical experience."

The duets were loosely arranged blues in which, according to guitarist Richard Lieberson, the two musicians "transcend their disparate backgrounds to create a two-guitar sound that has rarely been equaled for sheer excitement." For the most part Lang stayed in the background, playing his unique rhythm and feeding Johnson changes, while Lonnie played high-register, finger-picked blues lines remarkable for their fluency, variety and shifting rhythmic base. Lang did come out front for occasional leads, as in the introduction and third verse of "Blue Guitars," second and third verses of "Midnight Call," and the intro and first verse of "Blue Room." These duets are infectious, provocative music, as fresh and vigorous today as when they were recorded.

They have also proven a lasting influence on the jazz world, spawning what amounts to a sub-genre, and in later years many another jazz guitar duet has borne the banner and created memorable, lasting music: Carl Kress and Dick McDonough, Kress and George Barnes, Barnes and Bucky Pizzarelli, Chuck Wayne and Joe Puma, Herb Ellis and Joe Pass, Ralph Towner and John Abercrombie. Several of Lang's own solo pieces, such as "Melody Man's Dream" and "Perfect," seem to exhibit Johnson's influence in their timing and emphasis on high-register lines.

"He didn't tell me what to do," Johnson said. "He would ask me." And Johnson does seem to have been the driving force of the duets, with Lang quite content to give him rhythmic and harmonic support. It is probable that Lang recognized Johnson's superior facility in the idiom; still, comparison with Lang's own blues leads discloses more similarities than differences, shared strengths above relative debility. The two had considerable common ground.

"Lang was the finer musician," Sam Charters wrote in *The Country Blues*, "and had probably more knowledge of the guitar's harmonic possibilities than any musician of his period, but Lonnie had an emotional sense and emotional intensity that shaded Lang's brilliance. Their duets were always marked with a careful respect for each other's abilities."

In June 1928 Lang joined the Dorseys and other well-known jazz musicians as sidemen on the second version of Emmett Miller's "Lovesick Blues," a session of some historical interest. The enigmatic Miller was the first country singer to record with horns and drums, also the first to employ the bluesy, yodeling style (present on the original 1925 version of "Lovesick Blues") later closely associated with Jimmie Rodgers. The song's lyrics were by Irving Mills, who went on to write such standards as "Mood Indigo," "Caravan" and "It Don't Mean a Thing If It Ain't Got That Swing." Copied from a 1939 Rex Griffin version of the song (itself a virtual duplication of Miller's own) "Lovesick Blues," yodels and all, became Hank Williams's smash debut at the Grand Ole Opry in 1949.

Not much is known or remembered of Emmett Miller. He first recorded in 1924, dropped out of sight sometime around 1929, then emerged briefly in 1936 to cut four sides for Bluebird. In his book *Country: The Biggest Music in America,* Nick Tosches writes, "The mongrel jazz-country music of Bob Wills is rooted strongly in the work of Emmett Miller."

That 1928 release of "Lovesick Blues," incidentally, was backed with "Big Bad Bill Is Sweet William Now," a song that enjoyed recent revival in the work of Ry Cooder and Leon Redbone.

At the time of the duets with Lonnie Johnson, Lang was already a featured solist in the prestigious twenty-nine-piece Paul Whiteman Orchestra. Whiteman was practically the monarch of popular musical entertainment in the period that stretched between declining interest in "hot" jazz and the arrival of the swing bands; and he paraded, in the words of Frank Tirro from his *Jazz: A History,* "an endless supply of popular songsters, semiclassical arrangers and composers, vaudeville tricksters and name jazz musicians before the public." Whatever his aesthetic shortcomings, and these were many indeed, Whiteman seems to have had genuine feeling for his musicians; he was a good manager and an honorable man. He provided a shelter for many fine musicians, Bix, George Gershwin, Lang and Venuti among

them, and probably did more to promote general acceptance of jazz than anyone else of his period.

Lang had worked with Whiteman in the past. He and
Venuti joined the orchestra briefly in 1927, and throughout
that year Whiteman called upon Lang for special recording
needs, often bringing in Carl Kress when Lang was not
available. He and Venuti rejoined Whiteman in 1929 and
remained a year, featured on many recordings, concerts
and radio broadcasts, even in *The King of Jazz,* the first
all-Technicolor movie. Lang also played frequently behind
Whiteman vocalists Mildred Bailey and Bing Crosby.

Frank Trumbauer remembers Lang carrying the entire
Whiteman library in the form of cues on the back of a small
business card. Whiteman himself, ten years after, had this
to say in *Down Beat:*

> Eddie played with our band over a long period of time
> during which I had less trouble with rhythm than at any
> other time. . . . No matter how intricate the arrangement was,
> Eddie played it flawlessly the first time without ever having
> heard it before or looking at a sheet of music. It was as if his
> musically intuitive spirit had read the arranger's mind and
> knew in advance everything that was going to happen.

Lang and Crosby became close friends during their
Whiteman days, Eddie eventually marrying a friend of
Crosby's wife Dixie Lee. Kitty Lang had been with the Zieg-
feld Follies and was Eddie's second wife, remaining with
him for the few years he had left. It was for Kitty that Lang
wrote his solo piece "Rainbow Dreams," recorded in 1928.

By 1930 the Whiteman Orchestra was having trouble
meeting its nine-thousand-dollar weekly payroll and began
trimming sails. Crosby left the organization in the spring of
that year, Lang and Venuti departing shortly thereafter.

"Singers replaced big bands as the chief purveyors of
popular songs," Russel Nye comments in *The Unembarrassed*

Muse: The Popular Arts in America, and in 1931 Lang became full-time accompanist to Crosby. Crosby had called Eddie Lang "the best musician I know." Now Lang dedicated the majority of his time and professional activity to supporting the rapidly rising Crosby, working four theater shows a day, nightly radio broadcasts and frequent Crosby record dates. When Crosby went to Hollywood with a $300,000 contract for five films, Eddie went along, even making a brief appearance in *The Big Broadcast of 1932.*

Lang did find time to work other dates during this period. He recorded with a jazz-oriented vocal trio, the Boswell Sisters, displaying on releases such as "Mood Indigo" and "There'll Be Some Changes Made," according to Richard Hadlock, "a new feathery touch, combined with the steadfast four-four rhythmic flow, that was signaling the coming of swing music and the end of the 'hot' era." He also recorded with his pal Venuti as part of the Venuti-Lang All-Star Orchestra, which included Benny Goodman and Jack Teagarden. The four sides cut by this band are generally considered classics, a fair summation of the past decade's achievements and a preview of music soon to come.

In 1932 Lang recorded, with Carl Kress, his only guitar duets aside from those with Lonnie Johnson. The two sides, "Pickin' My Way" and "Feelin' My Way," exhibit Lang's characteristic strengths and demonstrate, too, that he was still developing as a guitarist. Kress would be instrumental in extending the guitar duet as a recognized jazz form into present times, pairing with Dick McDonough from 1934 to 1937 and, after McDonough's death, with Tony Mottola; then again, in 1961, with George Barnes. "Pickin' My Way" was recorded in 1937 as "High Flyer Stomp" by an early western swing group that at one point included legendary steel guitarist Bob Dunn—some measure of Lang's pervasive influence.

Eddie Lang died at about age thirty, on March 26, 1933.

Hitler established the Nazi dictatorship in Germany that year, and a favorite song on radio and in musical shows was "I've Got the World on a String." Lang's chronic sore throat had worsened and begun to affect his general health. He entered the hospital for a routine tonsillectomy and, while still under anesthetic, developed an embolism from which he died without regaining consciousness.

Lang of course left a gargantuan legacy. Almost single-handedly he legitimized the guitar and created roles for it in solo, accompaniment and ensemble settings. His novel use of chord voicing and arpeggio figures alternated with single-string lines formed the basic vocabulary of jazz guitar, and other techniques appropriated elsewhere (the glissando and gruppetto from classical music, the smear and bent string from blues, artificial harmonics) built on that foundation, setting guitarists' future directions. He had earned a great deal of respect for his instrument and, among other musicians because of his professionalism and complete musicianship, for jazzmen as well.

A recurrent criticism has been that Lang did not swing, and his playing does seem stiff by today's standards, but little more so than that of contemporaries; contentions that Lang's playing did not survive its time certainly seem unfounded. Marty Grosz says,

> The Chicago guys felt that Lang didn't really swing, and I'm inclined to go along to an extent. . . . But I think we can overlook that for the nonce. In his way he did so much, and it sounds so damn natural and easy. And he was first; he had to think the whole thing out for himself. It's always more difficult to lead the way. Hence modern bass players can play rings around Jimmy Blanton—but Blanton was first and had the soul. Same with Lang.

Joel Vance summed things up nicely in a review of current jazz reissues for *Stereo Review:*

It has been said that Lang didn't "swing," and he probably didn't possess the rhythmic feeling inherent in many jazzmen. But he was not unduly concerned about this—nor should we be. Lang was more interested in the harmonic and compositional potential of the guitar and, in an almost atavistic sense, in the *honor* of the instrument. He thought like an Italian and played like an American, and while his music may not always have been "pure jazz," it was always successful as music in ways that antedate and transcend jazz.

And *that,* finally, is the genius of Sal Massaro.

THE WIZARD OF THE STRINGS:

Roy Smeck

ASKED IF HE PLANS ANOTHER ALBUM, Roy Smeck says, "I
think that's all. The last one was very tough at my age.
Who's ever had an album come out at eighty years old—you
know anyone?"

The album is *Roy Smeck, Wizard of the Strings* (Blue Goose
2027) and it showcases Roy on guitar, Hawaiian guitar,
ukulele and tenor banjo. He has been playing for 66 years.
One of the pieces on the album he learned in England in
1937, when he played for the Queen's coronation; five
years earlier he had played at Franklin Roosevelt's Inaugu-
ral. He also helped open Radio City Music Hall. And in
between he put out fifty-one instruction books on stringed
instruments; had instruments named after him by Gibson,
Bacon & Day and Harmony; and made a dozen or so shorts
and a couple of feature films, including one of the first
sound films for Warner and another for Paramount which
split the screen into four parts and showed Roy playing a
quartet with himself, probably the earliest example of multiple tracking.

"I played a bar mitzvah Saturday night," Roy said recently. "Played the uke and harmonica together, imitated a
train, turned the uke upside down and played it, did some
of my solos. I just keep saying to myself, How long can I

keep this up?" He's also been playing colleges recently, generally to standing ovations, and a show at Amherst led to a public-television documentary. "I didn't want to go at first," Roy says of the college gigs. "I didn't think they'd like me." A couple of new books have come out and Roy still teaches about thirty students a week, from twelve years old to eighty-two. When I last spoke with him he'd just written two new banjo instrumentals and told me proudly of the letter he'd gotten from President Reagan thanking him for a copy of his "Jelly Bean Rag."

Roy is animated and self-assured. He has no illusions about his career, only a fine sense of his place in American music. He is understandably proud of things he did for the first time, of having instruments named after him, of being the only one ever to record two ukulele solo albums, and he returns to such landmarks repeatedly in conversation, as a man will who has done something quite out of the ordinary. He responds to questions with a smoothness of delivery polished by many years of interviews, often launching into his answer before the question is finished; some seem set pieces, recited almost without conscious thought. He recalls with ease dates that he met other musicians or worked particular theaters and has a true vaudevillian affection for one-liners: "I've been married twenty-five years and all I have is a ukulele"; "I was my own quartet but I only got paid for one." Yet he clearly recognizes that his music, his way of making music, is past.

"As far as the Hawaiian guitar and the ukulele and tenor banjo—they're gone. Look at all the players that are gone. I get scared when I lie in bed sometimes and just think of it. I know I'm next." There are no tenor banjo, ukulele or Hawaiian guitar teachers in New York, he says, and if people want to learn those instruments they have to come to him. Recently a fifteen-year-old boy heard one of Roy's ukulele albums and fell in love with it. When he went into a music store to buy a ukulele, he also found one of Roy's instruction books. Then he looked in the Yellow Pages for an instructor and found Roy's name. "I never saw anybody so enthused about the ukulele, and so excited," Roy said. "That kid was just on the phone about an hour ago. He said, 'I want to take three times a week. I'll be in Thursday, then I'll be in Monday. . . .' "

So perhaps by apprenticeship, and certainly by example, Roy will manage to carry on at least some part of his music and the tradition of his instruments.

That music is the important thing, and one has to resist losing it in a welter of generalizations. But it does seem that Roy Smeck's career parallels very closely the development of popular music in America in this century and comprises a fair history of American popular musicianship as well. He could hardly have thought to make much of a living at it when he began playing: there was no tradition of professionalism or virtuosity, no body of established styles, and the popular music itself was a peculiar stew of ragtime, riverboat and Tin Pan Alley. Yet from the first Roy displayed a professionalism that carried him through every shift and vicissitude of musical fashion. He pioneered in areas that later became critical to the shaping of our music —records, overdubbing, method books, movie soundtracks —and day after day, year after unfailing year, brought music and the concept of a professional musician before thousands of people, helping form their attitudes, expectations and tastes. Roy was a contemporary of Eddie Lang, but he was also a contemporary of the great comics and always as much entertainer as musician. His music is diverse and nonconforming, distinctly American both in form and delivery.

Roy Smeck was born in 1900 in Reading, Pennsylvania, but his family soon moved to Binghampton, New York, where

Roy was brought up. His first instruments, learned from an uncle, were Jew's harp and harmonica, then (a very popular instrument around the turn of the century) Autoharp. His father had an old Stella guitar and taught Roy the three chords he knew and used to accompany folk songs. Roy was about fourteen at the time; with his good melodic sense and ear for chords, that was all the start he needed.

"If my father hadn't played those three chords, I wouldn't be here today," Roy told *Guitar Player* magazine, "because there were no guitar teachers in Binghampton then, and the local music store had only one book, *Guckett's,* which only showed the C, F and G7 chords. I, of course, bought the book."

By age fifteen Roy had dropped out of school and was working in a shoe factory. He played tenor banjo with a drummer and piano player also from the factory and backed up a lot of accordion and mandolin players on his guitar at Italian weddings and the like. His habit of taking his uke to work with him ("I even took it to bed with me") and conducting jams in the men's room eventually got him fired.

"When the boss heard my playing, he said, 'Roy, the next time you play your uke and take the employees away from their jobs, you're going to be fired.' Well, shortly thereafter, I made *sure* that I got fired. I wanted to play in vaudeville."

Roy was still working at the factory, playing, and practicing seven hours a day, all at about age sixteen, when he began having nervous problems. He got, he says, so that he didn't even know his own name, finally collapsing completely. At that point, on his doctor's advice, he quit playing for six months. His father took all his instruments into the basement and chopped them to bits. "It takes a lifetime to master one instrument, and I was trying to master five; that's why I got sick," Roy says now. Told at last that he could begin practicing an hour a day, Roy got new instruments and did just as the doctor said, practicing an hour a day—on each instrument. "I knew if I played all those instruments that I would be more valuable as a vaudeville act."

He soon got a job in a Binghampton music store and spent his spare time there working out solos and practicing. He learned the "Hilo March" and a hula called "Drowsy Waters" on Hawaiian guitar, picked up some banjo tunes from other players and records, learned "12th Street Rag" on ukulele, "and before I knew it I had an act."

Around 1921 Roy worked for a time with the Paul Speck Orchestra, one of the most popular big bands of the period. Roy played banjo in the band and did a fifteen-minute solo stint on the floor at intermission. Speck, whose band Eddie Lang joined shortly thereafter, was one of the first to tell Roy that he belonged in vaudeville, not in a dance band. He also suggested the sobriquet that Roy has used ever since: the Wizard of the Strings.

Roy polished his act daily, but his break came when the owner of the store where he was working mentioned Roy to salesmen who passed word on to agents for the RKO vaudeville circuit. They came to the store, heard Roy and arranged an audition for him at the Hamilton Theater at 146th and Broadway in New York, following which Roy was given a twenty-six-week contract. At $250 per week he began playing RKO theaters throughout the country. He was twenty-six years old.

Roy's stage act at this time adhered to a basic pattern, he later recalled. First a "southern medley" on banjo "to wake them up," then an imitation of two or three banjos playing at the same time followed by an original boogie or other composition for banjo; next a switch to Hawaiian (and later Spanish) guitar for a selection of numbers such as "St. Louis Blues," Prelude in C$^\sharp$ minor, "Hilo March" and a hula; then to the ukulele for "12th Street Rag" and a medley of favorites like "Five Foot Two," "Ain't She Sweet," or "Stars and Stripes Forever" (complete with drum sounds) and a final duet with ukulele and harmonica.

Roy had picked up the multiple-banjo effect from vaudeville headliner Joe Roberts. Roberts was originally a violinist, coming to banjo only after an accident hindered his bowing, and applying violin technique to the instrument. "Through that," Roy explains, "he was playing way ahead of the instrument's time. He would come out on stage with his banjo and ask the audience, 'What overture do you want to hear?'" Roy saw Roberts in 1918 or 1919 and was captivated by his routine of sounding like two banjos while playing only one. He went backstage after the show and Roberts told him, "Do you have twenty-five dollars on you? I'll play it here, in the dressing room, just once; if you don't get it, that's it!" Understandably, Roy's father would not allow this extravagance (Roy's salary at the factory was eighteen dollars at the time), so Roy returned to the theater with his banjo stuffed with towels, used a business card for a pick and, after two matinees in the balcony, had it: a combination of chords for rhythm and single notes played with tremolo. Today Roy imitates the sound of *three* banjos while playing only one.

His biggest influence as far as banjo, however, was Harry Reser, "my inspiration and the greatest tenor banjo player in the world." They first met when Roy played Reser's Cliquot Club radio show and quickly became friends: "I was afraid to play the banjo in front of him, but he loved the way I played the Hawaiian guitar and the uke." Roy believes it was Reser's technique that set him apart from other banjoists, that no other could play with his speed, clarity and precision. He was also, in his original compositions especially, quite imaginative, as Roy's recently published transcription of twenty-three Harry Reser solos from Mel Bay attests. Reser and Roy coauthored two or three books in later years, and Reser eventually did the arrangements and played ukulele for Roy's album *South Sea Serenade* in the fifties. Also in the fifties, Roy put out the first album of tenor banjo instrumentals; he would do two more and play banjo on individual cuts of other albums as well.

Roy learned Prelude in C♯ minor from virtuoso accordionist Pedro Diero when they shared the bill in Erie, Pennsylvania. They sat together in the dressing room between shows, with Diero carefully teaching Roy all the chords needed to play the piece; Roy's ear did the rest. This Rachmaninoff piece became the first number Roy played professionally as a Spanish guitar solo. Eddie Lang recorded his own version of the piece in 1927.

Roy's ukulele work was influenced by Johnny Marvin, another vaudeville headliner who recorded for RCA. "He played 'Stars and Stripes Forever' and imitated the drum sound," Roy told *Frets,* "but when I heard him play '12th Street Rag,' that really inspired me to play the uke better and better. . . . Though the ukulele was a very popular instrument then, few people soloed on it. It was used for accompanying singers." Roy became the first musician to record an album of solo ukulele, in fact two, *The Magic Ukulele* and *The Magic Ukulele of Roy Smeck,* both on ABC Paramount, with guitarists such as George Barnes, Tony Mottola and Joe Puma as sidemen. The uke is featured prominently on the new album too, and much of the accompaniment is by Dick Plotka, playing the baritone uke invented by Eddie Connors, one of Roy's oldest friends, for Arthur Godfrey.

American music, at the time Roy's career began, was feeling the crosscurrents of many trends and influences.

The term vaudeville had gained currency in the late 1800's to identify variety entertainment. In 1865, in an effort to attract women and children, Tony Pastor prohibited smoking or drinking in his Paterson, New Jersey, theater, and gave door prizes (dress patterns, grocery staples, toys, pots and pans). He was also the first to send vaudeville entertainers on tour. Both of Pastor's ideas took, and soon American stages were filled with "rope dancers, hat-spinners, knife-throwers, bird-whistle imitators," as well as serious singers, musicians and actors. Just about anything unusual could have a chance on vaudeville circuits—one act consisted of two mechanics who disassembled and reassembled a Ford onstage in eight minutes flat—and some acts, like the Englishman in Turkish costume who could whistle through his navel and Enoch the Fish Man, who played trombone under water, were quite bizarre.

"Vaudeville," writes Russel Nye, "was the ultimate democratic theater, simple, uncomplicated and direct, with neither continuity nor implication," obviously the direct ancestor of television.

Around the turn of the century, vaudeville theaters commonly used a brief motion picture, often a travelogue, to clear the house between shows. As the new century rolled on, however, the motion picture assumed ever greater emphasis, until finally, by about 1920, the practice had reversed itself and many managers were using vaudeville acts to clear the house between showings of feature pictures.

"The cancerization of vaudeville, due to the Depression and talking pictures, was almost complete by 1930," Roselyn Yoder writes in *U-2 Can Be a Fake Ukulele Player*, "with many actors selling apples on street corners. But Eddie Cantor's name was in lights at the Palace, and Rockefeller planned to build a super-theater with the most elaborate stage show ever, to be called Radio City Music Hall, a real cathedral. . . .

"You won't remember these days unless you'll admit to being past that half-century mark, but it was the longest era of no war, and the greatest era of music, this century will ever know."

The phonograph and then radio had transformed American music, popularizing new styles, necessitating an endless supply of tunes, universalizing the music America heard. Regional musics began to vanish, as did home and community music-making in most cases, and everyone in the country heard pretty much the same thing. Simultaneously the new industries had created a product and the audience for it, and to feed that ever-swelling audience, they began pulling in every kind of musical style, using every angle, trick or gimmick imaginable. The period was an incredibly rich and productive one, broadly eclectic, sometimes silly.

The tenor banjo was introduced in the early twenties as a more appropriate and viable instrument for current music than the mandolin, which had enjoyed huge popularity from about 1900 to 1920 but was now passing from favor. It was quite easy for the mandolin or violin player to cross over, as the instruments were tuned to identical intervals, and tenor banjo quickly became the standard rhythm instrument for combos and dance bands, remaining so throughout the decade. In the thirties, under the influence of Eddie Lang's virtuoso playing and, again, changing musical fashion, banjoists became guitarists. Roy was one of the few who retained the tenor banjo alongside guitar.

Bacon & Day brought out its Roy Smeck model tenor banjo in 1926, one of the finest and most ornate ever produced. Day had seen Roy on stage in Boston and worked out promotional arrangements with him. "Whenever I played a city that had a store carrying their banjos, I had to give a banjo demonstration in that store," Roy says. "That was part of our agreement." The Roy Smeck model was made of rosewood, elaborately hand-carved and engraved, often gold-plated—a truly striking instrument. Roy still has the one presented to him by the company; this model today is a prime collector's item.

Hawaiian music came to vogue about 1898, when the United States assumed control over the Hawaiian Islands, and continued its popularity well into the forties. Following World War I, returning soldiers and sailors brought ukuleles home with them and the little instrument spread rapidly: sheet music included ukulele chords; top singers recorded with ukulele accompaniment; everyone was strumming the uke. Rather like radio, the instrument made music accessible to all.

Roy still plays the Martin uke he's had for forty years. "It's the very best," he says. "I did my movies with it. I don't think they make them with an ebony fingerboard and pearl inlays like this one anymore."

After learning the basic hula strum, Roy went on to create his own arsenal of complex strums and picks, so that he often sounds like two or three ukes playing together. He also developed tricks such as using his fingers on the body of the instrument to imitate tap dancer Bill Robinson's style while simultaneously playing melody and rhythm, playing the uke upside down and backward, and a vibrato achieved by holding the ukulele up and swinging it from side to side like a bell.

"I always ended my shows with it," Roy remarks, "because I could do so much with the uke. There was nothing I could do with the other instruments to top my uke playing."

Hawaiian guitar had come to America also and, like yodeling years before, gained popular acclaim. With the end of the war, troops of Hawaiian musicians began touring the United States, and record companies quickly became involved. Irene West's Royal Hawaiians, for Victor in 1912, were among the first to record; Sol Hoopii was almost certainly the most popular and influential. (Bob Kaai may have been the finest, but recorded far less.) Hawaiian guitarists fronted dance orchestras, showed up on movie soundtracks and country recordings and themselves made hundreds of recordings. The 1942 Decca catalogue listed more than five hundred Hawaiian titles.

As it declined in popularity the Hawaiian guitar developed in two directions: it moved into country music (retained as the Dobro, with gradual addition of strings, more sophisticated tunings and finally, changer mechanisms, it evolved into today's pedal steel guitar); and it sidestepped into the slide or "bottleneck" style of playing among southern bluesmen. Blind Lemon Jefferson may have been the first to record in the style with "Jack O'Diamond Blues" in 1926; others such as Bukka White, Ramblin' Thomas and Kokomo Arnold used the style almost exclusively, while Robert Johnson extracted from it an unparalleled power and sensitivity. On the country side of things, early players were Cliff Carlisle, Frank Hutchison and Jimmy Tarlton. Bob Dunn was the transition figure between the older, Hawaiian-derived steel styles and the single-string, jazz-derived style of playing in country music; he was also probably the first amplified steel guitarist. The first electric guitars were in fact Hawaiian ones, and musicians of the time referred to "Spanish" or "Hawaiian" guitars to distinguish between them.

Roy names the Royal Hawaiians as his earliest influence on the Hawaiian guitar; shortly after hearing their first records, he raised the strings on his standard (Spanish) guitar in order to play Hawaiian style. He told *Frets,*

> The man who really caught my ear was Sol Hoopii. He was a Portuguese Hawaiian. I first heard his music blasting from a record store in Chicago. I had just finished giving a concert, and I heard this music while walking down the street and just had to find out who that great Hawaiian guitarist was. He had such a beautiful tone and great technique. Then I started

learning from his records. Some years later, he and I were featured on the same album playing Hawaiian guitar. It was a great thrill for me.

Altogether Roy made over one hundred forty Hawaiian guitar records for sixteen companies. And he later made ten albums on Hawaiian guitar.

In 1931 the president of Gibson approached Roy about using his name on a Hawaiian guitar the company was going to bring out. This was one of the first guitars made expressly for Hawaiian playing, with a raised nut and without frets, and was issued in two models, the Roy Smeck Radio Grande and the Roy Smeck Stage Deluxe, at fifty and a hundred dollars, respectively. Like the Bacon & Day banjos, these guitars, incidentally among the first dreadnought-sized guitars, are highly prized instruments. Gibson also built for Roy what he believes was the first electric Hawaiian guitar: "I tried recording with it for Decca Records, but because it had no tone control the treble was very loud and sounded like a blast instead of something musical." By the time Gibson had perfected its electric lap steel, Roy was endorsing those from the Harmony company; some publicity photos do show him playing a Gibson electric Hawaiian, however.

He also recorded for a brief period with the Octachorda, an eight-string Hawaiian guitar in an E13 tuning, which was invented by Sam Moore. Moore, an ex-violinist and banjo player, had turned to Hawaiian guitar after losing mobility in his arm from a fracture. Roy met him in 1924 and cut his first record as accompanist to Moore's musical saw on "Dear Old Pal of Mine." He recorded an original Moore composition, an amazing piece called "Laughing Rag," in 1928. It was played on the Octachorda and required, Roy once stated, seven months of almost continuous practice. Roy used the Octachorda only for recording, sticking to the regular Hawaiian guitar for stage use; when the instrument was stolen in the late twenties, he never replaced it.

In 1928 Roy was living at the Knickerbocker Hotel in New York City. He became friendly with the manager there, Eddie Bell, who would come to his room sometimes and sing old songs while Roy accompanied him on banjo, guitar or uke. Bell was also a friend of Harry Warner, and when Warner told him they were planning auditions for the first sound picture, Bell said, "Look, we've got a guy here in the hotel you ought to hear." Roy was summoned to the hotel's Green Room at 2:00 A.M. for an audition with Warner.

The resulting movie, twelve minutes long, was titled *Roy Smeck in His Pastime*. It was made at the Manhattan Opera House on Thirty-fourth Street, and Roy earned $350 for it. He opened with the Octachorda, played a ukulele medley and harmonica-uke duet and finished on tenor banjo. With the film, Roy became an instant celebrity. He went back onto the vaudeville circuit, and when he played his first stop, Tulsa, Oklahoma, his salary was $1,250. "I didn't play any better for twelve-fifty than I did for two-fifty," Roy says today. But *his* name was on the marquee now, and he was the center of the show, with maybe a juggler, a singer or dancer, and a sketch to fill it out.

"For the next twenty years, from 1931 to 1951," Robert Yellin wrote in *Frets*, "Roy's name, playing, records, and instruction books seemed to be everywhere. Not only was he performing in vaudeville and demonstrating instruments at trade shows and music stores for Harmony, but in 1936, over WOR radio in New York City, he gave lessons for fifteen minutes a day on his instruments. It was calculated, by the amount of mail that came in, that Roy had between thirty-five and forty thousand students listening in."

The association with Harmony had begun in 1929 when

the president of the company approached Roy after he played the Oriental Theater in Chicago, inviting him out to the factory and asking to use Roy's name on a line of instruments. Harmony produced ukuleles, guitars, banjos, mandolins and electric Hawaiian guitars under the imprint, most of these of high quality. The earliest of the ukes bore seal-shaped sound holes and the designation "Vita-uke," presumably an attempt to relate the instruments to the "Vitaphone" motion picture which had brought Roy's name before the public. (Remember also that this was the heyday of the ukulele in America.) Roy refused to allow the company to bring out a solidbody electric guitar under his name, and those produced were what Roy still calls Spanish guitars, hollowbody (or semihollow) electric-acoustics. Roy continued his association with the Harmony company until 1971. "I am the only one to have my name on all the instruments I played," he says.

Roy's radio show, abandoned after a year because of the pressures of being almost continuously on the move, ran five days a week for fifteen minutes at a time and featured Roy giving instruction on a different instrument each day. It *was* quite popular, as well as innovative, and doubtless helped steer Roy toward his later work as a teacher. About the same time, a nineteen-year-old named Al McBurney, who was playing banjo with a local dance band, asked Roy to teach him Hawaiian guitar. Roy took him down to the Lyon & Healy music store and got him a Roy Smeck guitar, Roy Smeck picks and Roy Smeck bar. (The guitar, of course, had Roy Smeck strings on it.) As Alvino Rey, Roy's student became very popular as a bandleader, recording artist and "singing guitar" accompanist to the King Sisters; he also, in the late twenties, wrote some of Roy's arrangements for him.

The Warner film was responsible for Roy's tremendous output of instructional material as well. William J. Smith came to him a little after the film's release and asked if he could use Roy's name on a series of instruction books. The first was on ukulele, followed by guitar, Hawaiian guitar and tenor banjo. Roy had little direct involvement in these books, as he still could not read music, but some of the material was transcribed by others from his playing. The books were highly successful; Montgomery Ward picked up the guitar book and distributed it all over the country. Roy went on to do books of guitar and ukulele solos for Irving Berlin songs, a book of Scott Joplin rags arranged for tenor banjo, a series of guitar arrangements of W. C. Handy's blues. Roy still has a photo of himself and Handy together, Handy holding his own aged guitar.

Fifty-one books have come out under Roy's name, and many remain in print. His *4400 Chords* for Robbins Music has sold an average one thousand copies a month for the past twelve years. And it may be from Roy's instruction and song books that his name is best known to contemporary musicians.

Roy did learn to read music in later years when things slowed down a bit. "Once when I was playing Chicago, a fellow came backstage to ask some questions from my guitar book," Roy told *Frets,* "but I couldn't answer him because I didn't read music. . . . I got out of it by showing him a few tricks on the guitar. You can imagine how embarrassed I was." Roy remembered that and in 1952, beginning to teach full time, he also began teaching himself to read music.

It was about 1931 that Roy started thinking of the guitar as a solo instrument, and "Slippery Fingers" for Victor was one of his first recorded pieces in this vein. His friend Nick Lucas had recorded solo guitar, and Eddie Lang had cut some guitar solos, though generally with piano accompaniment from Frank Signorelli or Arthur Schutt. "My style of playing," Roy says, "was directed toward being a soloist who didn't need accompaniment," and with this he helped pioneer an area of guitar which in recent years has become a profound one, leading to soloists such as George Van Eps, Jimmy Wyble and Lenny Breau.

Roy's move toward a self-sufficient solo-guitar style obviously stemmed in large part from his vaudeville setting, where he would have no sidemen. That much of his early study and playing was done alone may have contributed as well. His early turn to ukulele-harmonica duets and the multiple-banjo effect—even his urge to play so many instruments, to be as it were an orchestra in his own right—bear witness to an orientation for entertaining completely, and for extrovert (display) above introvert (ensemble) playing. Whatever their practical or psychological points of origin, Roy's development and widespread exposition of solo guitar are a major legacy.

Roy worked the London Palladium in a show called "Swing Is in the Air" in 1937, then toured England and Ireland, playing for the Queen and proving popular with British audiences. He also recorded six albums for Decca Records while in England and appeared on BBC-TV in 1938, when there were a total of five hundred TV sets in London. "I didn't even know what television was," Roy has said, "but they put makeup on my face, gave me an interview and I played my instruments."

He returned to the United States that year and continued concert tours throughout the country until 1951. He had already made a number of shorts for various studios—eventually about a dozen, plus a couple of features—and in the late forties, for Paramount, became the first musician to cut a multiple track for a movie soundtrack. The film split the screen into four parts, with Roy playing a different instrument in each quadrant. He played the instruments individually, then all together, swapping solos back and forth on "Farewell Blues." Whenever one instrument took a break, the other Roy Smecks would look that way on the split screen. Roy says that was hard, that he'd take a break and look the wrong way, "but the hardest part was, we all had to end together." The film took a week of afternoons to complete.

Roy performed before six thousand people at the opening of Radio City Music Hall in a show about clocks all over the world, representing (naturally) the banjo clock. His banjo head was painted as a clockface and a strobe light was used. "I imitated a clock and played 'Three O'Clock in the Morning' like two banjos playing at once; that's how I got in," Roy says. He also played ukulele in the show.

Throughout the forties and fifties Roy recorded soundtracks for cartoons and movies from RKO, Universal, Paramount and other major studios. He played harmonica, Jew's harp, banjo and guitar on Gene Autry songs, worked with Gene Raft and the Three Stooges, recorded with legends such as Carson J. Robison and Vernon Dalhart. In the studios, in fact, he got to work with most of the great players: Dick McDonough, Carl Kress, Al Caiola, George Barnes, Harry Reser, Sol Hoopii.

In 1972 Roy Smeck told *Guitar Player,* "I haven't recorded in about three years; today most everything is rock and roll." At that time he had made over five hundred records on Edison, Diamond Disk, Victor, Columbia, Okeh, Decca, RCA and ABC Paramount, including seventeen albums. Some of the best of the early cuts were made available in recent years by Nick Perls, who also sponsored the new album, on *Roy Smeck Plays the Hawaiian Guitar, Banjo, Ukulele, and Guitar* (Yazoo 1052); Perls tracked Roy down after hearing his "Laughing Rag." The new album was his first in twelve years and, Roy insists, his last. A variety of fifties' recordings still turn up in used-record stores, pawnshops, flea markets and the like, most of them excellent.

Roy toured extensively for the USO throughout 1951,

but when he returned home the following year he found many theaters closed and the last tatters of vaudeville gone; it was virtually impossible for a touring musician to make his way. "I wondered what I was going to do," Roy says. "I started teaching the four instruments I played, plus mandolin, showing my students tricks and things, and I'd spend four, maybe five hours a day teaching myself to read music. I was learning on their time." One performing outlet Roy did have in the fifties was television, and he appeared on all the major variety shows: *Jack Paar, Steve Allen, Ed Sullivan, Milton Berle,* even *Captain Kangaroo.*

Roy carries about thirty students now, advertising in the Yellow Pages but receiving most of his students by word of mouth. Using his own books, he starts students off reading single-note melodies, then accompanies them with chords, switching off after a bit so that they play chords while he does the melody; finally he shows them how to play using a combination of notes and chords. He teaches five days a week, mostly in the afternoons and early evenings; among his students are a psychiatrist, the fifteen-year-old ukulele enthusiast, and an eighty-two-year-old who keeps asking when she's going to learn to play like he does. ("That, I can't answer.") After teaching is done for the day, Roy sits in a favorite chair and composes.

Roy Smeck is a signal figure in American music and the history of guitar in this country. His career has spanned and absorbed many thoroughgoing changes in popular music and entertainment. A contemporary of Nick Lucas and Eddie Lang, he was of the first generation of American guitar virtuosos. He is certainly our strongest link with the near-lost traditions of Hawaiian guitar, ukulele and tenor banjo in this country, each an important part of our musical heritage. He has pioneered in areas critically important to us and our music today: soundtracks, film, solo guitar.

While by publication, endorsement, direct instruction and, most of all, his constant example, he is probably the greatest popularizer of the guitar and other stringed instruments we have had.

His weaknesses too—restriction to three-minute song forms, penchant for (as distinct from reliance upon) novelty and trick sounds, redundancy—are typically American. But his guitar playing on numbers like "Slippery Fingers" is the equal of Eddie Lang's and other contemporaries, and his Hawaiian guitar is often reflective of the best Hawaiian players (Bob Kaai, Sol Hoopii) in its precision, control and expressiveness. The metronomic flurries of notes in pieces like "Nifty Pickin' " and "Tiger Rag" leave little doubt about technical proficiency. Failures are not of taste, but preference. If anything, it is in expressiveness that we finally find Roy lacking, too often breaking away from emotive lines for pyrotechnic display—but we are of course judging by the standards of our own age, discrete from his.

In some respects Roy Smeck seems caught in the same middle ground that Lonnie Johnson occupied, too slick and commercial-sounding for folk-oriented listeners, too diverse and inelegant for "serious" musicians and listeners. (Their careers quite incidentally began about the same time and were similarly lengthy.) And just as with Lonnie, I feel certain the contributions and permanence of Roy's music will become clear as the grip of time relaxes.

The year 1979 was the second for the Greater Southwest Guitar Show, which began as a display of vintage instruments and information sharing but was fast becoming a circus as trendy solidbody guitars and absurd prices drove away instruments of true interest and value, as well as many spectators. I was wandering the aisles there, the snicker-snack of commerce all about me and silent tills ringing in every head, watching the hustlers in tour jackets and promo T-shirts pass up a small booth of fine old steel guitars without notice and rush toward any Martin in view (Martin had just reduced its lifetime warranty to one year). I was growing rather depressed.

One booth at the far end of the hall had a display of hand-painted Harmony and Silvertone guitars from the forties, old ukuleles painted with Hawaiian scenes, a souvenir hula girl and a Harmony Roy Smeck guitar. In inquiring about the price (being told, refreshingly, it was not for sale), I mentioned that I vaguely knew Roy and was immediately set upon by luthier Mike Stevens, whose personal guitar it was, who greatly admires Roy and wanted to share his enthusiasm with me. In that crowded hall, with the tour jackets and plastic shoes swirling about us, Mammon stomping hearts flat and the Scylla and Charybdis of supply and demand, for a moment there was an intimate, casual musical community between the two of us.

That is what Roy Smeck stands for.

CHARLIE'S GUITAR:

Charlie Christian

THE COUNT BASIE BAND came to Oklahoma City. It was 1937: the big bands would play a town several weeks, then swing back out onto the circuit. In June blues legend Robert Johnson had his final recording session with Columbia's Don Law down in Dallas. Two years before, steel guitarist Bob Dunn slapped a homemade pickup on a cheap Mexican guitar and became the first musician to play electrically amplified guitar on a country record.

The Spanish Civil War was in full swing, Edward Prince of Wales had just abdicated the British throne to marry American divorcée Wallis Simpson and become the Duke of Windsor, and on July 2, Amelia Earhart disappeared somewhere near Howland Island in the South Pacific. Hitler would invade Vienna the following year.

Traveling with the Basie Band as trombonist, arranger and guitarist was Eddie Durham, who within the year would play electric guitar on some of the most important jazz sides ever recorded: the Kansas City Five sessions with Basie on piano, Buck Clayton on trumpet, Jo Jones on drums, Walter Page on bass, Freddie Green on rhythm guitar; and the Kansas City Six sessions, which added Lester Young on clarinet and tenor sax.

Durham was born in San Marcos, Texas, in 1906. His

father was a fiddler who played square dances and worked with country-western groups; music came naturally to Durham. Beginning guitar and trombone at age ten, he was on the road at eighteen, and in 1928 joined bassist Walter Page's Blue Devils out of Oklahoma, a group that included Dallas trumpeter Oran "Hot Lips" Page, blues singer Jimmy Rushing, altoist Buster Smith and pianist Bill "Count" Basie. It was an exemplar of many territory "stomp bands" who dressed up the blues and took it uptown, polishing off the old rough edges and smoothing down the jagged, thrusting rhythms, creating a danceable form built chiefly around orchestral riffs.

The Blue Devils had their main rival in Bennie Moten's band out of Kansas City, and when Page's band broke up in mid-decade, many of the musicians went over to Moten, including Page, Basie, Rushing and Durham, the latter as chief arranger but also doubling guitar and trombone. Durham left the Moten band in 1933 and went on to work with Jimmie Lunceford and Andy Kirk. Moten died in 1935, and after a brief period under his brother, Buster, the band folded. Several of the musicians returned to Kansas City and eventually joined Basie at the Reno Club there, a workhorse, nickel-beer establishment. That December John Hammond first heard the Basie Band—on his car radio, broadcasting from the Reno Club over experimental station W9XBY—and began writing about the band in *Down Beat* and the *Melody Maker,* finally persuading a major booking agency to take it on.

Durham was one of the first guitarists to solo in a big-band setting, and he continually worked to deal with an implicit problem, that of volume. He'd earlier tried using megaphones, slipping homemade resonators (cones similar to those of loudspeakers) under the strings and other ploys. His 1935 "Hittin' the Bottle" with the Jimmie Lunceford Band was made on a National resonator guitar, the granddaddy of today's Dobro and steel guitar, and by 1937, when he joined Basie, he was playing electric.

Durham met Charlie Christian in a pool hall in Oklahoma City, and the story he's repeated over the years has varied little, even if other sources do seem to contradict it. The version here is from an article on Durham by Joel Siegel and Jas Obrecht which appeared in *Guitar Player* magazine in 1979.

> Charlie was only playing a little piano then; he wasn't playing guitar. He asked me to give him some pointers, like what to do if you want to play with class and go through life with the instrument. He wanted to know technical things, like how to use a pick a certain way. So I showed him the way to sound like I did. I said, "Don't ever use an upstroke, which makes a tag-a-tag-a-tag sound; use a downstroke." It takes an awful fast wrist to play a downstroke—it gives a staccato to sound, with no legato, and you sound like a horn. . . . At first Charlie didn't even own a guitar, and so I said, "Well, you bring one." I'll never forget that old, beat-up five-dollar acoustic guitar he got. We used to sit in a pool hall —that's where we'd meet. I never saw a fellow learn so fast, nor have I ever seen anyone rise to the top so quickly. The next thing I knew, Charlie Christian was a star with the Benny Goodman band. If he were here now, nobody would be able to touch him with that style.

But Charlie Christian died in 1942, at age twenty-three. And Durham's memoir points up not only the magnitude of the musician but also the difficulty in finding the man. For Charlie, like Robert Johnson and Bix Beiderbecke, was the very stuff of legend, a virtual archetype: the implicit genius and meteoric rise; the driven, compulsive playing of a man who lived only for his music; the spectacular accomplishment and dramatic plummet. Around any such person, apocryphal stories gather in profusion.

There is very little written about Charlie Christian. There

is a great deal written about his music, his guitar playing, his contributions to jazz; but it is extremely difficult, perhaps impossible, to get any clear idea what he looked like, how he talked or how he might have passed the few hours a day he was not playing. It's as though the persona took over early, standing in Charlie's stead. Even Benny Goodman, whose band Christian routinely kicked into overdrive and helped bring into ever greater popularity, seems to have had little interest in Christian as anything other than a guitar player.

True, the music is the important thing, our clearest legacy. But music, like poetry or diplomacy, issues from the whole man in his environment. Charlie Christian was by no means an idiot savant, and the paucity of personal information, along with its often contradictory nature, is unfortunate.

No electric guitarist today, and few of any kind outside sternly classical discipline, is innocent of Christian's influence. Frederic Grunfeld in his fine book *The Art and Times of the Guitar* refers to "the great divide of the jazz guitar: there is the guitar before Christian and the guitar after Christian, and they sound virtually like two different instruments."

Christian was not, of course, the first important jazz guitar soloist. Lonnie Johnson was adding his fluid, blues-based single-string lines to jazz combos at least as early as 1927. Eddie Lang, with whom Johnson played a number of astonishing duets (in fact the first recorded jazz guitar duets), was regularly featured on recordings of the twenties and thirties by Bix Beiderbecke, Paul Whiteman and many others. Lang was the first to explore the harmonic possibilities of the guitar in ensemble jazz, and his sure harmonic movement, coupled with winsome single-string lines, is undoubtedly the real foundation of jazz guitar. From Paris, beginning in 1934, came the gypsy-colored jazz sounds of the maverick Django Reinhardt and Quintette du Hot Club de France: three guitars, violin and bass. Eddie Durham's development of the guitar as a solo voice and pioneering use of amplification were other beachheads. In March 1939 Floyd Smith attracted much attention with his popular recording of "Floyd's Guitar Blues"—a jammed tune tagged on to the end of an Andy Kirk session that Smith played on his Epiphone Electar lap steel (or Hawaiian) guitar.

"In the late thirties Andy Kirk used to feature Floyd Smith a lot," critic Ralph Gleason recalled. "He'd put him right in the front row and spotlight Floyd's solos. He was really a great, exciting player." Durham claims to have started Smith on guitar during the same trip he met Charlie Christian; again, this is doubtful in light of other sources —Smith seems to have been playing guitar professionally at least three years earlier.

Two other contemporaries are well remembered by jazz. Allan Reuss, born 1915 in New York, replaced George Van Eps with Benny Goodman in 1934 when Gene Krupa, Harry James and Ziggy Elman were all with the band; his rhythm playing was among the best, and his chord solo style contributed much to Goodman's records. Reuss later worked with Jack Teagarden's band and may have been among the first to attach an amplifier to his guitar for recording purposes. Oscar Moore, born in Austin in 1916, was a pioneer in accommodating the guitar to small combos. He played with Lionel Hampton just before Hampton broke up his own band to go with Goodman, then moved on to the Nat King Cole Trio. He was with the trio from 1937 to 1947, and its popularity was such that the bass-guitar-piano combo became a standard, used widely by others such as Oscar Peterson and Art Tatum. Moore's chief legacy was a new approach to rhythm. Rather than squared-off, percussive chords, he went for full, legato ones used intermittently. "He was actually comping at a time when

Charlie Christian was still chunking away," Barney Kessel says. And this approach to chords is implicit to contemporary jazz guitar.

Clearly, then, Christian wasn't the only player cutting new paths, and the question becomes one of degree, or intensity. Charlie really didn't seem to care too much about anything but playing. His seemingly endless stream of ideas fueled an entire generation of players; his drive and heavy riffs shored the rafters of many drooping sessions; his phrasing, fresh use of intervals and self-dependent lines paved the way for bebop and summarily liberated the guitar from its comfortable role as accompanist. Taking the southwestern blues and saxophone sounds he'd grown up with, Christian bent and shaped them into something truly novel, becoming *the* major soloist regardless of instrument. His playing went well beyond the guitar to influence pianists like Thelonious Monk and saxophonists like the great Charlie Parker—the mainstreams of jazz and popular music. It seemed almost that Christian tapped directly into some primal source of music. It seems that way still.

Charlie Christian was born in Dallas, possibly in nearby Bonham, in 1919. (The year 1916 has also been given.) His father was a trumpet player, his mother a pianist, and they seem to have been working together at a Dallas movie theater about the time of Charlie's birth. Blinded sometime after the family's move to Oklahoma City when Charlie was five, his father took to the streets as a singer and guitarist to support his family, eventually being joined by his sons. Clarence played violin and mandolin, Edward the string bass, Charlie another guitar.

Several sources suggest that Charlie began on trumpet, switching to guitar about age twelve because of a "chest condition." This is consonant with what we know of his medical history and with the assumption that his father would likely have started him on the instrument he himself knew best. At any rate, Charlie also seems to have played piano and string bass early on, and for a time in the mid-thirties he held down the bass chair with one of the best jazz ensembles in the Southwest. Eddie Durham recalls that Charlie was playing piano when they met in 1937. This, like much of Durham's story, seems unlikely; still, Christian's knowledge of harmony and practical theory was more in keeping with what one expects from keyboard players of the time than from guitarists. There's no doubt that much of what he did Charlie did by instinct and ear; there's no doubt either that this was buttressed by discipline and knowledge of fundamentals, perhaps acquired at least in part from his parents.

Novelist Ralph Ellison, a childhood friend of Christian's, remembers Charlie's first cigar-box guitar and once described what issued from that primitive instrument: "His own riffs . . . based on sophisticated chords and progressions that Blind Lemon never knew. No other cigar box ever made such sounds."

It seems, then, that Charlie was in fact playing guitar quite early. It also seems that tenor saxophonist Lester Young's playing may have been an early influence. Charlie's own sound was often likened to that of a sax, especially by people hearing him for the first time; the tone and lability characteristic of Young and other "Texas tenors" was in all his playing. Young and Christian eventually recorded together in 1940, and contemporary jazzman Lennie Tristano once stated that, to his thinking, Young and Charlie "were the only musicians to make records equal to their real power."

In the early thirties Christian played local clubs with his brother's band, the Jolly Jugglers, going on the road with Alphonso Trent for a stint as string bassist in 1936. By 1937, the year he met Eddie Durham, he had returned to

Oklahoma City and formed his own small combo. He also toured the Southwest with the Anna Mae Winburn Orchestra. Now playing electric guitar, in 1938 he rejoined the Alphonso Trent group for a tour of the Plains states. In Bismarck, North Dakota, a young guitarist named Mary Osborne heard him. She recalls hearing a sound like a distorted saxophone upon entering the club, realizing what she was actually hearing only when she saw Charlie: an electric guitar playing single-line solos, voiced in ensemble with tenor sax and trumpet. Years later, in an interview for *Guitar Player* magazine, Osborne said,

> The only electric guitar I'd heard was the Hawaiian. But some musicians told me to drop by a place called The Dome to hear this guitarist who was working with the Al Trent Sextet which was passing through town. The man was Charlie Christian. It was the most startling thing I had ever heard. I had listened to all the jazz guitarists of the time— Dick McDonough, Eddie Lang, Django—but they all played acoustic. And here was Charlie Christian playing Django's "St. Louis Blues" note-for-note, but with an electric guitar. I'll never forget that day.

She remembers the next day just as well, for she spent it scouring local stores in an effort to find a Gibson electric guitar like Charlie's. When she was finally successful, the guitar cost her eighty-five dollars, and for another forty-five dollars she persuaded a friend to build an amplifier for her. She and Christian eventually became close; and when Django was in America years later he came nightly to Kelly's Stables in New York City to hear the Mary Osborne Trio.

Christian's reputation appears to have been spreading throughout this period, and his local celebrity was such that one Bismarck store reportedly displayed the latest electric guitar model as "featured by Charlie Christian." Osborne remembers hearing many figures that night that would resurface in recordings with the Benny Goodman Band.

Charlie also seems to have developed his characteristic use of diminished and augmented chords during this period. He grew very fond of Django's playing, often quoting a Django improvisation verbatim on the first chorus of a solo before going on to his own playing for the second. It was a kind of reverence, but it was also lots of fun. In later years when Teddy Hill, manager of Minton's and a true friend to Charlie, would tease him, saying, "We're going to bring that Django over here, and he'll blow you right off that stand," Charlie would grin and slide a few typical Reinhardt lines out of his guitar.

Bassist Oscar Pettiford was playing with his father's band in Minneapolis in 1938 when he met Christian at the Musician's Rest, a popular watering hole and jam site. "We had a wonderful time blowing with Charlie," Pettiford says. "I never heard anybody like that, who could play with so much *love*—that's what it was, pure *love of jazz,* and great happiness just to be a part of this thing called music. We exchanged instruments: he'd play my bass, and I'd try his electric guitar. I hadn't heard about him yet, but Charlie told me, 'You'd better watch out for a guy named Jimmy Blanton.' I never forgot that."

Blanton and Pettiford, for the most part independently, liberated the bass in much the same way as Charlie did the guitar, playing hornlike lines and rapid runs that stretched far beyond traditional quarter-note concepts. Blanton, like Christian, died in his early twenties and is still idolized by bassists, much as guitarists idolize Christian. Pianist Dick Katz, who worked with Pettiford's small group and big band in the fifties, believes that "Oscar was the closest thing to Charlie Christian that we've had. He played Charlie Christian's style on the bass and the cello. Very, very close. Same rhythmic attack. There hasn't been a guitarist since Charlie Christian that played as much like Charlie Christian as Oscar did on his instrument."

Charlie may also have played with the Lloyd Hunter, Nat

Towles and Leslie Sheffield bands, possibly the Jeter-Pillars band out of St. Louis as well, during this period. In 1939 he was heard by Mary Lou Williams, pianist with the Andy Kirk Band, at the Ritz Café in Oklahoma City. Floyd Smith was the guitarist with Kirk and had just recorded "Floyd's Guitar Blues." Recalling the meeting, he said, "We played a one-nighter at the Oklahoma Ballroom, and after the thing was over there was nowhere else to go except the Blue Moon or Blue Grill or something like that. And Charlie was playing there. I had my guitar with me and we jammed upstairs. That's how I got to know him. . . . Mary Lou and I recommended Charlie Christian to Benny, and he got him."

John Hammond's account is somewhat different. His contributions to jazz as producer, publicist, mentor and scout are incalculable—according to Ralph Gleason, "Hammond had more to do with the evolution of popular music than any non-musician alive"—and one of the first sessions he supervised for Columbia Records in 1939 was a Mildred Bailey date with her Oxford Greys, including Mary Lou Williams from Kirk's Clouds of Joy. Kirk's band was then working the Apollo with Floyd Smith on Hawaiian guitar, and Hammond casually asked Mary Lou how she could stand "that horrible guitar."

Mary Lou shrugged. "If you really want to hear an electric guitar played like an acoustic guitar, you've got to go to the Ritz Café in Oklahoma City, where Charlie Christian works. He's the greatest electric guitar player I've ever heard."

Hammond was about to depart for California to produce Benny Goodman's first records for Columbia and decided to detour in order to follow up on Mary Lou's counsel. He wired ahead and was met at the airfield in Oklahoma City by the band members ("one of those old pregnant Buicks with six Negroes inside"), then escorted to the Humboldt

Hotel, where Christian had reserved a room for him and where Christian's mother worked as a maid. This is from *Hammond on Record:*

> The members of the band wanted me to come to the Ritz that afternoon. The band only worked three nights a week for two dollars and fifty cents per man per night, and they were off that day. At the Ritz I met Charlie Christian, a tall young man, thin, dark, and wearing a purple shirt and bright yellow shoes. I listened to him and knew immediately. He was great. He was unique. To begin with, he phrased like a horn, which no other guitar did in those days, and he had been influenced by Texans like Ben Webster and Herschel Evans. He was endlessly inventive, although he needed equally big talents to stimulate him.

Hammond called Goodman in California to tell him that he'd just found the greatest guitar player since Eddie Lang, an electric guitar player who would fit the small combo perfectly. Goodman's reply was, "Who the hell wants to hear an electric guitar player?" but Hammond persisted and finally convinced Goodman to fly Christian out for an audition.

On August 16, 1939, still wearing his purple shirt and yellow shoes, but with a huge hat and string tie added, Charlie walked into the middle of a session that was not going too well, and Goodman had no time for this apparition. It was only after Hammond's pleading that he agreed to let Christian "chord him" on "Tea for Two." Charlie never even had a chance to plug in his amp, and the audition was soon over. But Hammond would not quit.

That night the band opened at the Victor Hugo restaurant in Beverly Hills, and while Goodman was off having dinner, Hammond and the bassist from the band, Artie Bernstein, set up Charlie's amplifier on the bandstand. Just before they were to start, Charlie ambled from the kitchen and took his seat. Angry, but with little choice in front of the audience, Goodman called "Rose Room," a number he assumed Christian would not know. Hammond writes,

> I am reasonably certain Christian had never heard "Rose Room" before, because it was a West Coast song not in the repertoire of most black bands. No matter. Charlie had ears like antennae. All he had to do was to hear the melody and chord structure once and he was ready to play twenty-five choruses, each more inventive than the last. Which is what happened. Benny would play a chorus or two, Lionel would answer him, and their talent would inspire Charlie to greater improvisations of his own. Before long the crowd was screaming with amazement. "Rose Room" continued for more than three quarters of an hour and Goodman received an ovation unlike any even he had had before. No one present will ever forget it, least of all Benny.

Charlie's salary was set at $150 per week, and in October the Benny Goodman Sextet had its first recording session, which included a version of "Rose Room" and a song built chiefly around Charlie's guitar riffs, "Flying Home." An article appeared in the December 1 *Down Beat* under Christian's by-line, presumably a public relations release from Goodman, reviewing the contemporary guitar scene, exhorting guitarists to keep plugging (or plucking) away and reminding them, "A few weeks ago I was working for beans down in Oklahoma and most of the time having a plenty tough time of getting along and playing the way I wanted to play."

Charlie Christian had arrived, and would soon start dragging other guitarists behind him into the present.

"I memorized every solo he recorded. I can play them for you right now, and you'd think he was here, because I even memorized his phrasing." That's from Irving Ashby, himself an estimable guitarist who played with Lionel Hampton

Charlie's Guitar: Charlie Christian

and Oscar Peterson and replaced Oscar Moore with the Nat King Cole Trio. Ashby and Christian shared a room for a time when the Hampton and Goodman bands were booked into the same Chicago hotel during a room shortage. "There were other things I'll never forget from those few days. Like stepping out of the shower to find Charlie laying on his back, a pillow behind his head and his guitar resting on his belly. And, man, he'd be playing some things that would scare the average guitar player today."

In 1939 Tal Farlow, today a jazz legend, had been puttering about on mandolin for years while earning his living as a sign painter. He played by ear, mainly learning songs from the radio, and one night while trying to finish up a job in his workshop, he heard a Benny Goodman broadcast. He paused long enough to scrawl the name "Charlie Christian" in paint across the back of his bench, then went back to work.

> I was totally floored by Christian. It was the first time I had heard jazz lines played on the guitar and played loud enough to be heard through a band. A friend of mine, who worked in a music store, played the Goodman records for me when I went there. I bought the records and ran home to listen to Christian's solos. His style of playing had me so enthused that I went out and bought my own guitar. It was bought secondhand and cost fourteen dollars. I then proceeded to build a magnetic pickup for it from a pair of my father's radio earphones. Then, for twenty dollars, I got myself an amplifier from Sears, Roebuck. I then went about the serious task of learning all of Christian's solos from the records.

Farlow's litany is echoed by an entire generation of jazz guitarists.

Wes Montgomery got his first job just by playing Christian's solos, which he'd taken off records. He'd play one of the solos, then lay out. That was all he knew.

George Benson remembers that Charlie Christian playing with the Goodman Band were the first guitar records he ever heard and adds, "He was so great. Cats today are still trying to play his lines, but they can't capture his feeling." Sixteen-year-old Barney Kessel met Christian on the street in Oklahoma City one night in 1940 when Charlie had apparently returned to visit his family. They jammed the next day at the club Barney's group was playing, and the account of that afternoon, given many years later in Kessel's regular *Guitar Player* magazine column, is intriguing and valuable on several counts, not the least of which is its rare glimpse at Christian, not as legend but person, just another guitar player.

Charlie showed up with a couple of friends, a pianist and drummer, and they set to it.

"At that time he had a white, natural-finish Gibson guitar with an old screw-type pickup mounted diagonally in relation to the strings, rather than straight across. His amplifier and case were made out of what they called 'airplane cloth,' with red and orange stripes, and the amp was painted bright red; a real eye-catcher."

Kessel's comment that Charlie played at high volume met with the explanation that he thought of it not as loud but as a full sound; that he didn't want a thin sound but one that was alive and vibrant. He told Kessel that swing was the important thing when playing jazz; no matter what else, you had to get some fire going, some emotion. At one point an inadequate tenor sax player none of the musicians knew came into the club and started jamming. After just a few minutes Christian looked at his watch, said he'd have to be going and packed his guitar away. He unpacked it only after the sax player, thinking the session over, had left. Later Charlie told Kessel that if you couldn't have fun, enjoy the playing, then you shouldn't.

Eventually the session wound down and, as Charlie prepared to leave, Kessel thanked him repeatedly for the opportunity to jam with him, saying he'd never forget this day.

"He walked away a few steps, then turned and smiled. I can recall today his last words to me and just the way he said them, they inspired me so much. I lived on these words for a long, long time, and they helped me to build a sense of worth in myself. He walked away just a few steps and turned around and said, 'I'm gonna tell Benny about you.' "

The aftermath of this meeting was a rededication on the sixteen-year-old guitarist's part to making his way as a professional musician, and a realization that he'd have to go beyond his emulation of Christian to the sources of music within himself.

Back at the Goodman Band though, despite Charlie's newfound security, interaction with some of the finest musicians of the day and a galloping reputation, things were far from ideal. If Horatio Alger began the story, Nelson Algren continued it. Benny still would not allow the amplified guitar with the big band, and though he used Charlie in recordings, the band guitar chair was generally held down by Arnold Covarrubias or Mike Bryan. Also, the "colored" stars were relegated to the chamber group that staged brief concerts during the big-band breaks. These various quintets and sextets included Count Basie, Jo Jones, Cootie Williams, Georgie Auld and many other outstanding musicians; at the time of Christian's debut with the band Lionel Hampton, Fletcher Henderson, Nick Fatool and Artie Bernstein comprised the Benny Goodman Quintet.

Charlie could not have been other than frustrated by this situation, and though he certainly recognized his good fortune, begrudging no one and apparently never voicing complaint, it's obvious some other musical outlet was essential to Charlie. He found that outlet at Minton's, a jazz club and after-hours jam site that became the crucible for a wide-ranging revolution in jazz. So after Charlie finished playing with the Goodman Band, still in uniform most nights, he'd pack up his guitar, grab a cab and head uptown to Minton's. He didn't need an amp: as far as Teddy Hill was concerned, the club belonged to him, and an amp was bought and kept there expressly for Charlie's use. Charlie rarely left the bandstand until the last musician had packed away his instrument. And soon the long nights, short days and plains between began taking their toll.

Minton's Playhouse came on the scene in October 1940 when Henry Minton, one-time saxophonist and in fact the first delegate from Harlem to Local 802 of the musicians' union, refurbished a decrepit dining room in the Hotel Cecil on West 118th Street, opened it as a jazz club and brought in Teddy Hill as manager, giving him free rein. Hill had grown up with jazz in New York City. He'd toured the South and Midwest with Bessie Smith while still a teenager and fronted his own band from 1935 to 1940, a band that traveled to France to play the Moulin Rouge and included among its alumni Kenny Clarke, Roy Eldridge, Chu Berry and Dizzy Gillespie.

Hill hired Clarke, Joe Guy, Nick Fenton and Thelonious Monk as the house band, but he threw the stage open to all musicians, and Minton's quickly became an oasis for new music at a time when jazz jobs of any sort were scarce. After-hours sessions might find Don Byas, Georgie Auld, Ben Webster, Hot Lips Page, Lester Young, Earl Hines, Jimmy Blanton or any of a dozen other musicians dropping by to blow after their regular gigs. Christian became a regular, as did Dizzy Gillespie and Charlie Parker. Teddy Hill set the whole thing up but never influenced the musicians in what or how they played. In fact he often cooked up batches of food for them, even supplied free drinks. Sidemen from all the black bands that came to town to play the Apollo on 125th Street would drop by after the shows there for some freestyle blowing. Monday nights, which most musicians had off, were especially fecund as Minton's pulled them in from Fifty-second Street, Harlem clubs and name bands downtown. On Mondays Charlie Christian was on the bandstand from the first note to the last.

It may be that in retrospect we tend to overcelebrate the role of Minton's in the evolving jazz, that it was something less than the glamorous sharing of minds we perceive at this remove. Certainly other clubs were active—Monroe's Uptown House where the musicians often ended up after the 4:00 A.M. closing of Minton's, for example—and elements of the new styles were being worked out independently by several musicians. Thelonious Monk said, "Nobody was sitting there trying to make up something new on purpose. The job at Minton's was a job we were playing, that's all." But the club irrefutably provided two essentials: freedom for musicians to play as they wanted and an engaged audience (many musicians themselves). Difficult to find in any era, these alone assured its magnetism and made Minton's a watershed for radical harmonic and rhythmic developments just then rising to the surface of jazz currents.

Tiny Grimes, who played with Art Tatum and on Charlie Parker's first records, remembers, "Another club I went to was called Minton's—it was up in Harlem—and there I met Charlie Christian, Dizzy Gillespie, Charlie Parker and all those guys who were playing bebop. Charlie Christian used to play on my guitar; he was the only one who could use that little four-string."

Drummer Kenny Clarke in turn recalls a day he and Christian were visiting a friend who was a dancer and played ukulele. Clarke was fooling around with the little instrument when Charlie took it from him and said, "Look, Kenny, you can make all the chords you want to on this if you just stretch your fingers right." Clarke experimented for a while, found something that sounded good, then went upstairs to his own hotel room and wrote it down. Eventually, he says, it became "Epistrophy," a number generally attributed to Thelonious Monk, which remains a favorite with jazz players.

The music issuing from Minton's came to be known as bebop. It was a flat-out reaction against the kind of swing music Charlie played with Goodman, an effort to realize jazz as chamber art rather than dance music, and it brought incredible dissension to the jazz world.

"We'd play 'Epistrophy' or 'I've Got My Love to Keep Me Warm' just to keep the other guys off the stand, because we knew they couldn't make those chord changes," Kenny Clarke has remarked. "We kept the riff-raff out and built our clique on new chords."

Elitism was certainly a characteristic of the musicians playing bebop though, as Clarke's remark suggests, it was more by way of challenge than blind, a direct line of tradition from the cutting contests back in New Orleans at jazz's inception. The Minton group was ready to acknowledge kindred spirits; but if these guys couldn't keep up with them, then they needed to head home and woodshed a while. And many did just that.

The key to bebop was increased freedom for the combo and the individual player. The rhythm section liberated itself from the rather plodding swing beat and went for a smoother, more legato effect, chiefly by shifting the downbeat from the bass drum to the cymbal and dropping all emphasis on the second and fourth beats; the bass and snare were now used for accents, the result being a kind of shimmering, floating quality. Horn men and pianists used more abstract chords, shifting accents from measure to measure as well as within the measure, abjuring one-to-one correspondence of scale to chord or melody line to rhythmic table.

First, then, the song was reharmonized. A player faced with four beats of C, for example, might begin on C9 and move into Am9, using substitute chords that have common tones. He then plays off these new chords, obviously with greater option as to appropriate tones and scales. The melody beloved by early jazzmen may be obscured or lost in a flurry of notes. And this is the backbone of modern jazz.

An early and excellent attempt to achieve historical perspective for the style appeared in *The Record Collector* in 1948–49 and is reprinted in *The Art of Jazz,* edited by Martin Williams. Written by Ross Russell in the peak years of controversy, the piece remarks:

> The guitar was an important part of the Goodman Sextet and Christian's playing on records like "Till Tom Special" actually foreshadowed bebop line phrasing and harmony. Christian's important role in the Minton laboratory is also well known. Many musicians feel that if Charlie Christian were alive he would have solved the problem of integrating the instrument with the bebop section. However, many of the guitarists who have followed after and been influenced by him play exciting bebop solos.

From this we infer that Christian's contributions to the emergent style were freely recognized, also that following his death the guitar underwent a brief period of decline, presumably until other guitarists began to catch up with him.

"Half-dead," John Hammond wrote, "Charlie Christian could outplay most musicians he met"—more observation than romantic conjecture.

Sometime in 1940 while the band was playing Chicago, Charlie started coughing badly and was sent by Benny to Michael Reese Hospital where routine X-ray disclosed a spot on one lung. Charlie had known he was infected with tuberculosis, but apparently received treatment and believed himself fully recovered; he had not mentioned this illness to Hammond or Goodman. The doctors at Michael Reese warned him to take care of himself, but felt he could have an active, full life.

Still, the regimen of convalescence—regular hours, rest, conservation of energy—conflicted mightily both with Charlie's personal habits and with the requirements of his music. In the spring of 1941, seriously ill now, he was admitted to Seaview Sanitarium on Staten Island.

Dr. Sam McKinney, a Harlem physician and devoted jazz fan, took interest in Charlie's welfare and began making weekly visits to the sanitarium, apparently supervising his care. Teddy Hill went out each Sunday with specially cooked chicken and chocolate cakes sent along by "Mom" Frazier, whose restaurant at 121st and Seventh Avenue was a gathering place for Harlem musicians; Charlie was a favorite of hers.

The guitarist began showing improvement after several weeks. But Charlie had other, less benign visitors at Seaview and stories yet circulate of Charlie being spirited away by fellow musicians for late-hour parties. One winter night he slipped out to join these "friends" and pushed himself too hard, getting overheated and exhausted. Dr. McKinney learned of the infractions and ended them, but it was too late: Charlie had contracted pneumonia and in his weakened state, with the added complication of tuberculosis, could offer little resistance.

"Charlie was forever grateful to Benny for rescuing him from obscurity," John Hammond wrote. "He was a sweet, loving man, as Lester Young was, with few defenses against the world. His only resource was his music and when he was unable to play he was unable to live."

Hammond returned from California in February 1942 to receive a call from Seaview telling him that Christian was acutely ill. He went out right away and realized the dark was crowding close.

Charlie Christian was amazing. I first heard him around 1941 or '42. There were ten-cent vending machines then, like jukeboxes but with pictures. You put in a dime or a quarter and you could see the most popular people of the day. That's how I first saw Duke Ellington, Louis Armstrong, Count Basie and Louis Jordan. And that's how I saw Charlie Christian. I was still in Indianola, Mississippi, at the time.

To me, Charlie Christian was a master at diminished chords. A master at new ideas, too. And he was kind of like a governor on a tractor. If a tractor is bogging down in the mud, the governor will kick in and give it an extra boost. Christian was the same way—when the band would hit the bridge, he would keep the whole thing flying and get it really taking off.

These comments are from B. B. King in selecting "My Ten Favorites" for *Guitar Player* magazine, and they converge toward a definition of Christian's style, at least those elements of it that proved the foundation upon which George Barnes, Herb Ellis, Barney Kessel and others would fabricate modern jazz guitar throughout the early and mid-forties.

For as Christian told the young Kessel, first you have to swing. And Charlie did, relentlessly. But he also could take twenty-five choruses and never let up; he was that boundlessly inventive.

"Charlie's greatest asset," Al Avakian and Bob Prince wrote in liner notes for a 1950's Columbia LP of Goodman Sextet recordings, "was his command of rhythm. He had a natural drive to swing at all costs, and this, coupled with his spontaneous exploration of rhythmic principles, led him to a flexibility of the beat that was unique. This flexibility became a prerequisite in all forms of jazz to follow."

His solos typically contrasted tight riff figures with flowing lines. They exhibit miraculous manipulation of tension and release and give his solo playing a self-sufficiency unparalleled at the time they appeared and for many years after.

In all Charlie cut twenty-five sides with the Goodman Sextet or Septet. He was also on most full-band recordings but was rarely featured in that context, two exceptions being "Solo Flight" (Charlie's showpiece) and "Honeysuckle Rose." Columbia has collected most of these, along with three jams in a Minneapolis nightclub circa 1940 and a "Charlie Christian Jammers" cut titled "Waitin' for Benny," on *Solo Flight* (Columbia G 30779), which is readily available. *"Solo Flight,"* Pete Welding wrote in a *Guitar World* survey of Christian on disc, "is the essential Christian album for anyone wishing to investigate his brilliant, fiery, still fresh-sounding music."

Jazz Archives' *Charlie Christian-Lester Young: Together, 1940* (JA-6) offers five cuts with Young and Christian along with eleven Goodman cuts, five of them duplicates of *Solo Flight* material, the others rehearsal or alternate takes of issued Goodman Septet recordings. Charlie's contributions to the 1939 Carnegie Hall "From Spirituals to Swing" concert are available on a two-record set under that title from Vanguard (VSD 47/48). In February 1941 Charlie recorded on acoustic guitar—producer Alfred Lion would not allow amplified guitar—with the Edmond Hall Quartet: Hall on clarinet, Meade Lux Lewis on celeste, Israel Crosby on bass and Charlie. Four sides were cut for oversize 78s, and in 1968 the entire session was issued on Blue Note as *Celestial Express* (Blue Note BST-86505), now out of print.

Jazz fan Jerry Newman set up his bulky, rather primitive recording equipment in Minton's in 1940 and thus afforded our only signature of Charlie playing live with the house band. These acetates are very important and have surfaced periodically on Vox, Newman's own Esoteric label and Everest. "On these," Welding says, "can be heard the living proof of John Hammond's assertion that Christian could solo, with unfettered creativity, at great length." Bill Simon goes still further: "Charlie 'wails' on chorus after chorus with those long, full-blown lines, those simple riffs and those complex strung-out changes. Here was the beginning of 'bop,' with Clarke dropping 'bombs' in unorthodox places behind Charlie's own shifting accents, and Monk beginning to play his own strange harmonies and 'comping' for the soloists."

An interesting sideline here is *Tony Rizzi's Five Guitars Play Charlie Christian,* an album devoted exclusively to harmonized versions for five guitars of Charlie's solos, taken note for note from the Goodman recordings.

Charlie Christian died on March 2, 1942, at the age of twenty-three. Three months earlier Pearl Harbor had pulled America into World War II; Orson Welles's *Citizen Kane* had come out the previous year, and Raymond Chandler's third detective novel, *The High Window,* was scheduled for summer publication. Charlie was buried, Hammond tells us, in the plainest wood coffin. But the only box Charlie could ever be in, really, was his guitar, and stories abound concerning it.

In 1950 Mundell Lowe, a fine player who later turned to the studios and composition because of dwindling opportunities for jazz guitarists, was playing New York clubs in a quartet with former-Stan Kenton-guitarist Sal Salvador when Christian's guitar came into his possession. "It was a great guitar," he says. "It was an ES-150 with Gibson's first bar pickup on it. I had John D'Angelico make it blond and put a D'Angelico neck on it. I don't have any idea where that guitar is now, but if I ever find out. . . ." The guitar was later stolen.

Roy Clark never owned Charlie's guitar, but he does believe he got a rare chance to play it. "It was about seven years ago," he told *Guitar Player* magazine.

> I was working in Oklahoma City, where Charlie Christian lived. A guy named Benny Garcia had acquired Charlie's guitar. It had been neglected in an attic somewhere, and

Benny got it all fixed up. He brought it to me one night to play. He brought Christian's amp, too. The guitar had that filed bar pickup on it, and there was a big bubble in the back of the body. But I could just *feel* the vibrations in that guitar, like Charlie's music was still in it somewhere. It was a beautiful instrument.

The Gibson pickup mentioned in both these stories is today still called the "Charlie Christian pickup" among guitarists.

Sal Salvador tells about a time he approached Dave Barber, then Peggy Lee's accompanist, and asked him how to get ahead in the business. Barber told him: Go home and practice, and when you get good enough they'll find you.

And that's the real fascination of Charlie Christian. He came onto the jazz scene playing full tilt, with the power and directness of a natural force, a wind that snapped and burned and never let up, but after a bit passed on. He leapt from tiny clubs in Oklahoma City to Carnegie Hall virtually overnight, just another version of the good old American dream in his purple shirt and yellow shoes, with his guitar and amp, at the back, please, of the bus.

"Where did he come from?" Teddy Hill asks, still trying to understand how something like Charlie happened. "When we were kids growing up here in New York, we watched Benny Carter grow from a squeaking beginner to a master musician. Or take Dizzy. When he joined my band after Roy [Eldridge] left, he played just about like Roy. . . . Then Dizzy began to work out those new things with Monk and Klook [Kenny Clarke]. . . . The point is, we could see him grow. But what about Charlie? . . . Where did he come from?"

And the simple answer is: we don't know. I don't believe we ever will. But I rarely hear an electric guitar without wondering.

KING OF THE
HILLBILLIES:

Riley Puckett

THE SPECTRUM of country guitar styles is a broad one, running from simple strummed accompaniment to note-for-note picking of fiddle tunes in the manner of Doc Watson or Tony Rice, and from the old-time finger-picking of Sam McGee to the jazz- and classical-influenced fingerstyle playing of Chet Atkins: it incorporates the take-off solos of swing players like Eldon Shamblin alongside contemporary rock licks. And it's probably with country music that the guitar in this country has its longest and closest association.

Before the turn of the century, however, the guitar was not much used in popular music of any sort. Banjo and fiddle were the favored folk instruments, and the guitar existed primarily in northern enclaves as a "parlor" instrument, often joining with the mandolin in small string orchestras that played light classical music. By 1894 Sears was offering several guitar models in its mail-order catalogue, though, and this rather quickly distributed the instrument throughout rural America. A separate, folk tradition for the instrument developed chiefly from Mexican music in the Southwest and the blues and ragtime music of southern blacks, but it was spurred on by the vogue for Hawaiian music after 1898. The Spanish-American War also introduced many servicemen to the instrument in the early

1890's, as they witnessed its widespread use in Cuba.

When the guitar was seen in rural America in the days before World War I, it was generally in the hands of a black player. "Black people were about the only people that played guitars then," Sam McGee remembered. But by the early 1920's southerners had formed their own version of the northern orchestras.

Charles Wolfe writes in *Tennessee Strings,*

> The guitar was quickly adopted as vocal accompaniment and then integrated into the instrumental dance music of the fiddle and the banjo. Thus the classic country string band was formed: the fiddle to play the melody lead, the banjo to pick a melodic counterpoint and the guitar to form a rhythm and bass. This was an instrumental lineup that functioned much as the trumpet, clarinet and trombone functioned for New Orleans jazz, and the string band was to have as much influence on American culture as the New Orleans music.

Riley Puckett is a somewhat obscure figure in American guitar, known primarily to scholars and fans of old-time music. But Doc Watson repeatedly names him as a prime influence on his own playing, and it is in Puckett's playing that we find the direct antecedent of today's bluegrass guitar styles. Puckett was an integral part of the most popular and influential string band in history, and in his own right the first genuine country singing star, recording over two hundred songs, including early versions of yodels later covered by Jimmie Rodgers, for whom the yodel style became a trademark. Consistently cited by contemporaries as a serious, dedicated musician, Puckett was in fact among the earliest true professionals of country music, simultaneously representing its folk origin and prefiguring its commercial future.

The first high-powered radio station in the South was Atlanta's WSB, which was also probably the first to feature country music. Owned by the Atlanta *Journal,* this station began broadcasting on March 16, 1922. "For approximately one year before the first recording expedition went to Atlanta searching for folk talent," Bill Malone notes in *Country Music, U.S.A.,* "singers and string bands had been appearing on WSB, providing a reservoir of talent for any recording scout who might venture into the city."

The audience for folk music in the central Georgia region was large. In the final two decades of the nineteenth century, fiddling had begun to gather considerable attention as a folk art, and fiddling contests were held throughout the South in increasing numbers. One of the largest of these was the annual Atlanta contest established by the Georgia Old-Time Fiddlers' Association in 1913, making Atlanta a strong center for old-time music. "Unique in all things," the *Journal* wrote in 1915, "Atlanta has nothing more distinctive than this"; when WSB went on the air in 1922, the station found both a ready market and established pool of talent. Local favorite Fiddlin' John Carson, for example (who became in 1923, more or less by accident, the first old-time artist to record), was well known for his participation in Georgia political campaigns.

The situation in Atlanta formed a ready-made opportunity for the recording industry. Companies originally tailored their products to the middle and upper classes—light opera, parlor music, dance bands such as Paul Whiteman's —but as sales declined with the proliferation of radio stations, these companies began casting about for new markets. Carson was recorded by Okeh in June 1923 as a favor to a local client. Ralph Peer, a giant in field recording and later discoverer of both the Carter Family and Jimmie Rodgers, was the company representative, and he thought the results pretty dreary stuff, assigning no catalogue number and going ahead with pressings only because the local client had preordered the records. Within weeks the record was selling in the thousands; within the year, record companies were recording southern music extensively. These "race" and "hillbilly" records were generally produced rather cavalierly, and without much attention paid to sound quality, in quickly outfitted hotel rooms. Frank Walker, who recorded Riley Puckett and the Skillet Lickers Band, recalled these sessions in an interview with Mike Seeger.

> We recorded in a little hotel in Atlanta, and we used to put the singers up and pay a dollar a day for their food and a place to sleep in another little old hotel. . . . You would have to go from one room to another and keep your pen working and decide we won't use this and pick out the different songs that they knew. . . . So, when you picked out the three or four that were best in a man's so-called repertoire you were through with that man as an artist. . . . It was a culling job, taking the best that they had. You might come out with two selections or you might come out with six or eight, but you did it at that time. You said goodbye.

Walker cowrote, with Dan Hornsby of WSB, the skits such as *Corn Licker Still in Georgia* that proved so astonishingly successful for the Skillet Lickers, and Riley Puckett seems to have been a favorite of his, the rare "hillbilly" unbound by his repertoire and capable in fact of performing any music. Walker concentrated on the country artists but rather incidentally provided also a fine documentation of bluesmen (Peg Leg Howell, Barbecue Bob, Blind Willie McTell) working in the rich Atlanta tradition.

The early hillbilly entertainers, then, were transition figures, folk performers who very gradually began adapting their traditional styles and repertoire to the expectations or demands of record companies. But throughout the twenties and much of the thirties the music remained largely a regional phenomenon and, free of commercial control, a venerable tradition of singing and string-band music that radio and the phonograph were content simply to exploit and popularize.

In this regard, Alton Delmore's impressionistic account of his first encounter with these new professionals is a fine one. In his autobiography, *Truth Is Stranger than Publicity,* Delmore wrote,

> While we were waiting to get in to see the man, we were gawking at the recording stars. They were an interesting sight. Something we had not expected to see. They wore the best of clothes and had diamond rings on their fingers and presented an atmosphere that simply bewildered all four of us boys. . . . These people had something and were not the kind of folks they sounded like on the records we had at home. There was Clayton McMichen and he really was a dandy. All tailored up in the finest clothes, and they fit him perfectly. We had listened to his records and he sounded like a true mountaineer. And Riley Puckett, who was blind. But he dressed immaculately and clean as a pin. He couldn't see but his knack for good-looking clothes must have been instinctive.

The Delmore Brothers themselves became important transition figures in the second generation of country stars who carefully crafted and polished their work for the new medium of radio. In contrast to most string bands of the time, they featured guitar leads; they also incorporated huge portions of southern black blues, and in songs like "Freight Train Boogie" reached toward country rock.

The hillbilly string bands so popular on radio during this period were direct descendants of folk entertainers who for many decades before the 1920's routinely played at house parties, barn dances, church socials and political gatherings. Uncle Dave Macon, who, according to Charles Wolfe, more than anyone else "took the nineteenth-century folk music and turned it into twentieth-century country music," was forty-eight years old and had been entertaining at picnics and social occasions for most of them before he demanded fifteen dollars to play at a party given by a farmer he thought somewhat arrogant. He received it, and became a professional rather quickly thereafter.

Riley Puckett and Gid Tanner had been fixtures at the annual fiddling contest since they first teamed up in 1916 and brought the house down with their version of "It's a Long Way to Tipperary"; with their recordings of March 7 and 8, 1924, just after Fiddlin' John Carson's records became a hit, Puckett and Tanner may have been the first recorded string band. They were also regulars on WSB, and by 1926 joined other WSB performers Clayton McMichen and Fate Norris to begin recording as Gid Tanner and His Skillet Lickers. That first year their material consisted wholly of traditional pieces like "Turkey in the Straw," "Alabama Jubilee" and "Bully of the Town." The last, backed with "Pass Around the Bottle and We'll All Take a Drink," sold an amazing two hundred thousand copies that year.

Not surprisingly, the huge success of the Skillet Lickers was followed by a scramble to record other old-time bands. Few of these recordings came to much, the bands generally exhausting their repertoire rather quickly and failing to develop any following, but some that did become popular on record remain important today. The Carolina Tar Heels featured harmonica instead of fiddle lead (a common occurrence in early bands) and the singing of Clarence Ashley, later a mainstay of the sixties' folk revival. The East Texas Serenaders recorded for Columbia from 1927 to 1931 with fiddle, guitar, banjo and cello, including "rag" material in their repertoire and prefiguring the shift from traditional fiddle-band styles to western swing styles. Charlie Poole and His North Carolina Ramblers recorded their first song for Columbia, "Don't Let Your Deal Go Down," in 1925. Poole's technique was a direct precursor to modern bluegrass banjo, and his vocals were far more polished than those of his string-band predecessors, foreshadowing the singing stars soon to dominate country music.

Again, it is important to emphasize that all these bands developed from pre-guitar banjo and fiddle duos, and in all of them the fiddle was emphatically featured: this was the guitar's first foothold in country music, but little more than that.

In 1925—the year of Lonnie Johnson's first recordings and the year Eddie Lang accompanied Bix on the classic "Singin' the Blues"—way down in Georgia, Riley Puckett's career was well underway. He was a guitarist, an unusual guitarist who sometimes substituted complex bass runs for straight rhythm and so started the guitar on its way to becoming a lead instrument in country music. He lent that guitar to the vastly influential, fiddle-led Skillet Lickers Band. And on his own, he became country music's first singing star.

Born May 7, 1894, in Alpharetta, Georgia, a small town about fifteen miles northwest of Atlanta, Riley Puckett was blinded at the age of three months when an eye infection was mistakenly treated with lead-acetate solution. In 1901, aged seven, he entered the Georgia Academy for the Blind in Macon, where he learned Braille and, apparently, some rudiments of music at the piano. (This was incidentally the same school Willie McTell attended in later years.) Puckett left the school after five years, moving with his parents to Atlanta.

The years up until 1922 are, like much of Puckett's life, pretty much a blank to researchers. His father died early on, leaving Riley and his brother James, Jr., to be brought up by their mother, Octavia. In his teens, about 1912 or 1913, Riley taught himself five-string banjo, almost certainly with the idea of supporting himself as an entertainer; for the blind, then, there were few other choices. Eventually, as the guitar gained some favor in string bands, he picked that up as well, and by the end of the decade was playing on street corners and working occasional dances and parties. (Guitarist Ray Brown recalls as a child leading both Puckett and bluesman Blind Boy Fuller through the streets of Atlanta.) Though he did some carpentry and reportedly knew telegraphy, Puckett's chief income was always from music, and by about 1920 his high, clear tenor voice was gaining recognition.

"Puckett had a strong, clear, pleasant voice," Norm Cohen writes in his study, *Riley Puckett: "King of the Hillbillies."* "He enunciated clearly and was easily understood. . . . He did not have a highly decorated style, as did his fellow Georgians, John Carson or, to a lesser degree, Gid Tanner. Nor did he have the almost conversational presentation that Clarence Ashley or Doc Walsh could slip into. . . . His voice was, though less mellow and more piercing, practically that of a pop singer of the day. And in that regard, it fitted his repertoire."

On September 28, 1922, Puckett joined Clayton McMichen's Hometown Band as a guest on its regular WSB broadcast. WSB's powerful transmitters carried its shows throughout the United States, and the station's audience, particularly in the South and Midwest, was large. The Atlanta *Journal* noted the following day, "Already favorites at WSB, the Hometown outfit scored a knockout by introducing Mr. Puckett as one of their stars Thursday night." Puckett was invited back repeatedly, both to guest with the McMichen band and to perform as a soloist. Norm Cohen observes that musicians such as those in the Hometown Band were patently attempting to make their reputations with contemporary music of the day as much as with the older traditional material, a critical point in regard to Puckett's own career.

The following year, Puckett joined McMichen alumni Ted Hawkins (an early country mandolinist) and Lowe Stokes (fiddler) to form the Hometown Boys and began regularly playing social affairs around Atlanta. They became quite popular, in mid-June beginning regular broadcasts over WSB. Announcing their Saturday night broadcasts, the *Journal* noted Puckett's "fine tenor voice" and remarked that the band now included "the best of the new numbers along with the ancient favorites." A subsequent review of the premier program commented that Riley's "peculiar method of handling his guitar perhaps has something to do with the unusually fine harmony he gets from it."

Puckett quickly became a local favorite, shuttling from one appearance to another, sometimes with the band and sometimes as a solo act. Charles Wolfe notes that of three songs singled out by the *Journal* at this time as his most popular ("Johnson's Old Gray Mule," "My Buddy" and "You've Got to See Mama"), one was a traditional piece, one a sentimental song from the 1890's, the other a twenties' jazz tune—bespeaking the rather incongruous repertoire he would continue throughout his career.

Puckett was also yodeling, something he may have picked up from the founder of the Georgia Old-Time Fiddlers' Association, "Professor" Alec Smart, "the Georgia mountaineer yodeler." The two musicians sang a number of duets over WSB, at least two of which Puckett later recorded solo. "Strawberries," a specialty number of Smart's, Puckett covered at his first session in 1924. "Sleep, Baby, Sleep" was cut the following September. It was intended to follow up on Riley's "Rock All Our Babies to Sleep," probably the first country song to feature yodeling, from the earlier session. Three years later "Sleep, Baby, Sleep" was the song Ralph Peer culled from Jimmie Rodgers's repertoire for his debut record.

In his admirable biography, *Jimmie Rodgers*, Nolan Porter-field writes,

> It has been thought that Rodgers's version was only a pale imitation of Riley Puckett's 1924 recording, but in fact the two performances have little in common except the title and a similar tune. Jimmie was obviously familiar with Puckett's recording, but his lyrics are derived from other sources and modified to highlight his fluid, melodic yodel. Puckett's raw, often hollow falsetto suffers by comparison, and his rendition lacks the driving clarity of Rodgers's, although these flaws may be attributed in part to the acoustical process by which the earlier record was made.

Yodeling had become popular on the British stage in the early nineteenth century and from there had passed into American minstrelry, Tom Christian being the first min-strel to introduce it. Daniel Decatur Emmett, author of "Dixie," wrote many classic yodeling songs. George P. Watson became the first yodeler to record, cutting cylin-ders for the Edison Company in 1897, among them both English and German versions of "Sleep, Baby, Sleep." (The song itself had been a hit for S. A. Emery as far back as 1869.) Yodeling records were very popular for at least the first two decades of the twentieth century. Nick Tosches notes that a 1917 Columbia catalogue includes a section of them, with many selections by George Watson, and that a 1920 Victor catalogue lists seventeen yodel songs. Jimmie Rodgers of course became famous for his "blue yodels," and the tradition extended into the fifties with "Lovesick Blues," Hank Williams's debut song at the Grand Ole Opry in 1949, itself a cover of maverick Emmett Miller's 1925 recording. (A later version from Miller included the Dorsey brothers and Eddie Lang as accompanists.)

In 1924, close on the wake of Fiddlin' John Carson's successful records with Okeh, Columbia joined other companies in the rush to record hillbilly artists. It was only natural that Frank Walker would approach Gid Tanner, a long-time rival of Carson's at the fiddle contests, and in February test pressings were made in Atlanta with Tanner and his contest associate, Riley Puckett. The following month the duo traveled to New York, cutting seventeen tunes for Columbia, fourteen of which were released between May 1924 and June 1925. Their first session yielded a cover of Carson's "Little Old Log Cabin in the Lane" (the historic first country recording), vocal versions of "Casey Jones" and "Steamboat Bill," and spirited traditional pieces like "Johnson's Old Gray Mule" and "Old Joe Clark." The second session the following day saw Puckett's version of Smart's "Strawberries," more fiddle tunes such as "Buckin' Mule," "Black-Eyed Susie" and "Give the Fiddler a Dram," and the first yodeling song in country music, "Rock All Our Babies to Sleep." (As with "Sleep, Baby, Sleep," Jimmie Rodgers recorded his own version of this song in 1932, with fiddler Clayton McMichen, who had just left the Skillet Lickers, as a sideman.) Of the seventeen sides, two were Tanner solos, six were solos by Puckett, the others duets. "All but one of Puckett's solos," Norm Cohen notes, "were pop songs from the 1890–1920 period. Tanner's selections, and the duets, were of a much older vintage."

The Tanner-Puckett sides became Columbia's first country records and almost certainly the first string-band records as well. Released in the label's regular popular series alongside recordings by Ted Lewis and Paul Whiteman, they were sufficiently successful that Columbia invited Tanner and Puckett back for another session that September. By the end of the year Columbia had instituted its 15000-D hillbilly series, and the majority of cuts from the second sessions would issue thereon.

For these sessions, held September 10 through 12, Riley

brought his banjo along and recorded with it for the only time in his career. He and Tanner cut several traditional fiddle-banjo duets such as "Cripple Creek," "Sourwood Mountain," "Cumberland Gap" and "Bile Dem Cabbage Down," Riley also accompanying himself on banjo for a rendition of "O! Susannah." He switched to guitar to cover a couple more Carson tunes, "You'll Never Miss Your Mother Till She's Gone" and "When You and I Were Young, Maggie," also singing "Jesse James" and "Swanee River"; then he and Gid rounded out the sessions with "Blue Ridge Mountain Blues," "Railroad Bill," "John Henry" and "Arkansas Traveller."

Altogether thirty-six sides were cut, twenty-six of them, in their mixture of traditional and popular material characteristic of Puckett's general repertoire and career, released. Puckett in fact dominated the session: ten tunes were by him alone, while another ten featured him with Tanner's uncredited fiddle accompaniment. These were the sessions that produced, on the first day, "Sleep, Baby, Sleep," and it is interesting to note that Columbia advertised these records nationally, apparently believing their appeal transcended regional popularity.

With the inception of a hillbilly series, Columbia felt it more practical to go to the singers than to bring them to New York, and with Frank Walker in charge, began visiting Atlanta twice yearly for field recordings. The first of these trips was in September 1925. Of forty-six sides recorded then, twenty-four were hillbilly—and fourteen of those were by Riley Puckett. Charles Wolfe remarks that pressing orders for Riley Puckett records at this time were second only to those of superstar city vocalist Vernon Dahlhart.

Also in 1925 Puckett was involved in an automobile accident that hospitalized mandolinist Ted Hawkins for six months and necessitated a homebound convalescence for Riley. His nurse during this time became his wife on May

18, 1925, and in June he and Blanche traveled to New York at Columbia's expense, a combined honeymoon and business trip. (Of the twenty selections recorded June 15 through 17, however, only seven were released.) In November 1930, a daughter was born to the couple. Blanche Bailey (remarried and still residing in Atlanta) denies persistent rumors that she and Puckett quarreled incessantly and that she later left him.

Gid Tanner was a Dacula, Georgia, chicken farmer as famous for his clowning as for his fine old-time fiddling. He was a natural entertainer and a fixture at fiddle conventions for more than thirty years, winning his last contest in 1955 at the age of sixty-nine.

Clayton McMichen came to Atlanta as an automobile mechanic in 1921, but soon found music more profitable. While he played the old-time tunes, his personal taste ran to jazz-tinged popular music. He had recorded for Ralph Peer in 1925 without great success. In 1926 he was working with banjoist Fate Norris.

Riley Puckett was a popular singer throughout the South, but had failed to gain any significant national following.

It was Frank Walker who brought these musicians together and, despite profound basic differences in taste and orientation, continual squabbling and interpersonal problems, kept them together for five years. Walker felt that a combination of Puckett's singing, Tanner's comedy and traditional fiddling and McMichen's virtuosity would be a sure thing—and he was right. The Skillet Lickers took off like a skyrocket. Essentially a pickup group assembled for recording purposes, they soon made string-band music the dominant form of country recordings.

From 1926 until 1931, the Skillet Lickers cut over one hundred thirty sides for Columbia, this single band and its offshoots accounting for a full 20 percent of all records issued on Columbia's old-time series. The first sessions included only Tanner, Puckett, McMichen and Norris, but before long McMichen brought fiddlers Lowe Stokes and Bert Layne into the group and soon the Skillet Lickers were joined on sessions by a bewildering array of fiddlers, banjoists and other musicians: Gid's brother Arthur, fiddler Bill Helms, Ted Hawkins, guitarists Mike Whitten, Hoke Rice and Gus Adams, and many others. They recorded in every permutation as the Skillet Lickers, and a number of spin-off bands (McMichen's Melody Men, Fate Norris's Playboys, Lowe Stokes's North Georgians) were also recorded. The first records were released as from Gid Tanner and His Skillet Lickers with Riley Puckett, then upon McMichen's demand for equal billing, Gid Tanner and His Skillet Lickers with Riley Puckett and Clayton McMichen.

Probably 20 percent of the sides were devoted to comedy skits such as the ongoing (eventually fourteen-part) *Corn Licker Still in Georgia,* which presented a group of moonshiners given to playing music between stints at sugaring the still, feuding with the sheriff and so on. These skits were largely the work of Frank Walker and Dan Hornsby, though band members helped out with ideas. Walker also encouraged the use of two and sometimes three unison fiddles on the old breakdowns, a distinctive Skillet Licker sound that presaged western swing's multiple-fiddle stylings.

Despite their tremendous success on record, the Skillet Lickers made most of their money from tours and personal appearances, and from 1926 to 1930 various bands toured the South under the Skillet Licker name, sometimes with Riley, Gid and Mac, sometimes with only one or two of them. Riley Puckett seems to have received equal billing with the band in every case and to have had a substantial part of the program to himself. Often these tours would take the form of fiddling contests; Bill Helms has described them.

These conventions would last usually three days in one place, and the last night was usually contest night—you fiddled off and they had prizes for guitar players and banjo players. Top man got the prize. . . . We drew huge crowds; around in those days people in this part of the country didn't have anything to go to. Oh, they had these silent movie theaters, but a lot of the old-timers didn't care nothing about that; they was crazy about hillbilly fiddling and banjo picking, and, man you'd fill every place you went to up. Once me and Gid and Riley went out through north Georgia and Gid'd booked the route for us. Some towns, they'd just have a store, post office and blacksmith shop—that was your city. But we never played a place up there that we didn't get the people inside. Adults was a quarter, children fifteen cents. We'd pick up as high as three or four hundred dollars in one place. . . . They'd be coming to hear us, down out of those mountains, on mules and horses, wagons. Used lanterns in those days, didn't have any electric light at all. Old kerosene lanterns: you could see 'em like little bugs at night coming way back 'cross those mountains there, coming down there toting that lantern along, have it in the wagon with them, so they could see which way they were going. I'd never seen nothing like that before.

By 1930 the band's traditional material shared time with increasing quantities of popular numbers, and personal rifts were growing ever wider. The Skillet Lickers were preparing to disband in fact when the Depression hit, crippling the recording industry for some time. Gid Tanner went back to chicken farming. Clayton McMichen went on to form the first of several groups with the "Georgia Wildcats" name and eventually to work with Jimmie Rodgers. Riley Puckett continued to work with one or the other of them—with Gid and Bill Helms on radio in Columbus and Cleveland, with McMichen at fiddlers' conventions and other stations—and to record as well, though with far less frequency. While with the Skillet Lickers, Puckett had recorded as many solo and duet sides as band sides, everything from guitar solos ("Fuzzy Rag" and "The Darkie's Wail") to his usual "heart songs" and numerous duets with McMichen, Hugh Cross and others. It was with Cross, a Tennessee singer who was one of the first to record "Wabash Cannonball" and anticipated in his repertoire the future turn of country music away from old ballads to love songs, that Puckett recorded "Red River Valley," one of his biggest hits. Frank Walker claims to have brought the song to him, one he remembered from his childhood in upstate New York as "Bright Mohawk Valley," democratizing the location for broader appeal.

McMichen would always give credit to Riley Puckett's singing and guitar playing as the source of the Skillet Lickers' success, even though in later years, frustrated by his inability to break out of the old-time fiddler's mold, he would claim, "The band stunk." Gordon Tanner, who still plays the old songs down in Dacula, believes that his father's clowning and jokes were what carried the band, and he may be right.

Charles Wolfe says,

> They exhibited a marvelous sense of comedy, both in vocals and in skits; they preserved numerous rather unique old tunes; and they exemplified a spirit that infected a whole music and our image of it. And much of this was Gid's contribution. He was perhaps the only one of the main band members whose personality fit the persona created collectively on the records. In recent years, researchers were able to get to three of the Skillet Lickers—Stokes, McMichen and Tanner—before it was too late. The interviews are oddly characteristic: Stokes wanted to talk about fiddling; Mac wanted to talk about himself; and Gid wanted to talk about his dogs.

It seems, then, that Gid was the central figure of the Skillet Lickers Band in ways obscured by changing musical fashion and by Puckett's and McMichen's subsequent popularity.

Joe Miller began playing guitar in 1930 after hearing Riley Puckett on record, trying to sound just like him, and later worked with Tanner and Puckett when they came home during the Depression. Miller says,

> Clayton McMichen once said that Riley's picking and singing was what made the Skillet Lickers' recordings go over with the public. I fully agree. I've seen Gid and Riley rival each other in shows, each trying to capture the limelight, and they really did some fantastic performances for the stardom of the show. These two men loved each other as much as any two I ever saw. This, with their deep respect for each other, is what held them together for so long, even after the band disbanded. Gid Tanner was one of the finest men I ever knew, strictly sober and honest, and the best comedian I ever knew. And Riley was the best guitarist for band work, as well as singing, I ever knew.

The Skillet Lickers left a legacy of over one hundred thirty records, many of which sold over two hundred thousand copies and one of which, "Down Yonder," remained in print as late as 1950, amassing sales in advance of one million. The band's importance is without parallel, yet it remained, as the editors of *The Illustrated History of Country Music* point out, "an unstable compound of brilliant, creative egos: Gid was too old-timey, McMichen was too pop-oriented and Puckett was too experimental in his guitar runs. They bickered constantly and often toured separately, yet like the latter-day Beatles, they were less impressive as individuals than as a band."

For a period in 1932 Puckett joined McMichen and several others in a revival of the Skillet Lickers over station WCKY in Covington, Kentucky, just across the river from Cincinnati. McMichen left with his new Georgia Wildcats band for Louisville radio station WHAS the following year, however, and Puckett returned to Atlanta.

Victor's new Bluebird label began recording the top acts from Columbia's defunct country series in about 1934, and Tanner was asked to revive the Skillet Lickers for them. Riley, Gid, Gid's son Gordon and mandolinist Ted Hawkins traveled to San Antonio for lengthy sessions that produced some of the band's most popular recordings as well as some of Puckett's finest solo work, among them his versions of "Chain Gang Blues" and "Ragged But Right" and a new version of "My Carolina Home" with Gid and Gordon Tanner playing twin fiddles. At age seventeen, Gordon had been playing just over three years.

"I thought I was mainly going out there to help with the driving, but I ended up leading the band," he says today. "It was my daddy, Riley, myself and Ted Hawkins. We didn't do any rehearsing; they just called out the numbers and we played them."

Today, though he still plays the traditional songs, Gordon Tanner's style perhaps more closely resembles McMichen's jazz-tinged, swing-influenced fiddling than his father's.

"Gordon Tanner did most of the fiddling on the session," Charles Wolfe notes, "and Ted Hawkins often took the lead with his mandolin. The result was a loose, pleasant string-band ensemble sound, quite different from the sound of the Columbia band. The sessions were produced by Victor's southern regional manager, Elmer Eades, an easygoing man who later recalled the session as a wild, freewheeling affair." Each of the forty-eight sides cut at the session was released, among them probably the Skillet Lickers best-selling titles: "Down Yonder," "Back Up and Push," "Soldier's Joy" and "Flop-Eared Mule."

And so the Skillet Lickers departed the country music scene as they entered it: full of energy, raucous, eccentric, exceptional.

* * *

Two volumes of Skillet Lickers recordings are currently available on County Records (County 506 and 526), as is a fine solo Puckett album, *Waitin' for the Evening Mail* (County 411).

Rounder Records carries two others, *Gid Tanner and His Skillet Lickers* (Rounder 1005) and *Gid Tanner and His Skillet Lickers: The Kickapoo Medicine Show* (Rounder 1023).

Another album devoted to solo work is *Riley Puckett* on GHP LP 902, and Skillet Lickers albums now out of print have appeared on the Voyager label and from the Folk Song Society of Minnesota.

Further collections, one hopes, will be forthcoming.

Clayton McMichen's lifelong frustration and discontent are manifest in Charles Wolfe's statement that "when Mac was playing on tour with Jimmie Rodgers in 1929, helping Rodgers create songs like 'Peach Pickin' Time in Georgia,' he was most widely known as a key member of the Skillet Lickers, a great old-time string band whose sound was at least a generation earlier than the kind of semi-pop country that Rodgers was trying to develop."

For almost a quarter century McMichen dominated southern fiddling, winning at least eighteen national fiddling crowns and playing a major role not only in the development of modern fiddle styles, but in the commercialization of country music itself. He was a restless, serious musician, forever trying new combinations, new musical styles; even playing a traditional number like "Fisher's Hornpipe" he might take it through four or five keys and spend a chorus or so improvising on the melody.

Bill Monroe recalls that Mac was the best of the old fiddlers and says, "If you check the way I would play a fiddle number like 'Fire on the Mountain' and check the way Clayton plays it, you'll find it note for note the same way," implying a powerful influence on bluegrass styles. There are strong echoes of McMichen, too, in the western swing of Bob Wills and Milton Brown, and Mac was somewhat bitter in later years at the popularity of these musicians. He was bitter about many things, in fact. He felt that people repeatedly forced him into their preconceived notions of an old-time fiddler, and that his serious music was ignored, never given its due. His Georgia Wildcats band, an early version of which recorded for the first time at the last Skillet Lickers session, produced some fine records, hosted many excellent musicians (Merle Travis among them) and continually worked to introduce contemporary pop, jazz and swing sounds into country music. This met with limited success, but when the idea's time came not too long thereafter, Mac and his bands had laid important foundations.

McMichen retired in 1955, but was coaxed back into playing during the early-sixties' folk revival. He was frequently cross with those who spoke only of his work with the Skillet Lickers and knew of or cared nothing at all for his more progressive music. But he toured the folk and later bluegrass festivals, and as late as 1968 won the Kentucky state fiddling championship. He died in 1970.

"McMichen," Charles Wolfe summarizes, "was a victim of one of country music's first and most enduring stereotypes: the wise-cracking hillbilly fiddler. Unlike Bob Wills or Roy Acuff, he was never really able to transcend this, and most of his repeated attempts to do so were not commercially successful."

Restless, relentlessly eclectic in a decidedly non-eclectic period and swimming upstream of the Depression, Clayton McMichen never found the acceptance and success he deserved; and he was continually puzzled at this. One suspects that with time, however, he will be universally acknowledged as a major influence in the history of country music.

The final Skillet Lickers session prompted a three-year association between Puckett and Bluebird, and in July 1934, four months after the San Antonio sessions, Puckett cut his first records for the label. Several of them also featured vocalist Red Jones, while others included a fiddler (possibly Bert Layne) and at least one had Ted Hawkins on mandolin. The tunes were mostly popular or sentimental songs: "I Only Want a Buddy Not a Sweetheart," "The Isle of Capri," "Caroline Sunshine Girl," "When I Grow Too Old to Dream" and a version of "St. Louis Blues" titled "Puckett Blues." In three sessions Riley recorded twenty-six sides for Bluebird, but was unaccountably dropped after the February 14, 1936, session.

Puckett at this time was traveling with "Daddy" John Love, an original member of Mainer's Mountaineers now pursuing a solo career. He also worked with Bert Layne and His Fiddling Mountaineers, continuing radio work at WSAZ in Huntington, West Virginia, and in Memphis and Cincinnati. In the late thirties and early forties he organized his own tent show and toured widely throughout the South and into the oilfields of Texas and Oklahoma.

In September 1937 Puckett recorded twelve sides for Decca, now McMichen's label, in its New York studios. Red Jones joined him on several of these, and the material— "Poor Boy," "Moonlight on the Colorado," "The Longest Train," "Gulf Coast Blues," "The Cat Came Back"—was a mixture.

By contrast, his final Bluebird sessions (1939–41) emphasized current pop material such as "Oh, Johnnie, Oh," "Little Sir Echo," "Walking My Baby Back Home" and Bing Crosby's "South of the Border," though the sessions also included traditional songs. Frank Walker, recently hired to oversee Bluebird's field sessions, was almost certainly responsible for Puckett's return to the label and his influence may account also for the commercial emphasis. Ted Hawkins's mandolin was on all cuts.

Riley Puckett would not record again after the October

1941 session. He went back to Atlanta to renew his friendship and partnership with Gid Tanner.

"In 1940," Joe Miller recalls, "Gid Tanner, who had known me all my life, came to me and asked me to work with him and Riley on his show. I had seen Riley many times, and had visited with him in his home and played with him there, and he liked the style that I played, so we didn't need any practice, we just played like we had always been together."

They played local jobs, rarely traveling more than a hundred miles from home, and worked on radio in and around Atlanta. Miller remembers that Puckett was playing a National steel-body guitar at this time, rather than the Martin he's generally pictured with and used for recordings.

By 1946 Riley was living in East Point near Atlanta and playing with The Stone Mountain Boys over Atlanta station WACA. In July he developed blood poisoning from a boil on his neck that had become infected. He died at Gray Hospital on July 13 at age fifty-two and was buried four days later at Enon Baptist Church in College Park.

Eddy Arnold was the most popular country singer that year, and Hank Williams signed his first recording contract. Riley Puckett had ridden his guitar into a new world and finally left it.

It is difficult to assess Riley Puckett's guitar style at this remove. Guitarists accompanying fiddlers today are expected to play unobtrusive rhythm, something Puckett rarely felt obliged to do, and guitarists on their own of course are playing far wilder things than he imagined. Some of the fiddlers of his own time complained of the difficulty they had working with him, among them Lowe Stokes and Clayton McMichen, whose regard for Puckett as an artist nevertheless remained strong through the years.

For his solo recordings Puckett relied on a straightforward bass-and-strum accompaniment and seldom played single notes. Even in the early Skillet Lickers recordings he played single, forceful bass notes in time with Fate Norris's banjo rhythms. But as time went on, his work behind the band developed toward elaborate runs and oddly syncopated figures, dominating the band's sound in many respects by about 1929. On a 1928 recording of "The Farmer's Daughter," at one point McMichen urges Puckett to "put in that mean run." Even today this style is startling, attention-getting—which may explain it. This may ultimately have been Puckett's way of holding his own in that "unstable, creative" synthesis called the Skillet Lickers. Charles Wolfe's observation that Puckett even as a neophyte rarely played for dances, in which guitar was relegated to keeping time, and thus felt free to experiment with rhythm and accent, also merits consideration.

Norm Cohen describes Puckett's Skillet Licker style excellently: "His backup consisted essentially of single-note bass runs that were neither chordally nor melodically structured. When accompanying fiddle tunes he frequently made use of double- or quadruple-time runs. Only occasionally did he brush the treble strings."

Most contemporaries recall Puckett playing a guitar "strung hard" (with high bridge and action) and using only his fingers. "He used fitted steel picks on his fingers," Gordon Tanner told me, "but nothing on his thumb. He did all those runs with his forefinger; the thumb was used to locate the exact string." Gordon also remembers Puckett using a "high bass"—tuning the sixth string up from E to G to free the finger that would ordinarily have to fret it.

Gordon recalls further that Puckett always thought of himself as a professional and didn't always enjoy playing under casual circumstances. He told Joel Cordle for an article in *Bluegrass Unlimited,*

> If the neighborhood knew that Riley Puckett was at Gid
> Tanner's house they would just come in after supper. Well,
> don't count on Riley playing that night. He played if he took

the notion. If he didn't, he wouldn't take that guitar out. So my daddy, if people wanted to hear a little music, would have to scratch off a few tunes himself. Riley was moody; he was a businessman when it came to music. If they were to play at a show somewhere, that audience would never see him until he got on stage.

Gordon's comments are among the few we have that suggest a real personality, a face, for Riley Puckett. He seems to have been a loner, and more than one contemporary remembers him as moody and poor-tempered. (Lowe Stokes called him "the crabbiest guy you ever saw.") Some suggest that he led a rough and rowdy life, others that he was a family man who always stayed behind when the rest went out for a night on the town.

"My impression of Riley," Joe Miller writes, "was that he was a lonely man, and somewhat moody, but this I have experienced with other musicians. He expressed his feelings in his singing. I have worked with him when the audience was restless, but when Riley took his chair to play, everything would get still and quiet. When he stroked that guitar and started his song, children stopped crying and people were still all over the building. . . . He worked well with most musicians, and was jolly a lot of times, and then on the other hand he would be mostly silent."

The sketch that emerges, then, is not a surprising one, but the familiar likeness of an introspective, creative artist whose work absorbs and largely defines him. There was a considerable pride to the man; his sense of professionalism was a reflection of that pride and in some ways doubtless a shield as well. His occasional arrogance, moodiness and sudden joviality suggest that he may have felt set apart from others by more than lack of sight.

By the time Riley Puckett died in 1946 the guitar had come into its own as a lead instrument in country music. Maybelle Carter's "church lick" and Jimmie Rodgers's bluesy backup guitar led the way, urged on by Bill Boyd's

"Under the Double Eagle" (second in all-time popularity only to "Wildwood Flower") and a little later, Joe Maphis's amazing flat-picked fiddle tunes. Elements of Puckett's style seem to have been appropriated by Charlie Monroe and gone directly from there into bluegrass guitar.

Sam McGee played electric guitar very early on the Opry stage: "I got by with it about two Saturday nights; about the third one [Judge Hay] came in and patted me on the shoulder, 'Now, you wouldn't play that on the Grand Ole Opry. You know we're going to hold it down to earth.' " Even before Charlie Christian gained fame with Benny Goodman's Band, Les Paul's work with Fred Waring on network radio helped introduce the electric guitar; western swing players like Eldon Shamblin were playing their own Eddie Lang-derived jazz style probably as early as Christian. And 1946 seems to have been the year bluesman Lonnie Johnson switched to electric guitar.

Ernest Tubb brought the electric guitar to the Opry to stay when he joined in 1943, guitarist Jimmie Short playing a Martin acoustic with a DeArmond pickup. But Merle Travis was certainly among the first country players to adopt the amplified instrument, as he details in a 1980 letter to *Guitar Player* magazine:

> I was around when the electric guitar sneaked into country music. I was hooked the first time I heard George Barnes play "My Blue Heaven" on a show from Chicago called *Plantation Party*. I was in Cincinnati at the time broadcasting from radio station WLW, and I was playing a Gibson L-10 acoustic. Shortly after hearing George, I cropped up at the studio with a brand new Gibson amp and a DeArmond pickup. The welcoming words were, "Get rid of that damn thing."

Travis later got a Rickenbacker steel guitar from a friend named Bud Dooley, took the pickup off that and mounted it on his L-10. It was a great pickup, he says; he could definitely be heard. Eventually he had Gibson build his special Super 400 with two pickups, the guitar which has become a trademark for him. "But this," he says, "was after I had a brainstorm and drew a picture of a thin, solidbody guitar with all the tuning keys on one side. Paul Bigsby, my old friend whom I met when he was announcing at motorcycle races, built the strange-looking instrument." Bigsby, Les Paul and Leo Fender were all experimenting with the concept of a solidbody guitar about the same time. Paul had borrowed the Epiphone facilities in 1941 to create "The Log," a converted hollowbody. The Bigsby guitar was finished in 1947 and Fender began marketing his "Broadcaster" (the Telecaster's original name) the following year.

Also in the mid-forties—coals that would smolder and burst into bright flame twenty years later as the folk revival, retrieving and in many ways continuing the tradition of early country musicians like Riley Puckett—a group called the Weavers began recording folk songs and taking them before audiences all over the country.

Lonnie Johnson (COURTESY OF THE FRANK DRIGGS COLLECTION)

Eddie Lang
(COURTESY OF THE
FRANK DRIGGS
COLLECTION)

Roy Smeck (COURTESY OF ROY SMECK)

*Charlie Christian,
1940*
(COURTESY OF THE
FRANK DRIGGS
COLLECTION)

From left: Bill Helms, Riley Puckett, and Gid Tanner
(COURTESY OF THE JOHN EDWARDS MEMORIAL FOUNDATION)

Riley Puckett
(COURTESY OF
THE JOHN EDWARDS
MEMORIAL FOUNDATION)

T-Bone Walker (COURTESY OF THE FRANK DRIGGS COLLECTION)

George Barnes
(COURTESY OF
CONCORD JAZZ)

Hank Garland
(COURTESY OF THE
COUNTRY MUSIC FOUNDATION
LIBRARY AND MEDIA CENTER,
NASHVILLE, TENNESSEE)

Wes Montgomery (PHOTOGRAPH BY DUNCAN SCHIEDT.
COURTESY OF THE FRANK DRIGGS COLLECTION)

Michael Bloomfield
(PHOTOGRAPH BY
NORMAN DAYRON)

Ralph Towner (COURTESY OF ECM RECORDS)

Ry Cooder (COURTESY OF WARNER BROS. RECORDS, INC.)

Lenny Breau (PHOTOGRAPH BY DAVE BONNER. COURTESY OF ADELPHI RECORDS).

DADDY OF THE BLUES:

T-Bone Walker

DALLAS'S BLACK ENTERTAINMENT DISTRICTS were hotbeds of talent in the 1920's. Through them streamed processions of pianists, singers, bluesmen, string or brass trios, jug bands and early jazzmen, attesting to the wide variety of traditional and evolving styles then current in the region.

Coley Jones's Dallas String Band carried on one tradition, and its popularity rivaled the Mississippi Sheiks. Leadbelly, in and out of prison, was boss of the blues; every day Blind Lemon Jefferson started out at the Central tracks on Elm and walked uptown, playing and singing as he went, until he'd collected enough money in his cup to spend the rest of the day drinking. Boogie-woogie piano, often called "fast Texas piano," had originated in the area, and players such as Voddie White, Frank Ridge and Alex Moore flourished in bars and brothels. Young players of every sort came to Dallas to perfect their craft, and the territory jazz bands (Alphonso Trent, the Blue Devils, the Clouds of Joy) were all regular visitors.

Far-reaching influences were at work on a strong native blues tradition. Jazz had developed as musicians transferred vocal blues to wind instruments they found cheaply and in ready supply in pawnshops, relics of Civil War military bands; territory bands like Trent's and the Blue Devils often did little more than play straight blues against orchestrated riffs. Similarly, rural blues singers drifted to the city and began adapting their music to the new environment, pursuing a course roughly parallel to jazz.

In many ways Blind Lemon Jefferson typifies the rural bluesman. His blues were rough, idiosyncratic and personal, his guitar playing unschooled, his character coarse and unbridled. He scrabbled hard to make a bare living, playing not in clubs but on the streets and at all-night "country parties" outside town.

The urban bluesman in turn is well represented by a man who had much the same summary impact on blues as did Charlie Christian on jazz. He had followed Blind Lemon around as a child, and Jefferson had been a frequent visitor to his parents' home. He was the first bluesman to take up the electric guitar and the first to work with big bands. "I believe it all comes originally from T-Bone Walker," Freddie King told *Melody Maker,* himself one of the guitarists (Gatemouth Brown and Albert Collins are others) who carried on the Texas blues-guitar tradition. "B. B. King and I were talking about that not long ago and he thinks so, too."

Both Kings were still kids when T-Bone Walker was playing and recording electric, single-string lines with Les Hite's show band. Walker had carried the lean, biting Texas blues sound out to California with him, capturing faultlessly the inflections and phrasing of the voice in his playing, and thereby revolutionized blues and rhythm and blues. As with Christian in jazz, there was blues guitar before T-Bone and blues guitar after T-Bone, and they are discrete things. Despite early promise and a steady, lifelong career (as distinct from that of, say, Lonnie Johnson), T-Bone never achieved a great deal of commercial success, certainly not on the order of his successor, B. B. King, and was still playing clubs and festivals when he died at age sixty-four.

But he left his mark indelibly, and without him, as Rich Kienzle points out, there'd be no B. B. King, Eric Clapton, Mike Bloomfield, Johnny Winter, Steve Miller or Son Seals. Understandably then, T-Bone Walker's name comes up repeatedly in conversations with guitarists. In naming his ten favorite players, B. B. King told *Guitar Player:*

> T-Bone Walker has a touch that nobody has been able to duplicate. I've tried my best to get that sound, especially in the late forties and early fifties. I came pretty close, but never quite got it. I can still hear T-Bone in my mind today, from that first record I heard, "Stormy Monday," around '43 or '44. He was the first electric guitar player I heard on record. He made me so that I knew I just *had* to go out and get an electric guitar.
>
> T-Bone used to use a lot of horns, too—trumpet, alto, tenor and baritone. They made a beautiful sound, like shouting in the sanctified churches, in just the right places. He had a good rhythm section, too. And to me T-Bone seemed to lay right in between there somewhere. That was the best sound I ever heard.

Steve Miller, later a companion to Mike Bloomfield on the Chicago blues scene and following that an extremely popular rock musician, grew up in Dallas. His father was a pathologist and music enthusiast; Walker was ulcer-ridden and urbane. The two became friendly, and T-Bone often visited in the Miller home.

"I think T-Bone is the guy who really instilled taste into my head," Miller says. "I was listening to his music all the time. My dad would come home from work, and we'd put on T-Bone records while he had a drink before dinner. T-Bone was just a champion of taste. And I found that taste will carry you a lot farther than a lot of licks."

Mike Bloomfield remembered Walker's "Glamor Girl" as the first blues record he ever heard, and included a direct tribute to him on his album history of blues guitar, *If You*

Love These Blues. Texas guitarist Billy Gibbons of ZZ Top named Walker "an all-time favorite."

Fellow blues guitarist Lowell Fulson puts T-Bone and his contributions in good perspective. Fulson told *Guitar Player,*

> He brought the blues guitar back in style. Blues guitar players wasn't much back in those days; if you couldn't blow a horn, why, you was just out. And T-Bone came out with "Bobby Sox Blues" in '46, then guitar players were able to work a little more, get a decent price. I always give him credit, because he's the first man brought the blues guitar— matter of fact, brought the *guitar*—back in style, playing lead.
>
> Back in those times the average guitar player, if he was pretty positive into music, he wanted to be a Charlie Christian. When T-Bone brought the blues guitar out, you ought to have seen the guys going back and studying and playing and really trying to get their licks in, because the man was the only one being talked about.

T-Bone's career, like that of many others, declined with the advent of blues-based rock and, more importantly, the shift of black taste from blues to soul/Motown sounds. "Stormy Monday" remains, however, one of the top blues standards, possibly the most popular of all, thirty-four years after he recorded it, and his guitar playing has deeply influenced, either directly or indirectly, almost anyone who owns an amplifier.

Dignity is a word one hears often from friends and fellow musicians in relation to T-Bone Walker. It applies equally to his music and person. His shows were carefully arranged, and T-Bone's wife remembers that he always worked closely with his musicians, letting them know what he wanted, working things out with them. (For the most part this had to be done instinctively and by example, as T-Bone had no formal training.) He wanted everything just right. This attitude was reflected in his dress and grooming:

neatly cropped hair, small, trimmed mustache, long formal jacket and bow tie. His manner was quiet, gracious; everyone seems to have liked him instantly. He was a professional. And if during the course of performance he played the guitar behind his head, moved his hips in sharp counterpoint, did splits in anticipation of Chuck Berry's duck walk—neither that professionalism nor the man's dignity was in any manner diminished. These were as appropriate to his music as a deep bow or closed eyes to the concert pianist. *Energy*, by the way, is another word common in discussions of T-Bone.

"More of a ballad. That's the kind of blues I like to play," he said in a 1972 interview with Jim and Amy O'Neal of *Living Blues*. "And it's more smoother and more softer, more of an up-to-date thing. It's not a country blues . . . not a way downhome blues."

T-Bone stood, then, at several crossroads, rode point on many advances. But he never strayed far from the generative, common language. "I think they call mine Texas blues," he said. "They call Muddy Waters's Chicago blues or Mississippi blues. . . . I don't see where all these different names come from, 'cause they all sound alike." And though he recorded with jazzmen and often played jazz clubs, T-Bone never thought of himself as anything but a blues guitarist. "It's because I love the blues and I don't think I can play anything in the jazz world but the blues. And your blues is the foundation of your jazz. I think if it wasn't for the blues, there wouldn't be no jazz," he told the O'Neals. In that brief summation he harked back to his origins in the amazingly fertile Southwest, where Blind Lemon Jefferson, Charlie Christian and Buster Smith might have passed each other on the street, and wherefrom jazz began spreading from its hometowns, New Orleans and Chicago, into the wide, waiting world.

* * *

"Of course, the blues come a lot from the church, too," T-Bone told Nat Shapiro and Nat Hentoff for their book *Hear Me Talkin' to Ya.* "The first time I ever heard a boogie-woogie piano was the first time I went to church. That was the Holy Ghost Church in Dallas, Texas. That boogie-woogie was a kind of blues, I guess. The preacher used to preach in a bluesy tone sometimes. You even got the congregation yelling 'Amen' all the time when his preaching would stir them up—his preaching and his bluesy tone."

Walker, like most blacks of his period, was brought up in the church, and though church and the blues for some time had been natural enemies (older bluesmen such as Son House were forced to choose between the church and their demotic music), the two were beginning to intertwine; the eventual result was modern gospel and soul music. Not surprisingly, T-Bone's own playing was often likened to the tone and cadence of preaching. Both blues and black oratory were patterned on the call-and-response of the old field hollers, themselves derived from traditional African song forms. And music was an integral part of every facet of the black church, as indeed it was of African society.

T-Bone Walker grew up with music at home as well. His mother, stepfather and uncles all played guitar and often got together at the house to play for their own enjoyment; T-Bone's first intimations of his own talent came to him thus. "I think that the first thing I can remember was my mother singing the blues as she would sit alone in the evenings in our place in Dallas. . . . I used to listen to her singing there at night, and I knew then that the blues was in me, too."

Aaron Thibeaux Walker was born May 28, 1910, in Linden, Texas; the family moved to Dallas about two years later. He had no brothers or sisters and manifested classic only-child behavior, remaining with his mother until comparatively late in life: " 'Course I was one guy, you couldn't get me out of Dallas because there was nobody but my mother and so I wouldn't never leave. . . . If [bands] got any farther than Fort Worth, Texas, they'd lose me 'cause I'd go right on back to Dallas to my mother."

T-Bone spent some time as a child leading Blind Lemon up and down Central Avenue, doubtless learning some guitar along the way. In later years he cited Lonnie Johnson and Scrapper Blackwell as important early influences. He began playing at age thirteen, first tenor banjo and ukulele, then guitar, working local parties and, with his stepfather, making the rounds of drive-ins that sold soft drinks, where they went from car to car and played requests for a dime or fifteen cents. His first real job was a medicine show called Big B Tonic, which he joined when he was about sixteen.

The medicine shows were a training ground and livelihood for many country and blues musicians during this period. These shows relentlessly toured the South's endless stretches of small towns, getting people's attention with silent movies or stage shows, then hawking bottles of homemade tonic. T-Bone was with Dr. Breeding's Big B Tonic during his summer vacation, ten dollars of his fifteen-dollar-a-week salary being sent back to his mother and the rest paid directly to him. He worked with a comedian named Josephus Cook who did jokes and routines while T-Bone played tenor banjo and ukulele, the two of them singing numbers like "Comin' Round the Mountain" together. This was, of course, an echo of the minstrel shows so popular in the nineteenth century.

He must have liked that taste of show business, for not long after the medicine-show stint T-Bone ran away with a carnival, playing banjo in the small pit band that traveled with blues singer Ida Cox. His mother soon located him, however, and had him returned to Dallas to finish school. He then began playing with a group that eventually developed into his first professional band. It was with this group that he came to be known as "T-Bone," a corruption of his middle name first used by the band's manager and soon adopted universally.

"I played all over Dallas," he told the O'Neals.

When I was in school we had a school band, and then we changed the name of the band to Lawson Brooks. We had about sixteen pieces. The majority of us all come out of school together. We began to work around Dallas. Around a hundred or two hundred miles from Dallas, like Abilene, Texas, and Amarillo, and San Anton', and Waco, all in the district. And then we played Oklahoma City once or twice. Then I quit the band and gave the job to Charlie Christian. Charlie took the band over and then I moved to California.

The California move was not until 1934, however, and the years before that move were busy ones. T-Bone not only continued working with the Lawson Brooks Band, he also played with Coley Jones's Dallas String Band and the Milt Larkins dance band, won an amateur contest appended to the Cab Calloway show, even toured the South with an all-white band headed by Count Biloski, leaving it after trouble in Oklahoma City. For a time in early 1934 he worked as accompanist to Ma Rainey with the Haines Circus. A few years before that, in 1929, he had made his first recordings, for Columbia.

He would not record again for ten years, or under his own name until 1942. He was sixteen at the time of the Columbia session, and the name "Oak Cliff T-Bone" (after the community just south of Dallas where Walker lived) appeared on the record. Pianist Alex Moore has recalled some of the circumstances of that first recording. "See, when that jive was bein' put down back in the twenties, them recording guys had a place rented on Young Street, damn building looked like two blocks long. They were all down there, Okeh, Paramount, Decca, Columbia, different record companies. That's where T-Bone Walker first recorded at. 'Trinity River Blues.' I never will forget that song."

T-Bone himself was never too clear about the exact circumstances. "I don't know," he responded when the O'Neals asked how he happened to record at that time. "It's just a fellow happened to be coming through Dallas, and they recorded me with the blues, 'Trinity River Blues' and 'Wichita Falls Blues'. . . . I think we had a fellow named Doug on the piano. This was a long time ago. I can't remember all this."

He and Christian met in 1933, the year before Walker's move to California. "We'd go dance and pass the hat and make money," T-Bone said. "We had a little routine of dancing that we did. Charlie would play guitar awhile and I'd play bass, and then we'd change and he'd play bass and I'd play guitar. And then we'd go into our little dance."

Dancing seems to have been something of a specialty for T-Bone, and jazzman Buster Smith later remembered him for that as much as for his blues singing. Tap dancing was extremely popular at the time, of course, and Bill Robinson was a headliner wherever he traveled. T-Bone apparently abandoned dancing after his move to the West Coast, but the influence clearly shows in the splits, toe stands and posturing he was given to while playing, all of which have passed down (through Chuck Berry, Bo Diddley, Elvis, Jimi Hendrix, Pete Townshend) into the common vocabulary. "Swing the blues a little more," he would tell Lowell Fulson. "You can play it, swing it a little more. Put a little life into it, a little pep; rock into it. Tap your foot off of what you're doing."

The California move was prompted by T-Bone's marriage and difficulty getting enough work to support his family. He contracted to drive some cars out to the Coast for an automobile company, liked it there and decided to stay. "I just wanted to go somewhere, that's all," he said, trying to explain the urges that finally pried him away from Dallas. "You know, you just want to go out and see some parts of the world. And I picked California. So I been living there ever since. Los Angeles."

The black population in California increased dramatically in the thirties as migrants came from all over the Southwest hoping to find work in the fields of the San Joaquin and Imperial valleys, or in the defense projects of Oakland and Los Angeles a bit later. One large black community in Oakland on the eastern side of the San Francisco Bay hosted many expatriate Texans; Los Angeles became an important center of blues activity.

T-Bone soon found friends and began playing with different small groups in local clubs. He worked at a club called Little Harlem for five years, three nights a week at $3.50 a night, in a quartet with tenor sax, upright bass and piano. By 1936 and 1937 he was also working the prestigious Trocadero on the Strip in Hollywood, sharing the bill with such popular entertainers as Billy Daniels and Ethel Waters.

Four years before Christian's landmark recordings with Goodman, in 1935, T-Bone took up the electric guitar, probably the first bluesman to do so. "It was kind of hard getting used to," he said, "because it had an echo sound. I would hit a string and hear the note behind me." But amplification allowed him to cut through the other instruments while accompanying his singing, and that in turn made it far more practical for him to be out front of a band. Also, naturally, it necessitated refinements and adaptations in his style of playing to accommodate the instrument's sharply increased volume and sustain; what T-Bone developed then, basically a combination of single-string melodic work and arpeggio, formed the backbone of all subsequent blues guitar.

T-Bone had a peculiar way of playing, too, as individualistic as his sound. Riffing or playing chords, he held his
guitar like anyone else, sometimes swinging it from side to
side at the end of the strap. But right before taking the lead,
he'd tilt the guitar and push it out from him until it was
parallel to the floor, face up like a Dobro or a keyboard.
Then he'd wrap his wrist all the way under and over and
play it like that. Other times, overcome by showmanship, he
played the guitar behind his back, held it away from his
body with one hand, still playing, or knelt with the guitar
resting on the floor like a cello and played it with one hand
while waving to the audience with the other.

One of the people who caught T-Bone's act at Little
Harlem was future blues singer Jimmy Witherspoon. "I
always wanted to sing," Witherspoon told *Guitar Player* following Walker's death. "I told him I wanted to sing, and he
called me up. I was just an amateur, and he let me sing. All
I can say is that he's the Charlie Parker of guitars when it
comes to blues. And in jazz guitarists, he's right with
Charlie Christian. No one else can touch T-Bone in the
blues on guitar." The two bluesmen later recorded
together, an album titled *Evenin' Blues* for the Prestige
label.

Many others recall T-Bone's eagerness to help fellow
musicians. "He'd give me a lot of tips," Lowell Fulson said.
"One thing I liked about that guy, he didn't care who it was
—you take a lot of musicians, they'd get famous on certain
licks and tricks and they wouldn't tell you anything. Bone
didn't care! He'd show you anything; say, 'It goes like
this.'" Pee Wee Crayton says that T-Bone would often play
piano or bass along with him for hours in the forties, teaching him timing, changes, inflection.

In 1939 T-Bone joined the Les Hite Orchestra at the
Cotton Club in Los Angeles, subsequently touring with it.
(This was the same year Charlie Christian joined Benny

Goodman.) The Hite band played dance halls and club dates through the Midwest, including Joe Louis's Hurricane Club in Chicago, then the Apollo Theater in New York City, and settled in at New York's Golden Gate Ballroom. The following year, still in New York, T-Bone recorded with the band for the Varsity label, "T-Bone Blues" and "Mean Old World." "I was singing with the band, I wasn't even playing guitar," Walker remembered. "I did 'Mean Old World,' but I was doing things like 'Stardust' and 'Askin' on Me'—ballads. We stayed on the road about a year, then I quit Les Hite and went back to Los Angeles, to Little Harlem. I didn't leave no more, until the time that I came to the Rhumboogie, which was in Chicago. And this was where I really got my start—1942."

T-Bone *always* returned to Los Angeles, and for a couple of years after leaving Hite, until a wartime economy intervened, he toured with his own ten-piece band, using Los Angeles as his base. Declared 4-F, he played military bases in the Dallas and Chicago areas for the USO. Release of material recorded for the Black & White label (including his hit "Stormy Monday") had to be delayed because of wartime shortages of pressing materials.

In 1942 T-Bone began working the Rhumboogie Club in Chicago. Joe Louis, who knew Walker from his work with the Hite band at Louis's Hurricane Club and who owned part of the Rhumboogie, may have been responsible. T-Bone played the club frequently over the next three years, also recording (about 1945) on the Rhumboogie label. The first of Chicago's independent labels, Rhumboogie was started by the club's manager, Charley Glenn, chiefly to promote artists featured at the club, and only three issues are known. Each features T-Bone Walker backed by the Marl Young Orchestra. The first, "Sail on Boogie," reputedly sold over fifty thousand copies; Walker also cut "I'm

Still in Love With You" and a repeat of "Mean Old World" for the label.

That same year, aged sixteen, Riley B. King heard T-Bone Walker for the first time. "I lived in the country, and I went to town that particular day, to this little café, and heard this record playing. I went to the jukebox and saw 'the name 'T-Bone Walker.' And I've never forgotten it; it seems like yesterday." Walker was the first player he'd heard who had a distinctive sound on the guitar, King said. "I haven't heard nobody top that *sound!* It's a sound that anybody, me or anyone else, had to come by from him." King also noted that T-Bone was the first player he heard using ninth chords for blues, and that his control was of a type more generally associated with jazz players than bluesmen. "His touch was so clear. . . . Whenever he hit the strings he hit them with authority. It was almost a measured touch." What's more, King observed, T-Bone would play any guitar, any amp, and still get his characteristic sound.

Through 1943 and 1944, T-Bone worked the Trocadero, Capri Club, Circle Café, Casablanca Club and others on the West Coast; at San Diego's Silver Slipper (where he and Lowell Fulson, stationed at a nearby naval base, first met); and in Detroit clubs such as the Flame Show Bar, Twenty Grand and Frolic Show Bar. He was also with Fletcher Henderson's band for an engagement at the Club Plantation in Los Angeles.

In 1945 or 1946, wartime pressures abating, T-Bone again organized and toured with his own band, reducing personnel this time to a more manageable seven members. At about the same time records began appearing with some regularity. T-Bone told the O'Neals that "Stormy Monday" was recorded before the war; other releases also may have been on the shelf for a time before this. At any rate, he appeared on the Black & White label with Jack McVea's All-Stars, the Al Killian Quartet and other groups, and the following year on the Comet label out of Houston. There seems to have been a common source for all this material, with Capitol eventually acquiring control of the masters and leasing them to others.

"Stormy Monday" came out in 1947. "I haven't never had but one big hit," T-Bone said, "and it's bigger than 'St. Louis Blues.' Everybody's playing it. More and more are playing it now, and everybody knows about it, which is good." *Guitar Player* called it "a standard (if not *the* standard) of modern blues for three decades," adding that if the blues were still being sung in the year 2000, the song would probably *still* be a standard. T-Bone's fellow bluesmen were quick to agree.

"To me," B. B. King said, " 'Stormy Monday' tells such a good story, especially for the working man. It's a very unique song."

"It's true everyday life about the average guy," Lowell Fulson said. "It's smooth. It goes between a ballad and a blues. It's a type of tune that will fit in any kind of club."

And Jimmy Witherspoon continued, "It's just like a national anthem; it tells the truth. It tells the strife of working people getting paid on Friday, Saturday they go out and have a ball."

Originally titled "Call It Stormy Monday," the song was released as simply "Stormy Monday," a title already used by Billy Eckstine on a record with Earl Hines. As a result, royalty payments were misdirected and considerable confusion developed as to ownership of the song. Lengthy litigation ensued. "I think my first check was five thousand dollars," Walker said in 1972, "and the next one was thirty-five hundred. And I got a lot of checks like thirty-five hundred and so I got some money coming now. They got a hundred thousand dollars tied up that I can't get yet, not 'til they straighten this thing out. Which, that makes me very unhappy, 'cause I could use my money."

T-Bone's relations with record companies were never

good, and like many bluesmen he skittered from label to label throughout his career. Speaking of these companies or of his string of records, he continually referred to a faceless "them" or "they" with something more than the usual mistrust of artist for merchandiser, implying (though reference is never clear) an indifferent and possibly malignant force at work. "Well, they're all alike," he told the O'Neals. "They're after the money they can get, then they put your records up on the shelf. If there's no demand for 'em, they put 'em up. They deduct it from their income tax anyway. They can save maybe two thousand or three thousand dollars and deduct it from their tax and things. They don't care whether you make any money or not. They just go on and save the money for themselves." Just so, his account of the misadventures of "Stormy Monday" is riddled with inscrutable, apparently responsible "thems" and "theys."

An important point is brought out by Pete Welding in *Guitar World*.

> During this period black popular music was changing rapidly, and traditionally based blues, however masterfully performed or sophisticated in character, as Walker's were, had steadily lost ground to rock and roll and soul music. . . . Black popular music had simply passed him by. To young blacks, militant or otherwise, he and other entertainers of his generation were either "Uncle Toms," embarrassing reminders of times and conditions better forgotten, or irrelevancies, holdovers from a musical past and, thus, to be treated with some respect but largely to be ignored.

After the issues on Black & White, Capitol and Comet, T-Bone recorded for several years on the Imperial label out of Los Angeles ("They didn't do nothing for me"), then on Atlantic for about five years. During this period he appeared on Ed Sullivan's *Toast of the Town* over CBS-TV and worked club dates as far-flung as Philadelphia, Buffalo and

Providence, Rhode Island. He also began touring in rhythm-and-blues package shows. An early colleague on these shows was Lowell Fulson, who described one for *Guitar Player* following T-Bone's death.

> As I improved, agents began getting a package together called the Battle of the Blues. It seemed at the time, me and T-Bone was pretty good drawing cards for promoters. I'll never forget—they used to call us The Big Three: me, T-Bone and Big Joe Turner. We'd each play a separate set. I was the newest in the game, so I'd open the show. Well, Joe Turner, he didn't play an instrument, so he'd come on in the middle (instead of having both guitars together). Then T-Bone played on the end. On the last set we'd all get together and have a jam session. I really enjoyed working with those men.

T-Bone's health was declining rapidly, however, and in 1955 he entered the hospital for a gastrectomy. He later claimed the operation was a tremendous boon to his career, estimating he'd lost close to a hundred thousand dollars in prior years from shows he'd been unable to make because of pain and sickness. The ulcers returned in the last years of his life, and Jimmy Witherspoon recalls that T-Bone was often in severe pain, unable to eat and able to drink only a little milk.

Shortly after recovering from the operation, T-Bone went into the Blue Mirror Club in San Francisco and remained there for four years, from 1956 to 1960. In the early sixties he worked the Five-Four Ballroom in Los Angeles, San Francisco's Sugar Hill and at least two clubs, the Atmosphere Club and the Longhorn Ranch Club, back home in Dallas. He was also a regular on West Coast television in this period. Sam Charters, with his customary disdain for newfangled blues (the sort of attitude that plagued Lonnie Johnson), describes these appearances in his book *Country Blues*.

Only a handful of singers have emerged as blues singers of any stature out of the hundreds of "downhome" singers who have recorded since the war. One of the most popular singers of the late 1940's was a Texan named Aaron "T-Bone" Walker. . . . He wasn't much of a blues singer, but he was a hard-working entertainer. He made several television appearances in the 1950's as " . . . a singer whose singing goes right to the heart of this thing we call the blues." The curtain would open on T-Bone wearing a gold lamé jacket and holding a jeweled guitar plugged into a long cord that T-Bone had to keep stepping over during his performance. He usually sang a fast "jump blues" ending up in a rhythm dance, with a split while he played the guitar behind the back of his head as the climax.

In 1962 T-Bone first traveled abroad as part of a rhythm-and-blues package show, discovering audiences in England and Europe (as have so many other blues- and jazzmen before and since) more sympathetic than American ones to his music. He returned again and again over the following years, recording with expatriate pianist Sunnyland Slim in Hamburg, and in Paris, on the Polydor and Black & Blue labels. He toured with the American Folk Blues Festival in 1963, 1968 and 1972, in shows that included Muddy Waters, Victoria Spivey, Lonnie Johnson and many others, and which, according to Big Joe Williams, "packed London Stadium." In 1965 he toured England with a group called the T-Bones: "They were some admirers of mine, crazy about T-Bone Walker and had never saw me." The following year he returned with the Jazz at the Philharmonic shows.

"I spend quite a bit of time over there," Walker said a few years before his death, "because I think we get a little more work, and the people seem to enjoy it better." He then was touring with a new band, mostly quite young, and playing coffeehouses as often as clubs; as with many bluesmen, the faces in his audiences had changed from all black to virtually all white. "I do know that the college kids and the kids over there have started to studyin' blues for a long time before the kids in America. Like the English kids. They had quite a few blues bands and they were doing all blues, by me and Muddy Waters, and by all the cats from Chicago and Texas, and they were doing a good job of it."

At home during the late sixties and early seventies, T-Bone frequently traveled with the Johnny Otis Revue and played prestigious clubs such as Shelly's Manne Hole, the Ash Grove and Max's Kansas City. He also played Carnegie Hall a number of times and appeared regularly on the festival circuit: the Monterrey and Pacific jazz festivals (1967), the Watts Summer Festival (1968), the Ann Arbor Blues Festival (1969), the Berkeley Blues Festival (1970), the Nice (1971) and Montreux (1972) jazz festivals. Records continued to emerge on Atlantic, Bluestime, Bluesway, Wet Soul, Reprise and other labels. In 1970 his *Good Feelin'* on Polydor received a Grammy as best ethnic/traditional recording of the year.

On New Year's Eve, 1974, T-Bone suffered a severe stroke, dying of associated pneumonia on March 16, 1975, at Vernon Convalescent Hospital in Los Angeles. His funeral was attended by over a thousand people, and dozens of musicians volunteered their services for the memorial concert (originally planned as a benefit) held two months later at the musicians' union auditorium. There in his beloved adopted Los Angeles, guitars made of flowers stood at each end of his coffin and a wreath from Ray Charles read, "The Bone is gone, but the melody lingers on."

T-Bone Walker liked to say that all he ever did in his whole life was play music. And that music goes on today, like a great river flowing through all the amplifiers and sound systems, along mile upon mile of guitar cord and out of records everywhere in the world, through blues and rock and jazz and hot country licks—it just keeps rolling on.

FURTHER ADVENTURES
OF CAPTAIN GUITAR:

George Barnes

In 1947 a lanky young guitarist from the Tennessee hill country, who'd been fired from most of his jobs because of the weird way he played, came to Chicago to record. The producer on the session was RCA Victor's Steve Sholes, who later installed that same lanky young guitarist as head of the newly built Nashville RCA studios. The guitarist, of course, was Chet Atkins.

"I said I wanted an accordion, bass, piano, fiddle and a good rhythm guitar," Atkins remembers. "I tried to write some songs to have ready for the session. He [Sholes] told the people in Chicago to get the best musicians they could find, and one of them was George Barnes for rhythm. Here I go, my first recording session and scared to death, and I have George Barnes."

Invisible to the public for much of his career, Barnes wielded great influence on other guitarists and, both directly and by implication, on the directions of popular music as well. Atkins's youthful, legitimate awe reflects a general attitude toward George Barnes and his amazing versatility. At seventeen a staff member of the NBC studios in Chicago, he had followed Lonnie Johnson about as a child and pioneered in the use of guitar for country swing; he was authentically at home with blues, country, popular music and straight jazz.

"George Barnes was my idol—he would play with such drive and dynamics," Roy Clark says. "He played sort of conventional, but with great tone and feel. He played right on top of the beat, and I loved that."

Barnes's primary outlet for many years was studio work, first with blues singers and country groups, then with popular singers such as Frank Sinatra, Bing Crosby and Patti Page. For a time in the fifties he even worked as a rock and roller. But jazz, the older, melodic jazz that came out of Chicago about the same time as he did, was always his first love, and over the years he borrowed time from family and daily career to work in several very important jazz guitar duos and in other jazz settings (and capacities) which helped advance markedly the visibility and viability of guitar players.

At the time of George Barnes's death he had returned wholly to that first love. "I'm doing exactly what I want to do," he told *Guitar Player* in 1975. "I'm not doing any commercial music, with people telling me how to play. I'm playing the tunes I like, the way I want to play them, and I'm performing with guys I love to work with." Though his influence is universally acknowledged, in the years since his death there's been a curious silence. No retrospective has appeared in any of the jazz or guitar publications, and like many other players in this book (Lonnie Johnson, Eddie Lang, Riley Puckett), George Barnes has become simply *donnée,* "given," part of the set of assumptions upon which a structure (be it geometrical problem, fiction or drama, guitar playing) proceeds.

Barnes's death following a heart attack in 1977 brought to an end over fifty years of almost continuous involvement with music. Born in 1921 (the following year would see the first recordings of Fats Waller and of the Mound City Blue Blowers; Bessie Smith's earliest records would appear in 1923), George came from a family of professional musicians. "At age six," he remembered in the *Guitar Player* interview, "I began to play the piano and I knew that was the instrument for me. But when the Depression came, we lost our piano as well as our house." There was an old Silvertone guitar left, though, and George picked it up. He was nine then; his father helped him find his way around the instrument.

It wasn't a particularly popular instrument at the time. Les Paul has said, "I found a Chicago musicians' union book from 1929 not too long ago, and I think there were maybe six guitar players listed." The earliest intimations of the guitar's ascendancy came with Eddie Lang about 1925 or so but even here, as Steve Calt points out in the notes for Yazoo Records' *Eddie Lang: Jazz Guitar Virtuoso*, "While Lang's artistic significance was by no means lost on his peers . . . it was his commercial misfortune to specialize on an instrument that had no real following."

Barnes seems to have realized quite early, and intuitively, what critic Ralph Gleason once said took him years to learn, "that Robert Johnson was just as important as Charlie Christian, but different." He knew that he wanted to be a jazzman when he first heard Bix and Venuti on the radio; then about the same time he met Lonnie Johnson. "When I was young, I hung around with Lonnie Johnson," he said, "and he taught me how to play the blues." Barnes must have learned quickly and well. He was soon recording with major bluesmen such as Bill Broonzy, Washboard Sam and Blind John Davis. A few years later Hughes Panassie, knowing only Barnes's work as sideman on these recordings, referred to him in the French publication *Le Jazz Hot* as "the great Negro blues guitar player from Chicago."

When Barnes joined the musicians' union in 1933, at age twelve, he'd already been playing electric guitar for two years, clearly a pioneer in that regard. He formed his first group, the George Barnes Quartet, a couple of years later, recording with the quartet ("I'm Forever Blowing Bubbles" and "I Can't Believe That You're in Love With Me") in 1937 for Okeh. In 1938, the year before Charlie Christian joined the Benny Goodman Band, Barnes joined the NBC staff in Chicago, at seventeen the youngest conductor-arranger in its history. He remained with NBC until he was drafted in 1942.

Down Beat's December 1939 issue carried a piece attributed to Charlie Christian (presumably a public relations release from the Goodman office) reviewing past difficulties of guitarists and suggesting that electrical amplification had given them a new lease on life. Among the guitarists mentioned were Allan Reuss, one of the first to attach an amplifier to his instrument, and Floyd Smith, who'd come out with "Floyd's Guitar Blues" in March of that year. "Then," the article goes on, "there's Georgie Barnes, the seventeen-year-old Chicagoan, who, with an amplified instrument, set that town on its ear at Chicago's Off-Beat Club last spring. Barnes has just been added to the staff of the Chicago NBC studios. A year ago he had a tough time booking his own Chicago Heights combo for Saturday nights."

The guitar, then, was definitely on the rise, to what heights no one at the time could have imagined. Still, as Barnes said, "there were few guitarists then who soloed. I didn't want to play rhythm; I wanted to play melody. I heard many records by Django, but I couldn't relate to his playing because he sounded foreign to me. The musicians who influenced my playing the most were the horn and reed men I played with while I was growing up in Chicago."

Chicago in fact focused much that was happening in music at this time. A massive diaspora was beginning as increasing numbers of southern blacks migrated toward Kansas City, St. Louis, Detroit, New York and, perhaps most of all, Chicago. The white jazz bands (Original Dixielanders, New Orleans Rhythm Kings, Tom Brown's) all headed north shortly after the war; King Oliver left New Orleans behind in 1917, the year Storyville was closed; and by the early twenties even Jelly Roll Morton had abandoned the South. Large black communities, with active club scenes and a burgeoning demand for jazz musicians, developed in northern cities.

In all these cities, but particularly in Chicago, black and white musicians worked together at the new music, pushing it beyond its old limits, shaping and refining it, so that by the mid-twenties jazz had a secure commercial base in virtually every northern city. And from these cities men such as Louis Armstrong, Earl Hines, Bix Beiderbecke, Jimmy McPartland, Fats Waller and Duke Ellington began spreading their gospel across the land.

The music that developed was actually a couple of generations removed from the uncomplicated jams of the New Orleans bands. That early spontaneity was retained for "hot" solos of the type Bix became famous for, but for the most part backgrounds were tightly written, the arrangements conceived around repetitive rhythmic riffing and harmonies extended far beyond the typical I-IV-V (tonic-dominant-subdominant) blues progression.

By the thirties college students were staying up until the small hours to catch Benny Goodman's *Let's Dance* broadcast from the West Coast, and swing records were sailing across the counters like Frisbees. Victor alone, in 1936, sold nine hundred thousand dance records, almost 80 percent of its total output, and a new company, Decca, lowering its price from the standard seventy-five cents to thirty-five cents, was an instant success. "The thirties," Russel Nye writes in *The Unembarrassed Muse,* "were perhaps popular music's most prosperous era, through movies, radio, records, jukeboxes, clubs and dance halls; a band like Goodman's or Dorsey's could gross half a million dollars a year."

It was a long way from Buddy Bolden and spasm bands, but it was a remarkably straight line.

The thirties were also a period of expanding radio coverage of country music as stations in the South and Midwest recognized the popularity and appeal of hillbilly music and (more to the point) the money to be made from its sponsorship. New 50,000-watt powerhouse stations reached out to scattered rural audiences all over the country and as far away as Canada, Hawaii and Cuba. In the Southwest, jazz and big-band swing crossed with indigenous fiddle tunes, Mexican music and Texas blues to form western swing, with Bob Wills leaving the transitional Light Crust Doughboys in 1933 to form his Playboys and Milton Brown departing the same group a year earlier to organize his Musical Brownies.

For almost twenty years, because of its recording activity and perhaps most of all because of the presence of WLS, Chicago was a major center for country music. Atlanta's WSB had set the trend for country programming beginning in 1922 with its broadcasts of Fiddlin' John Carson, Gid Tanner, Riley Puckett and other local musicians. In early 1923 Fort Worth's WBAP, initiated a few months earlier with the usual programming of popular, jazz, sacred and semiclassical music, broadcast ninety minutes of square-dance music to such enthusiastic response that this became an irregular feature of the station. But it was WLS that grabbed the ball and ran, its *National Barn Dance* the first such show to achieve longevity and national attention, broadcasting regularly from 1924 until 1960.

During those years WLS broke a lot of ground. Establishing an Artists Service Bureau, the station sent its performers out to the listeners in myriad road units—missionaries to far lands—blanketing the Midwest and adjacent southern states with touring country musicians. In 1932 WLS took over the Eighth Street Theater, broadcast the *Barn Dance* in two programs from it and charged admission. Alka-Seltzer picked up the show for sponsorship the following year, and a nationwide one-hour program went out Saturday nights over the NBC network.

Not until the late forties or early fifties would other stations, primarily WSM in Nashville, challenge WLS's supremacy in country programming, and then chiefly because the *National Barn Dance* fell to entropy, signing very few new stars in later years and varying little from its original format.

An early characteristic of *Barn Dance* programming was its inclusion of popular and sentimental songs alongside traditional country fare, in this reminiscent of Riley Puckett, Vernon Dahlhart and other of the first country music professionals. A group called the Prairie Ramblers, with which George Barnes appeared over NBC, typified this eclectic approach and evidenced the many crosscurrents at work on American music. "The Prairie Ramblers' repertory," Bill Malone writes in *Country Music, U.S.A.,* "one of the most diverse in country-music history, included mountain tunes ('Feast Here Tonight'), cowboy tunes ('Ridin' Ole Paint'), gospel songs ('What Would You Give in Exchange for Your Soul') and 'pop' tunes ('Isle of Capri'). It was in their instrumentation, however, that the 'swing' influence was most apparent: on their recordings they used, in addition to the conventional country instruments, the piano, clarinet, and saxophone."

In 1933, the year that the *National Barn Dance* connected with NBC and the year that George Barnes joined the union, the Library of Congress began its systematic recording and documentation of southern folk music, first under the direction of Robert Winslow Gordon, later John and Alan Lomax.

In these same years Chicago harbored a rich community of blues musicians. The "race" market had boomed from

1927 to 1930, doubling its previous output, with five leading companies recording on seven labels. With the Depression, however, recording declined sharply, and several companies succumbed. Despite this, Chicago remained important for its clubs and "rent parties" thrown, with live music and a small admission charge, to raise money for rent. By about 1934, the worst of the Depression past, recording activity resumed, expanding rapidly. Decca's 7000 "race" series helped greatly in establishing this new company; Victor's Bluebird label, beginning 1933, rode the crest; Brunswick's Vocalion label was also active. Tastes had shifted from country blues to the smoother, hybrid sounds of urban bluesmen like Tampa Red and Big Bill Broonzy, so there was little need for field recording in the South now and Chicago's position as the blues capital was reinforced. The end of the Depression, then, was the beginning of a period of intense development in urban blues.

Most Chicago bluesmen—Broonzy, Washboard Sam, Roosevelt Sykes, Memphis Minnie, Big Joe Williams, Sonny Boy Williamson, Lonnie Johnson, Leroy Carr, Victoria Spivey—worked with Lester Melrose, a man with roots in early jazz (he had recorded Jelly Roll Morton and King Oliver in earlier years) and a decided talent for scouting out marketable blues talent. "From March 1934 to February 1951," Melrose once said, "I recorded at least ninety percent of all rhythm and blues talent for RCA Victor and Columbia Records." He in fact developed the first musical assembly line, packing his artists all tightly together (Broonzy as guitarist on Lonnie Johnson's records, Lonnie Johnson as guitarist on Washboard Sam's records, Roosevelt Sykes as pianist on everybody's records) and slicing off individual records like portions of sausage or lunchmeat. Admirably efficient in terms of investment and product, artistically this proved stultifying, and many of the records suffer an ineluctable sameness. Still, these are the people who defined big-city blues, and theirs is a major legacy of American music.

No musician as precocious and permeable as the young George Barnes could escape the brand of all that diverse music flowing about and through him. "This was at the time that the Chicago sound in jazz was being formed and was strongly felt in the music world," he said in later years. "I was very fortunate to be a part of it. My single greatest influence was a famous Chicago clarinetist, Jimmie Noone. He also greatly influenced Benny Goodman. I was playing with Jimmie Noone when I was sixteen. His playing gave me a strong direction. Another strong influence was Louis Armstrong." If Barnes seldom chose to speak of music other than jazz, that music nonetheless was an abiding influence over the years in his work with blues singers, country groups, pop vocalists and other jazzmen. In America all musical roads lead to jazz, and Chicago in the time Barnes was coming up was a major switchyard, the biggest crossroad. Jazz was Barnes's point of origin and destination: there was considerable road between.

Following World War II George Barnes returned to Chicago and a full schedule of radio and recording dates. One of the shows he regularly worked was Dave Garroway's, and Garroway told the young guitarist that, with the television industry booming in New York, he could do far better for himself there. Barnes made the move in 1951, rapidly finding himself even more involved with recording than he had been in Chicago. A contract with Decca Records assured he would remain busy. "With them," he said, "I did just about everything: conducting, arranging, vocal backgrounds, my own albums and record dates. Probably the only thing I didn't do was sweep the floors." The range of his activities at Decca complemented his prior recording experience and already remarkable versatility, making him something of a self-contained musician, the complete studio wizard. He always believed that this total involvement with music in all its aspects explained the demand for his playing. "Not only am I a guitarist, but an arranger, conductor and recording engineer, with years of knowledge and experience behind me. I've also developed ways of accompanying artists that enhance and enrich their music. You have to know how a singer phrases so your accompaniment does not conflict. As an arranger, I have a whole different set of ears from someone who is just a guitarist." Another clue to Barnes's popularity at sessions is contained in his remark that "A musician should never just play for money alone. There are more rewards to music than money. Also, keep your musical ideas fresh by looking at each performance as a new experience."

Even with his incredibly full schedule, Barnes somehow found time (he always would) to play the jazz clubs. His first New York job was at the Embers opposite Tal Farlow, his own favorite guitarist.

Over the next twenty-four years Barnes played with Lena Horne, Frank Sinatra, Johnny Mathis, Ella Fitzgerald, Patti Page and dozens of others; it would be very difficult, he remarked, to find a singing star he hadn't worked with. More than two dozen albums came out under his own name, and in one eight-year stretch (1953–61) he recorded sixty-one albums with the Three Suns (a popular vocal group) alone. "They tell me down at the union," he said in *Guitar Player*'s 1975 interview, "that I have recorded more than any other person in their contract file. I don't know how many recording dates I've done, but one day I intend to add them up. I know the number is well into the thousands."

Barnes's work, though, was not limited to popular music. He continued to work with country musicians and in the early and mid-fifties became a stalwart at historic recording sessions recalled by Jethro Burns in an interview conducted by David Grisman for *Frets*.

> At the point we're talking about, we had all signed contracts with RCA—Chet, and Homer and Jethro. Every time one of us cut a record, why the other guys were sidemen on it. Homer and Jethro would have a background of Chet Atkins on guitar, Jerry Byrd on steel, Charlie Grillion on bass, and on a lot of things, George Barnes on guitar. George was the ultimate perfectionist. He was the kind of guy that would walk in and say, "Well, if you don't make any mistakes, there ain't gonna be any." He was that good. . . . Homer played rhythm, and Barnes and Chet just traded off leads. They stayed out of each other's way pretty well. I always liked to work with Barnes because he came up with all these real exciting runs. You were never sure where they were going to end, except they always ended right.

The description of these sessions reminds one of the Melrose blues machine, and the pairing of Chet Atkins with Barnes on twin leads foreshadows another such collaboration, that of Atkins and Hank Garland, which became a cornerstone of "the Nashville sound," the style (more properly, format) that brought country music uptown, greatly popularized it and eventually proved its vitiation, almost succeeding in tearing it from its roots.

Barnes's playing was also in demand for a new kind of session—rock and roll. This was years before the guitar revolution swept every kid in the country into his basement with electric guitar in tow; most of the vocalists and groups of the time didn't play instruments, or at best played them inexpertly. Yet from the first, with its origins in country and blues, rock and roll was guitar-based, necessitating heavy use of sidemen on recording sessions. For many years rock and roll paid the rent for most New York City studio and jazz guitarists.

"For almost every rock and pop date," Bucky Pizzarelli

recalls, "four or five guitars were used. On those dates I mainly played riffs or figures on a six-string Danelectro bass guitar. That was my main instrument then. I made zillions of rock dates with Al Caiola, Mundell Lowe, George Barnes, Kenny Burrell and Tony Mottola. Truthfully, I was on almost every hit rock and pop song recorded in New York City up through the mid-sixties: Dion and the Belmonts, Frankie Avalon, Fabian—I could go on for hours naming them." Pizzarelli later adopted another unusual instrument, the seven-string guitar, and with it joined George Barnes in an outstanding jazz guitar duo.

It's altogether fitting that George Barnes should have been part of early genre recordings that largely elicited the future popularity of electric guitar. He had played amplified guitar as early as 1931, before anything of the kind was commercially available, using a pickup and amplifier built for him by his older brother. "He did this for me," Barnes said, "because he knew I wanted to play solo lines which could be heard in a band. The first electric guitar came out the following year. National Dobro made them and one of those was my first real electric guitar. Nobody knows who had the first electric guitar; maybe I did. I knew the first time I played one that that instrument was going to take me through my career for the rest of my life."

If not the first to have an electric instrument, Barnes was certainly the first electric guitarist many players encountered. Merle Travis, working on Cincinnati's WLW, heard Barnes play "My Blue Heaven" on a show from Chicago called *Plantation Party* and wasted little time adding a DeArmond pickup to his Gibson L-10. Jazz guitarist Herb Ellis remembers that his first exposure to electric guitar also came via radio and George Barnes. "That's where I first heard it," Ellis told *Guitar Player*. "I got something from Sears, Roebuck, a really funky electric guitar, and I took that to college with me. Then I was able to get a better one, an Epiphone." Majoring in music at North Texas State, now renowned for its jazz department, Ellis was unable to play his guitar (there were no teachers, no curriculum) and studied instead on string bass; this was about 1941. While at NTSU Ellis first heard Charlie Christian.

An abiding concern among electric guitarists (as evidenced in the bewildering array of effects now marketed) lies in extending the tonal range and overall potential of their instrument, a concern George Barnes shared at least in part. Quite early on, he obstructed the f-holes of his fullbody acoustic-electric guitar in an attempt to eliminate feedback and achieve a purer tone. "I knew that if I had a live top with suspended pickups, I'd get a better sound," he told *Guitar Player.* "I realized a long time ago that f-holes cause feedback. Both George Van Eps and I discovered that about the same time. We did a concert together in Aspen, Colorado, and we both started laughing when we saw each other's guitar. He had put foam rubber in his f-holes to cut out the feedback, and I had taped over mine." Eventually this concept led to Barnes's designing, in 1961, a guitar *without* f-holes, its pickups suspended over triangular cutouts. The guitar, one of a kind, was built for him by Guild, using the finest imported woods, and he played it exclusively for the rest of his career.

Barnes also developed, again with Guild, an alto guitar called the George Barnes Guitar in F. "I made an album called *Guitars Galore* and I wanted the guitars to play the role of a big band. However, the guitar doesn't have the range for that. So I used the six-string bass guitar to cover the baritone range, the regular guitar to cover the tenor saxophone range and developed the guitar in F to play the alto saxophone range." Tuned a fourth above standard guitar (A-D-G-C-E-A), it was a transposing instrument, a first-position C chord actually sounding F, D chord sounding G and so on. Though it evolved from his background in jazz and swing, Barnes's use of this guitar, incorporating as it does ranges and functions earlier taken by tenor banjo, ukulele and tiple, tacitly acknowledges America's rich heritage of stringed instruments.

Another, far more personal factor in George Barnes's guitar sound was his picking technique, long a source of curiosity and controversy among fellow guitarists. "You get a better sound from the guitar by using only downstrokes," he said, something early guitarists such as Christian and Eddie Durham took as axiom, and he built his technique around that, using as many downstrokes as possible and falling back onto alternate picking only in cases of extremely rapid phrasing. This helped give him both a fat, full guitar sound and amazing drive and control, as did his manner of holding the pick with thumb, index and middle fingers. "By picking this way, all I do to change the dynamics and volume is tighten or loosen my grip on the pick. I don't have to pick harder and my wrist remains loose."

The guitar is, physically, a difficult instrument; to get past its cumbersomeness to the music inside requires considerable application. Things other musicians take for granted—legato playing, dynamics, even simply reading—can become awesome problems on guitar. (The piano has one way of playing D above middle C, and one way of voicing an ascending triad on that root; the guitar has many.) Yet the instrument is amazingly flexible, able to fill many needs in ensemble playing, and *basic* skills are acquired rather easily. For these reasons other musicians have tended to mistrust guitarists' credentials. George Barnes is an early example of the guitarist mastering his instrument and going far beyond the bounds of mere player, or technician, to total musician. And if this is today more rule than exception, it is because men such as Eddie Lang, Carl Kress and George Barnes set that precedent.

In 1961 the duo jazz guitar format begun by Eddie Lang

and Lonnie Johnson was extended and solidified when Barnes teamed with Carl Kress. Kress had worked with the Paul Whiteman Orchestra in the late twenties, recording extensively with Bix and Trumbauer, the Dorseys, Miff Mole, Red Nichols and others; by the early thirties he was the premier guitarist on American radio. He cut two duets with Lang in 1932, and in 1934 began a similar association with Dick McDonough.

"The two-guitar concept reached a new level of sophistication in Kress's work with fellow studio guitarist Dick McDonough," Richard Lieberson wrote in his article "Fifty Years of Jazz Guitar Duos."

> McDonough soloed in single notes and double-stops (playing two strings at once) as well as chords, and he played all the single-string lead on the duets. Recording together in 1934 and 1937, Kress and McDonough produced four classic duets, three of which were originals. The other was a stylization of Irving Berlin's "Heat Wave." Their duets are more structurally, harmonically and rhythmically complex than the Kress-Lang works. Unlike many loosely arranged pieces based on blues or standard chord changes, these adaptations are specifically suitable to guitar, with their modulations, tempo changes and rubato interludes. The guitarists play syncopations in imitation of band arrangements, and create three- and four-part harmonies not possible on a single instrument. . . .
>
> Aspiring jazz guitarists treasured the Kress-McDonough duets, which contain some of the best recorded examples of the chord-lead style of the thirties. George Barnes once recalled going to a fellow guitarist's house and listening excitedly to the just-released duets, which they played over and over.

Kress was a master of that chord-lead style, a kind of playing out of vogue for many years but attracting new attention because of recent emphasis on solo guitar, the playing of such people as Lenny Breau, Ted Greene and William Ackerman, and renewed interest in the style's all-time master, George Van Eps. Kress's tuning (B♭-F-C-G-A-D) was derived from the banjo, his original instrument, and while not particularly useful for melody work, was ideal for accompaniment. After McDonough's death, Kress worked for a time, in 1941, with twenty-one-year-old Tony Mottola, just then starting out in studio work. Two albums from Yazoo Records, *Pioneers of the Jazz Guitar* (Yazoo L-1057) and *Fun on the Frets* (Yazoo L-1061), contain examples of Lang-Kress, Kress-McDonough, Kress-Mottola and other duets.

It was Barnes and Kress who firmly established the jazz guitar duo, however. Previous duos had been occasional, performing only on radio or recordings; Barnes and Kress pursued theirs full time, even while meeting heavy schedules elsewhere, and took their playing into clubs and concert halls. They were also the first of the duos to employ electric guitars. Barnes told *Guitar Player,*

Carl Kress and I met in 1951, on *The Garry Moore Show.* I was seated in the audience and Carl was working the show. Garry introduced me to the audience and suggested that Carl and I play a duet. . . . Carl and I had a hard time finding time to play because he was busy with CBS, and my time was locked into Decca. Finally, ten years later, in 1961, we decided to work together. We were the first guitar duo to play steadily. . . . Carl and I were together for five years, until his passing in 1966, right after we returned from a concert tour of Japan with Mitch Miller. We played concerts all over the world. Carl was my closest friend. We really loved each other. We hung out together all the time, whether it be playing chess, drinking or going to hear other musicians. . . . He used a special tuning to give his chords a full, rich sound. . . . With this lower tuning, he could play more and fuller bass lines. However, this tuning was not very good for playing solo. He rarely soloed in single notes; instead, he soloed in chords. It was his unique tuning that brought about the development of the seven-string guitar. George Van Eps, who studied with Carl, was warned by his father not to study with him because he used an unusual tuning.

The Barnes-Kress repertoire consisted chiefly of standards and, unlike most duos since those of Lang and Johnson, featured improvised choruses, something Barnes excelled at. "The Barnes-Kress duets," Lieberson points out, "offer the best recorded examples of Barnes's gorgeous way with a melody, melodic inventiveness and overall command of the instrument." A typical piece would move from fully arranged passages through a couple of improvised choruses by Barnes into a Kress chord solo with Barnes playing a quiet bass line. The guitarists recorded four albums together: *Guitars, Anyone?* and *Smokey and Intimate* (both on Carney, LPM-201 and 202), and *Something Tender* and *Town Hall Concert* (United Artists UAS 6335 and UAJ 14033). They also produced an album called *Ten Duets for Two Guitars* (Music Minus One 4011), which makes it possible for student guitarists to play their own duets with Carl Kress, using Barnes's arrangement charts.

In 1966, much as Dick McDonough had collapsed twenty-seven years earlier (though of pneumonia) while they were working together at the NBC studios, Carl Kress suffered a fatal heart attack while he and Barnes were playing in Reno, Nevada.

Bucky Pizzarelli was one of the busiest studio guitarists in New York at this time, and he and Barnes had worked many sessions together. A few years after Kress's death, in 1969, Pizzarelli acquired a seven-string guitar and dropped by Barnes's studio to try it out. "We did some experimental recordings with it," Barnes said, "and we knew, right away, that we had a good sound. He had a marvelous facility for playing that instrument."

The seven-string guitar was developed in 1939 by

George Van Eps for his inimitable solo ("lap piano") style. Pizzarelli originated his own distinctive accompaniment style with the instrument, playing mostly with his fingers but occasionally using a pick to play chord solos in the Kress vein. Recent years have witnessed growing interest in the seven-string guitar among musicians such as Alan De-Mause and Lenny Breau. Traditionally the extra string is a low A tuned one octave below the fifth; Breau has added instead a high A above the first-string E.

"Bucky and I knew from the beginning that he wouldn't be satisfied to be my accompanist for the rest of his life," Barnes said. "He is too good a musician for that. We split up when he went to do concerts in Europe with Benny Goodman. But we had a marvelous three years together."

For a time after Pizzarelli left, another seven-string player, Art Ryerson, carried on with Barnes. His specialty was hot chord solos, and occasionally he'd accompany Barnes with chords played wholly as harmonics—a technique with its pedigree in Lang, first real exploration in Tal Farlow and eventual flowering in Breau's cascades of true and harmonic tones. Pizzarelli has continued his championship of the seven-string guitar in many contexts, with steel guitarist Doug Jernigan for example, and $2 \times 7 = Pizzarelli$ (Stash ST-207), his album of duets with son John (also playing a seven-string), ranks among the finest jazz guitar records.

Barnes and Pizzarelli worked a forbiddingly heavy schedule while they were together. In an interview with *Guitar Player* in 1974, Pizzarelli recalled their working methods and the manner in which their partnership evolved.

> There was a great rapport; he enjoyed soloing, and I was grateful that I had someone to play with so I could learn that seven-string monster. We started out playing local clubs in New Jersey, which then led to playing almost every night for three years.
> Nothing was ever written. We even rehearsed separately,

because we both had busy daytime schedules so could just play together at night. I would learn the chords to a song and George would learn the melody. Then usually when I soloed, I did so in chords while George would play the bass line. When he soloed single-string, I played the chords behind him. And when he put a fancy tag ending on a song, I'd try imitating it there on the spot. The more we played, the more we became familiar with our repertoire and each other's approach to playing. We had a couple of hundred songs in our repertoire, but from playing together every night for three years we became so familiar with it that we thought as one guitarist.

Barnes and Pizzarelli recorded one album together, *Guitars Pure and Honest* (A&R ARL-7100/007), and appeared together on *The Guitar Album* (Columbia KG-31045) with other guitarists assembled for a live Town Hall concert.

About 1973 Barnes and Ruby Braff, a cornet player sharing his deep affection for melodic jazz, formed the Ruby Braff-George Barnes Quartet, with Mike Moore on bass and a former Barnes student, Wayne Wright, on rhythm guitar. It is interesting that Barnes retained the familiar paired guitars in this larger group; interesting, too, that Wright later teamed with a guitarist in the Kress tradition, Marty Grosz (he even tunes his guitar B♭-F-C-G-B-D), to form probably the best traditional jazz duet working. In the Grosz-Wright duo, Wright balances Grosz's chord solos with single-string leads, but with Barnes he confined himself, like preamplification guitarists for many years, to playing strict time.

Assembled for the Newport Jazz Festival, the quartet went on in succeeding years to play festivals and concerts all over the world and to cut several excellent albums. Barnes recalled the group's origin in his *Guitar Player* interview.

George Wein, the producer for the Newport Jazz Festival, hired both of us to play there as part of an all-star band. Both

Ruby and I were disenchanted with that playing format. Each person in that kind of band just solos briefly. Each brief solo is followed by another brief solo. It's an atmosphere where both Ruby and I feel cramped. So we decided that we'd form our own group and play our own music. We called George Wein, before the festival, and told him that we wanted to work together. "Don't give us any more money," we told him. "We'll hire our own men and put our group together."

The quartet format was ideal for the sort of relaxed, eventual unfolding of a tune's possibilities favored by both Barnes and Braff, who often resembled one another even in the tone they got from their respective instruments. When Braff soloed, Barnes dropped back and played chords or accent lines. It was almost like having two horns up there with a rhythm section, except that Barnes's fluid hammer-ons and bluesy bends could come only from a guitar. Clement Meadmore wrote in *Jazz,*

> The brief but brilliant life of the Barnes-Braff Quartet can be traced on five LPs that make one wonder what drums are for. Three strings and a trumpet groove their ways through fifty of the nicest tunes in a most satisfying way. If I had to pick one LP, it would be their *Salute to Rodgers and Hart.* . . . If I had to pick a single track for sheer delectation, it would be "Lover," with its rarely heard verse introduced by a beautiful two-guitar arpeggio riff and stated by Braff with the subtlest of phrasing from Barnes. After this come two of the quietest unmuted trumpet choruses on record in any idiom, interrupted only by Barnes's positively singing guitar on the bridges. Sublime stuff.

In 1975 George Barnes moved to Concord, California, and settled into teaching, playing local jazz clubs and making frequent concert or festival appearances. Two Braff-Barnes albums came out on the specialty Concord Jazz label in this period, followed by two pairing Barnes with fiddler

Joe Venuti, then *Blues Going Up* and its posthumous sequel, *Plays So Good.* On these final albums, recorded live at Bimbo's in San Francisco, Barnes again featured double guitars (the other guitarist was Duncan James) in a quartet with bass and drums. These are arguably among the finest of his career.

"I've often said that there aren't enough lifetimes for me to do all the musical things I want to do," Barnes told *Guitar Player* the year he moved to Concord. "I recorded some classical tunes in the sixties. I'd like to do more of that. But, right now, I'm happier, musically, than at any other time in my life." On September 5, 1977, following a severe heart attack, George Barnes died, half a continent and half a century away from Chicago and the music that started it all.

JAZZ WINDS FROM
A NEW DIRECTION:

Hank Garland

ON ITS WAY UPTOWN, country music had passed from
Roy Acuff's East Tennessee mountain music to Ernest
Tubb's Texas honky-tonk and therefrom to Alabaman
Hank Williams's bare poems of longing and despair. Williams was the first country artist to attract significant attention from non-country, pop-oriented listeners, and
following his death in 1953, several singers came into
prominence who openly courted that new audience.

Eddy Arnold, another Tennessean, joined Pee Wee
King's Golden West Cowboys as a vocalist at age eighteen.
His style quickly developed in flexibility and sophistication
with this excellent group of musicians; in 1944 he left to
hold down a six-day-a-week job at WSM as "The Tennessee
Plowboy," his easy delivery and warm, clear baritone soon
making him country music's most popular singer. As his
popularity grew, in fact, he gravitated ever more toward an
urbane, almost crooning delivery, and by the fifties he had
phased out the Plowboy image for one of tuxedo and black
tie, nightclubs and Carnegie Hall. Somehow, though, he
managed to retain his country audience as he staked out
these new claims. "Today," Charles Wolfe writes in *Tennessee Strings*, "Arnold is recognized as often as a pop singer
as he is a country singer, and it was for this breakthrough

as much as anything that Arnold was elected to the Country Music Hall of Fame in 1966."

Tennessee Ernie Ford, born in Bristol where the Carter Family and Jimmie Rodgers first recorded, grew up with that region's rich Appalachian folk heritage but initially aspired to, and trained for, concert music. "You know I couldn't top Roy Acuff's stuff, and I couldn't beat [Perry] Como. So I mix 'em and people like it fine," he said, a remarkably accurate description. Early Ford hits such as "Mule Train" and "Shotgun Boogie" were strongly country flavored but featured slick band arrangements. With "Sixteen Tons" in 1955 he became a national figure and like Arnold hosted his own TV show for several years, yet his work retained both its strong country flavor and Nashville ties.

Meanwhile, another group of musicians dedicated itself to preserving the rural sound and roots of country music—the basic string band and high, lonesome mountain vocals—in a body of music that came to be known as bluegrass, after Bill Monroe's Bluegrass Boys. Monroe had formed the band in 1938 after dissolution of a successful duo with his brother Charlie, and with it joined the Opry the following year. In 1945, a time when bluegrass was gathering force from many directions, he added fiddler Chubby Wise, Lester Flatt and Earl Scruggs. With radio stations in Knoxville and the Bristol-Johnson City area supporting the music, and especially with the establishment of businessman Jim Stanton's independent Rich-R-Tone label, East Tennessee became a center for bluegrass activity. The music remained largely underground for some time, surfacing during the sixties' folk revival and proving in recent years a rich artesian well that's brought arresting work from bluegrass-spawned musicians such as the Red Clay Ramblers and David Grisman.

Despite the rising popularity of singers like Arnold and

Ford and the appearance on pop charts of songs like "Chattanooga Shoe Shine Boy" and Floyd Tillman's "Slipping Around," Nashville was not fully aware of crossover potential until release of Patti Page's "Tennessee Waltz" in 1950. Written by bandleader Pee Wee King and vocalist Redd Stewart after noting the popularity of Bill Monroe's 1948 "Kentucky Waltz," the song was intended as the B side of Page's record but became a national hit within the first month of its release, in the next six amassing sales of over four million records and becoming possibly the biggest hit in popular-music history. The *New York Times* noted that "New York's writers of pop tunes look in envy and calculation at the 'country' songsmiths. . . . There's a revolution brewing in the music business."

By the mid-forties Nashville was on its way to becoming an important recording center. Engineers at WSM, turning out record transcriptions of radio shows, had developed considerable technical skill, and in 1945 three of them (Aaron Shelton, George Reynolds and Carl Jenkins) opened a studio in the former dining room of the old Tulane Hotel. Intended as a part-time endeavor, Castle Studio quickly became so busy that its owners were forced to draft other station engineers to help them, and eventually WSM grew concerned, pressuring its staff to abandon outside work. The studio closed in the early fifties, but by then momentum was established. Steve Sholes began recording in Nashville for RCA Victor in 1946, and in 1950 Capitol became the first major studio to locate its director for country music there; Mercury followed suit two years later. Introduced in 1948, LPs rapidly became the standard of the industry, greatly increasing demand for writers, publishers, musicians, technicians and other support personnel, so that by the end of the decade Nashville boasted a huge pool of talent and ran many of its bustling studios on a twenty-four-hour basis.

Two men central to this transfiguration are Owen Bradley and Chet Atkins. Bradley had worked extensively as a musician and arranger, and in the late forties became musical director of WSM, also working as assistant to Paul Cohen of Decca Records. In 1952 he began making documentary films on his own in a small downtown studio, but he regularly spent his evening hours recording singers like Ernest Tubb and Kitty Wells there. The facilities were cramped and inadequate, so, with a guarantee from Decca of one hundred sessions a year, he built another, larger studio, going on to record Marty Robbins, Johnny Cash, Sonny James and other emerging stars. An old quonset hut, which he used to continue his filmmaking, stood nearby, and about 1955 he outfitted it with a three-track recording console, discovering that the hut had superb acoustics. It quickly became legendary, and when Bradley sold the quonset hut to Columbia in 1962 for three hundred thousand dollars, Columbia built its entire complex around it. Three years later an old barn Bradley found about twenty miles outside the city and converted to a studio became another favorite, booked solid by top producers and stars. Bradley's technical expertise and experiments with sound modification (he built an echo chamber for use at the studio) made important marks on Nashville recording; even more, the informality of his sessions—in large part legitimized jams among musicians used to working together and devoted to keeping the singer out front—set the style for what's now known as "the Nashville sound."

Born in East Tennessee, Chet Atkins followed the example of his brother Jim, a singer-guitarist with the popular Les Paul Trio, into professional music. Beginning as a fiddler on Knoxville radio, he soon switched permanently to guitar and put in ten years as a sideman with various radio and traveling acts. He first went to Nashville while playing with the Carter Family (Maybelle and daughters), but found his guitar talents and versatility netted him a great deal of session work. He worked the Opry, sessions with Hank Williams and many others, then drifted into helping organize sessions for RCA Victor's Steve Sholes, who had first recorded him (though without much success) a few years before. By 1957 Atkins was in charge of Nashville operations for the company and was himself producing sessions for most major stars. His own eclectic listening and playing habits—he was as likely as not to follow a Travis-like version of a country standard with some classical guitar or a jazz piece—became reflected in what he recorded, modernizing and helping popularize country music as never before. Steel guitar and fiddle vanished to be replaced by lush arrangements of horns and strings; piano was given a major role; lavish use was made of vocal backgrounds, overdubbing and other production devices. In later years Atkins grew to mistrust his efforts at slicking up the music, telling *Rolling Stone* in 1976, "I've said that I hope country music doesn't completely lose its identity—and I apologized for anything I did in taking it too far uptown, which I sometimes did because we were just trying to sell records."

Country music had been almost wiped out with the advent of rock about 1954, and it was in trying to meet the challenge of this wild new music that it changed so substantially. Ironically, the rock and roll that almost destroyed country music came largely from *within* it, from young musicians like Sid King and His Five Strings, Bill Haley, Buddy Holly and Elvis Presley, who infused the basically country music they were playing with heavy doses of the black rhythm and blues they'd also grown up with in the South. "We played country music, we were raised on country music," says Sid King, who with His Five Strings was probably one of the first to play rock and roll. "But we liked to listen to rhythm and blues a whole lot, people like Fats

Domino or Jimmy Reed, the Drifters and the Clovers, and it definitely influenced what we wrote and recorded."

At a time when traditional country music had gone begging before the onslaught of rock, then, the new "Nashville sound" grabbed it by the bootstraps and yanked hard. There's some question whether this intercession actually improved or damaged the music, but whatever else, it retrieved the industry when things looked their darkest. (It also set the scene for the eventual fusion of rock and country more than a decade later when Waylon Jennings, Willie Nelson and the boys started swimming upstream against that staid, slick Nashville sound, precipitating the much-adoed "Outlaw" revolution.)

Of course few things are quite that linear, and as Bill Malone points out in *Country Music, U.S.A.*, "Much of what occurred in the late fifties came not from outside pressure but from within the music, as a result of the logical development and refinement of instrumental techniques."

Nashville's session men by this time had become remarkably adroit, inventive and multifarious musicians, pushing hard at the boundaries of country music, and when they played together for pleasure, they often turned to a kind of loose, easy jazz. Several of them, Atkins included, periodically got together at a Nashville nightclub, the Carousel. "This group of musicians," Malone writes, "performing on most of the recordings aimed at popular audiences, produced a distinctive instrumental pattern widely referred to as 'the Nashville Sound.'" Other members of the group were pianist Floyd Cramer, drummer Buddy Harmon, bassist Bob Moore, guitarist Grady Martin—and Hank Garland.

Walter Louis Garland was born November 11, 1930, in Cowpens, South Carolina. His father bought him a used guitar for about four dollars when he was six years old.

"There was a man living down at the end of River Street in Cowpens who knew how to play," Garland told Rich Kienzle for a *Guitar Player* article published in January 1981 (by far the most comprehensive work on the guitarist to date), "so I went down to his house and said, 'Tune this thing up for me and show me how to play it.' He tuned it up and started giving me lessons on the thing. I went on to play whatever I could think of or hear. Whatever I heard on the radio I tried to copy."

Hank learned basic chords and positions from that neighbor, Mr. Fowler, and most of the rest he worked out for himself. His advice to young guitarists now is to find a good teacher; you've got to start off right, he says, so you'll know the possibilities. His own preoccupation with technique was profound in later years, but so were the natural resources that carried him to that preoccupation: his phenomenal ear and feeling. "Old Hank," Atkins says, "you know, he'd play harmony to anything I could do, first take. Hank was the type of guy where you could play a lick and it would come back at you like an echo. He copied everything he heard. You'd do 'brrr,' and he'd do 'brrr'—he'd do the same thing."

Hank's first influence, like most country guitar players of the time, was Mother Maybelle's lead lines on the Carter Family recordings. He also listened regularly to seventeen-year-old Arthur Smith, then playing over WSBA in Spartanburg, and so wanted to emulate Smith's electric guitar that at one point he hooked an electric cord to his guitar strings and plugged it into the wall, almost destroying his instrument. Still in his teens, Hank joined a local band headed by Shorty Painter. He got his first amplified instrument about then, an archtop Gibson or Epiphone with a DeArmond pickup and a small Gibson amp.

One day in 1945 Hank went downtown to buy some strings at Alexander's Music Store and was introduced to

Paul Howard, who was passing through town with his Georgia Cotton Pickers, a western-swing-style band that had helped break the Opry's ban on electric guitars. Howard was impressed with the fifteen-year-old's playing and offered him a job, calling a couple of weeks later to confirm it and telling Hank to come to the Tulane Hotel in Nashville. The young guitarist's boogie-woogie instrumental that first night at the Opry brought the crowd to its feet and Howard told him, "Kid, you have a job here as long as I got one."

Unfortunately, at fifteen Hank was too young to join the musicians' union and, because of child labor laws, unable to work full time. After eight weeks with the band he returned home to Cowpens with Howard's promise to hold a place for him. The day Hank turned sixteen, Howard called, and Garland rejoined the Cotton Pickers in Nashville.

Hank quickly met three friends who proved very important to his development as a guitarist. Chet Atkins, working then as a sideman with Red Foley on the Opry, describes his first meeting with Garland: "He was a little old, fat, red-faced punk, and he hadn't gotten all of his height yet. He was playing choruses that he heard on Bob Wills records done by Jimmy Wyble—the fellow who played like Charlie Christian. And he rushed an awful lot; he'd pick up tempo." Hank also met Ernest Tubb's lead guitarist, Billy Byrd, and established session guitarist Harold Bradley, brother of Owen Bradley. Before long Hank had moved into an apartment in Byrd's home and was spending all his free time jamming with Byrd and Bradley, learning about jazz. "We taught him songs and jazz licks and just a whole bunch of improvisations," Bradley says. "We showed him a lot of things we knew, and he just went on by us—just got into the jazz thing real heavy."

Chet Atkins heard Hank on record for the first time a year

or two later. "I was in Knoxville," he says "and I heard this chorus. I don't recall the artist now, but I remember then that I thought it was the greatest guitar chorus I'd ever heard, so I checked around and found out it was Hank who played it." He had told Hank that Django Reinhardt was the greatest guitar player in the world when they met in 1946, and Reinhardt became an important influence on Hank's emerging style. Bassist Bob Moore, with whom Hank roomed during this period, got up every morning at 5:30 to do a radio show with Lester Flatt and Earl Scruggs; when his alarm went off, Hank would get up too and be practicing before Moore finished his breakfast. Moore would do that show, then another one at noon, and when he got home Hank would still be sitting there listening to Django and playing along.

Garland had left the Cotton Pickers in 1947 for a three-year stint with Cowboy Copas, who himself had just left Pee Wee King's Golden West Cowboys after several successful recordings as vocalist with the band. Hank gained valuable experience doing some of Copas's earliest sessions; Kienzle observes that he probably also played on singer Autry Inman's 1948 recording "You Better Leave Them Guys Alone," the guitar solo thereon evocative of Les Paul or Django. Though he switched to Gibson by the end of the decade, Hank seems to have played a blond Epiphone Zephyr Deluxe during his tenure with Copas. His increasingly skillful guitar work was becoming well known and his reputation around Nashville growing daily, so that by 1949 he left Copas to begin free-lancing full time in the studios.

Before then he probably couldn't have seriously considered full-time studio work, but with the establishment of Castle Studio in 1947 and the continuing efforts of Victor's Steve Sholes and Paul Cohen from Decca, recording activity in Nashville flourished. A small group of musicians (Atkins, Harold Bradley, Grady Martin and Hank were the guitarists) formed around that activity, always available to augment, and increasingly replace, the singers' road bands for recordings. This was something new in country music, but a natural consequence of the music's centralization and growing sophistication. Hank began working Decca sessions for Paul Cohen and Owen Bradley and was soon in wide demand for his musical ideas as much as for his guitar playing. "He had a very good imagination for not only coming up with ideas, but also with arrangements," Harold Bradley recalls. Of course *arrangements* then meant (and for the most part in Nashville still mean) what are called "head" arrangements—loosely plotted outlines for instrument and vocal interaction. This wouldn't work with musicians unaccustomed to playing together and unfamiliar with one another's styles, but it is a magnificently efficient way of making records, and a busy producer like Paul Cohen could enter the studio with every prospect of cutting four or five strong sides in a single three-hour session.

About this time Paul Cohen grew fond of a song Hank had written as a finger exercise called "Sugarfoot Rag," recording it first as a solo instrumental and a little later, with lyrics added, in a version by Red Foley, with Hank playing the intro and solo. Paired with "Chattanooga Shoe Shine Boy," this version was released in early 1950 and accompanied "Shoe Shine Boy" to the top of the charts and sales of over a million records, itself hitting fifth place on the country charts for a brief period. Garland even received label credit on the song, a rare occurrence then and a certain indication that his value was freely recognized. The song also earned him the nickname "Sugarfoot" and a new string of sessions. Rich Kienzle writes,

> Garland did a number of early Nashville sessions, including a notable one with singer Eddie Hill in 1952. The song, "The Hot Guitar," featured Hank, Chet and Jerry Byrd

imitating other guitarists as well as themselves. The flipside cut, "Steamboat Stomp," was done with just Hank, a steel guitarist and a rhythm section. Having begun as a routine western-swing number, the song found Garland taking an incredible bebop guitar break in the middle which turned the tune inside out. Hank's jazz talents were crystallizing. Having already assimilated elements of Django, Christian and Barney Kessel, he now showed signs of Barry Galbraith and Tal Farlow influences in his playing.

For a few months in the early fifties Hank went on the road with Eddy Arnold. He soon returned to studio work in Nashville, but not until he'd had the opportunity to finally hear and meet, while in New York, some of the jazz guitarists he had been listening to so fervently, particularly Barry Galbraith, whom Hank credited with teaching him jazz rhythm playing. Self-taught like Hank, and almost the same age, Galbraith had started off as a banjoist and switched to guitar after hearing Eddie Lang play behind Bing Crosby in the early 1930's, working with the Claude Thornhill Band just before and after the war, and from 1947 until about 1970 as a top studio guitarist for NBC and CBS; in recent years he has worked primarily as a private teacher.

Meanwhile, Hank's enthusiasm was spreading to those around him. "Hank was the first guy to turn me on to Tal Farlow and Wes Montgomery," Harold Bradley says, and while Hank continued doing sessions with fiddler Tommy Jackson, Jim Reeves, Webb Pierce, Jerry Lee Lewis, Brenda Lee, Patti Page and many others, it was toward jazz that he increasingly steered.

Like many guitarists (Chet Atkins or Les Paul, George Barnes with his taped-over f-holes and custom-made Guild) Hank was a tinkerer, an experimenter, always trying different guitars, new ways of stringing or tuning them—anything to get a sound he wanted. For his solo on Patsy Cline's 1961 hit "I Fall to Pieces" he used an early echo device and was forever borrowing pickups and amps from Atkins just to see what he could do with them. Harold Bradley remembers that sometimes he'd use odd tunings, like using a wound G as his first string because he'd heard someone in Chicago do it and liked the sound. He bought a Gibson ES-150 from a cab driver in Nashville and another time tried out an L-7 with a "Charlie Christian" pickup for a while.

In 1955 Hank and Billy Byrd were sitting around the Gibson booth at the annual disc jockey convention in Nashville when they were approached by Gibson's sales manager, Clarence Havenga, who asked them what they would want in a guitar they couldn't find on any of Gibson's current models. They sat and talked with him for some time, saying they would like a guitar similar to the L-5 but with a thinner body and shorter scale than other jazz guitars. Havenga returned to Kalamazoo, Michigan, and months later sent them each a new Byrdland *(Byrd* plus Gar*land)* guitar. Hank began using this guitar for sessions and it has remained his favorite. (It is also the favorite of many jazz players, of James "Blood" Ulmer, and of rock guitarists Steve Howe and Ted Nugent.) Hank still has that Byrdland, stamped #2; he also owns L-5, L-7 and ES-150 Gibsons, two D'Angelicos, two Strombergs and a Depilar classical.

Like Chet Atkins, Garland took the rock and roll holocaust pretty much in stride. For an early Decca session with boogie-woogie pianist-singer Roy Hall, Bradley remembers, Hank told him he spent a lot of time listening to rhythm-and-blues station WLAC to get ideas and pick up on the feel of it; that session resulted in a tune called "Whole Lotta Shakin' Goin' On," turned into a rockabilly classic two years later by Jerry Lee Lewis. Hank also started using lighter strings and more treble on his amp to get a thinner, funky rock sound, appearing in this guise on such cuts as Jimmy Dickens's "I Got a Hole in My Pocket," Jerry Lee's "What'd I Say," Red Foley's "Crazy Little Guitar Man" and Eddie Bond's Mercury recordings—all cuts that largely defined Nashville's rockabilly phase. Hank had not abandoned his customary sound, of course; in fact in this same period he contributed a fine jazzy solo to Patti Page's "Just Because." But for a year or two rock and roll was happening, and was *all* that was happening, in Nashville as virtually everywhere else.

"After the initial trauma wore off," Kienzle writes, "some Nashville producers started to persuade as many country singers as possible to record rock and roll-flavored records. Everyone from Carl Smith and Red Foley to Little Jimmy Dickens, Webb Pierce, Johnny Horton and Marty Robbins jumped on the bandwagon—some of them reluctantly." This was not the ultimate answer, but it was an inevitable first reaction to rock's challenge, and the Everly Brothers, for whose recordings Atkins and Hank Garland often provided double leads, typify much that was going on at the time. Sons of old-time guitarist Ike Everly, they used contemporary moods and rhythms to deal with youthful topics in a style of singing descended directly from groups like the Blue Sky Boys and the Delmore Brothers. Their earliest records for Cadence in 1957 were received enthusiastically by both pop and country audiences, and their first for Warner Brothers in 1960, "Cathy's Clown," quickly became number one on pop charts; by 1961 the brothers had disappeared from country charts but continued a modest popular success into the late sixties.

Rather soon, instead of trying to chase rock and roll away, or failing that, to catch it, Nashville simply found another tree to climb in: the smooth, lushly produced "Nashville sound." Often Harold Bradley, Grady Martin and Hank would all work together on these sessions, each taking solos in line with his specialty—Grady the funky country tunes, Harold the pop songs, Hank the fast ones. Among hit records Garland worked on were Ferlin Husky's "Gone," Jim Reeves's "He'll Have to Go," Don Gibson's "Sea of Heartbreak" and "Just One Time" (both in tandem with Atkins), Kitty Wells's "Jealousy," Webb Pierce's "I Ain't Never" and "Tupelo County Jail."

From 1958 to 1961 Garland worked a number of sessions with Elvis, playing on "It's Now or Never," "Are You Lonesome Tonight," "Little Sister" and many others. Bradley remembers Hank using a Gibson ES-335 on many of these dates, borrowing Bradley's Fender Jazzmaster for "Little Sister" because he couldn't get the exact sound he wanted from his hollowbody electrics. Hank even played a few concerts with Presley, among them the 1961 Hawaii benefit show that proved to be Presley's last live performance for eight years. "In addition, Garland continued flexing his country-jazz muscles," Kienzle notes. "This is clearly evident in his work with jazz great Johnny Smith and Harold Bradley on Don Gibson's *Gibson, Guitars, and Girls* LP, which was recorded around 1960."

That same year brought three albums from Hank Garland. The Carousel Club in Printer's Alley had become a regular jamming spot for Hank and like-minded Nashville session men, and RCA made arrangements to record this casual band, along with Atkins and seventeen-year-old vibraphonist Gary Burton, live at the Newport Jazz Festival. Rioting disrupted the festival that year, however, and the musicians finally recorded on the back porch of the house they'd rented to live in during their time there. *After the Riot at Newport* was an album of loose jams, very much like what went on back home at the Carousel.

About the same time Hank recorded, again with Burton and regular playing partners, an album eventually released by Columbia as *The Unforgettable Guitar of Hank Garland;* with the support of Columbia's Nashville producer Don Law, Hank was subsequently signed by that label. His first album there, *Velvet Guitar,* turned out far too tame and pop-oriented for Hank's taste, though, and he pledged that on the next he would do exactly what *he* wanted to do, his own music. The next (and as it happened, last) album was *Jazz Winds from a New Direction.*

Jazz Winds featured Garland in a setting reminiscent of the fifties' Red Norvo Trios in which guitarists Jimmy Raney, Tal Farlow and Jimmy Wyble played such an important part. With only Burton, Dave Brubeck drummer Joe Morello and bassist Joe Benjamin, Hank ran six tunes through some solid, straightahead jazz guitar: "All the Things You Are," Irving Berlin's "Always," bop standard "Move," a Burton-Garland original "Three-Four, the Blues," and on side two, "Riot-Chous" (another original, a fast blues from Boots Randolph and Garland) and "Relaxing." "The LP turned many heads," Kienzle writes, "including those of jazz aficionados who couldn't believe that such a great guitarist could come from Nashville. All during this time Hank was still picking up direction, listening intently to Wes Montgomery and others. His fingerstyle chops were improving, and it looked like Garland was finally entering the world of jazz guitar on his own terms."

Bucky Barrett, who contributed a transcription of "Relaxing" to accompany Kienzle's piece on Garland and who has for several years been working on a book about Hank's playing, is now himself a versatile Nashville session guitarist. In 1980 he recalled for *Guitar Player* the first time he heard *Jazz Winds:*

> One night, while riding down the road, I heard a song on the radio in which the guitarist was playing some unbelievable things. I pulled over to the first phone booth and called the radio station to find out who it was. They told me it was Hank Garland's tune called "Riot-Chous." From that mo-

ment on, Hank Garland was my idol. He had a sound and touch that I had to have. He made the guitar sound so good. I immediately went out and bought the album, and slowed it down to sixteen RPMs, and started hacking away. I was so dumb I didn't realize you almost need a computer to figure out some of his licks.

Another young guitarist who heard *Jazz Winds*—the first jazz record, he later said, that really caught his ear—was George Benson, at that time seventeen years old and playing hard rhythm and blues in a hometown Pittsburgh band.

It indeed seemed that Hank Garland, at thirty years old, had come into his own, transforming himself in fifteen brief, busy years from a "little old, fat, red-faced punk" playing downhome guitar to a remarkable jazz musician. "It was almost as if Garland had smothered the 'hillbilly' stereotypes with chorus upon chorus of brilliant, bop-flavored jazz," Kienzle writes. "Before Hank Garland, the very idea of a steel guitarist such as Buddy Emmons recording with a jazz group—as he did in 1963 with his *Steel Guitar Jazz* album—or of mainstream jazz bassist Ray Brown and drummer Shelley Manne working with country mandolinists Jethro Burns and Tiny Moore, would have been all but unthinkable." Hank epitomized, he suggests, the popular image of Nashville pickers: able to walk into a studio, hear a run-through and come up with a strong guitar part on the spot; ready to leave a day's work in the studios to jam all night in Printer's Alley; always open to new sounds, new possibilities—a player "for whom the instrument was not just an end in itself, but a means to the end of creating music."

Other winds were at work as well, though—change winds. In the summer of 1961, near Springfield, Tennessee, Hank Garland was involved in an automobile accident. Severely injured, he at last regained consciousness to discover his motor functions and coordination virtually destroyed by extensive brain damage, the skills he had worked so long and hard to develop obliterated. Hank returned home to South Carolina and, encouraged by his family, began relearning guitar, playing scales and patterns endlessly in a struggle to regain control over not only the guitar, but himself. Finally, in 1976, at the Fan Fair Reunion Show in Nashville, he appeared briefly onstage to play "Sugarfoot Rag." Today he plays regularly with a rehearsal group in Spartanburg.

"We haven't had another one come down the pike who plays the lines that he played," Harold Bradley says. "We've got some guys who play fast, but they don't play the lines and they don't have the feeling, the soul."

Hank Garland represents many things: the growth of a specifically American industry, that of country music; a kind of brashness and bullheadedness just as distinctly American; the prodigy and then prodigious musician living for little else but his music, a "natural" who runs with every ball that comes near him. As much as anything else, Hank Garland, in his bluesy slides, bebop lines and unabashed country boogie, stands for the egalitarianism of our music, for the basic unity of all American music as it reaches back to the Delta and Storyville, to Texas and mariachi bands, back to the two-steps of Polish or Czech immigrants and the lonesome sound of yodeling, back to the sound of Hawaiian guitars and mandolins—and as it extends forward to whatever realms await us.

APOSTASY:

Wes Montgomery

"TO ME," Joe Pass once said, "there have been only three real innovators on the guitar—Wes, Charlie Christian and Django Reinhardt."

"From the beginning of his belated 'discovery,' the critical reception ranged from euphoria to hyperbole," Gary Giddins writes. "No one had ever heard a guitar sound like Wes Montgomery's. The decade had its share of gifted guitarists—Tal Farlow, Barney Kessel, Kenny Burrell, Jim Hall and others—but the consensus on Montgomery was 'not since Charlie Christian.' "

Wes Montgomery was born John Leslie Montgomery on March 6, 1925, in Indianapolis. He began playing guitar at age nineteen, just after he was married, first using a tenor guitar but quickly moving up to a standard electric. Asked in later years how he became interested in guitar, Wes responded, "Charlie Christian, like all other guitar players. There was no way out. That cat tore everybody's head up. I never saw him in my life, but he said so much on records. I don't care what instrument a cat played, if he didn't understand and feel the things Charlie Christian was doing, he was a pretty poor musician."

Wes could easily have been describing the effect his own playing had on other musicians, but he never really acknowledged that effect, remaining dissatisfied and insecure with his own playing and forever insisting that he *used* to play a lot better. He was not dissembling, but truly innocent of ego, thinking of himself as a tool for music rather than the other way around, and references here to the parity of music and to its emotional content are signal ones. "Like if you hear a classical guitar player," he once said, "he'll make you feel like 'What're you playing the thing you're playing for? *This* is what you should be playing.' . . . But if a jazz player is really playing, the classical player will have to respect him." Ralph Gleason remarked that when Wes hit the strings you could always feel it in your gut if you were anywhere within hearing. Wes himself said, "The biggest thing to me is keeping a feeling, regardless of what you play."

Wes set up his new guitar and amp alongside the record player and started listening closely to Charlie Christian records, trying to copy everything Christian did. After six or eight months he'd succeeded in taking all the solos from the records and got his first job with a local band, playing those solos verbatim. "I'd play Charlie Christian's solos, then lay out. Then a cat heard me and hired me for the Club Fourforty. I went on the stand and played the solos. The guys in the band helped me a lot about different tunes, intros, endings and things that they had. They wired me up on all those, but after that, that was it." Obviously Wes's keen, quick ear was asserting itself, and he progressed rapidly, working with various Indianapolis bands and touring for a time with one ("we starved"), then in 1948–50 joining Lionel Hampton's big band. Wes would always depend on his ear. He never learned to read or had any theory to speak of, yet he consistently played over the heads of other guitarists, turning out remarkably sophisticated harmonies and unremittingly fresh lines. Like Christian, Wes was a natural.

Wes himself later summed up these years. "I began working hard and experimenting with techniques, seeking out the ones that felt good and were most expressive of my thoughts. My explorations continued for quite a while. My technique improved, developing out of particular playing situations. More and more of *me* passed through my amplifier to those who took time to listen."

The most visible aspects of Wes's emerging style were his use of the thumb instead of a pick, giving a round, warm sound, and his use of octaves to double a lead line. "Montgomery created a relaxed, melodic style derived from Charlie Christian," Marc Gridley writes in *Jazz Styles*. "His tone was round and full, cleanly articulated, and not edgy or excessively percussive. He had a well-paced style where everything swung comfortably. Voicing lines in octaves was not new to jazz guitar, but Montgomery's use of this device did much to popularize the approach." Intuitively adopting unusual suspensions and modes, he combined single notes, octaves and chords in a fluid, highly personal manner. "What I do might not be right technically," Wes said, "but the music comes out all the same. . . . Because I had to play and tell my story." Just so, despite his innovation, it was the *intensity* of his music one responded to, the power and personality of it. When Wes hit a string you felt it, and it wasn't just a note, a C$^\sharp$ or a B$^\flat$, it was part of a story he was telling you. That big Gibson hollowbody *was* Wes Montgomery while he played it; there was no division between them.

Yet somehow Wes escaped the monomania and narrow focus that comes so easily to creative artists. He always asserted that music was but one aspect of his life. "What sort of person would I be," he asked, "if I'd devoted all my time to the instrument and then gave up music? There are other things going on, you know." He was a teetotaler, a family man with six kids he liked to be around and a strong distaste for the road life so much a part of the jazz world. "Wes was a marvelous man," guitarist Jimmy Stewart says.

"He was developed in other areas than music. His spiritual being was developed, he was warm and he loved to give his music. We can't ask any more of a human being than what he fulfilled within himself."

Despite two years on the road with Lionel Hampton and great local popularity, Wes was little known outside Indianapolis, where with brothers Buddy (piano) and Monk (bass) he'd become a vital part of the jazz scene, until 1959. Monk had started playing bass at age thirty after hearing Wes's group at a local jazz club and deciding he could do better than the guy then on bass. He started on a seventy-five-dollar Czech upright, then, after joining Lionel Hampton in 1951, switched to electric bass, finding that gave him the solid bottom he wanted even when he played it "melodically" like an upright. Thus he became if not the first jazzman to play the electric bass, certainly the first to record with it. In the mid-fifties Buddy and Monk gained some success in California as The Mastersounds, and it was during this period that not only Ralph Gleason, but many others, first encountered Wes Montgomery's astounding music.

"I heard a lot about Wes Montgomery before I ever saw him," Gleason wrote.

> His two brothers, Buddy and Monk, were in a group in San Francisco called The Mastersounds, and they kept saying, "Wait, wait until you hear Wes!" and they sure were right!
> Wes came out to San Francisco and played with them on Sunday afternoon at the Jazz Workshop, and that was it. The club couldn't wait to have him back.
> Eventually, Wes moved to the Bay Area and played with his brothers. He also worked a long engagement with John Coltrane and Eric Dolphy at the Jazz Workshop, plus an appearance with them at the Monterrey Jazz Festival, and then he formed his own group.

Wes and his brothers again played together in the mid-sixties, and many fine sides from them are collected on

Milestone's *Wes Montgomery: Groove Brothers* (Milestone M47051).

Following his brief period in Berkeley, Wes moved back home to Indianapolis and in 1959 was playing with Melvin Rhyne and Paul Parker in a guitar-organ-drums trio. He worked as a welder in a radio factory from 7:00 A.M. until 3:00 P.M., slept a few hours and played the Turf Bar from 9:00 P.M. until 2:00 A.M., then the Missile Room from 2:30 to 5:00 A.M.

Cannonball Adderley, on a one-night stand in Indianapolis, heard Wes with his group at the Missile Room. Adderley was one of the best post-Parker improvisers; he had worked with Miles Davis and John Coltrane, and had a habit of dropping bits of pop songs, long wails and blue notes into his playing, which was still pretty straight bebop. Impressed, he phoned the head of Riverside Records, Orrin Keepnews, to tell him about Montgomery. Keepnews was skeptical of Adderley's extravagant praise but recalled an article by Gunther Schuller in *The Jazz Review's* current issue and looked it up. Titled "The Indiana Renaissance," that article read in part, "The thing that it is most easy to say about Wes Montgomery is that he is an extraordinary spectacular guitarist. Listening to his solos is like teetering continually on the edge of a brink. His playing at its peak becomes unbearably exciting to the point where one feels unable to muster sufficient physical endurance to outlast it."

Spurred on by the article, Keepnews flew to Indy and immediately signed Wes. The first recordings were made in New York on October 5 and 6, 1959, with Wes's hometown trio. *The Incredible Jazz Guitar of Wes Montgomery,* with Tommy Flanagan on piano, Percy Heath on bass and Albert Heath on drums, was cut in early 1960. From that time on, until his death in 1968, Wes Montgomery was *the* American guitarist. "When Wes came on the scene," Ralph Gleason said, "he was so innovative and so powerful that he just swept the other guys away into the studios." From his initial celebrity among jazz fans Wes passed on to popular recognition. His albums were consistently at the top of the charts; he received awards from *Down Beat, Billboard* and *Playboy* as well as a Grammy; and he was profiled in *Time* and *Newsweek*. For a jazz guitarist that is unlikely territory, even today. At the time it was absolutely alien land.

Jazz critic Leonard Feather: "Montgomery's death roughly coincided with the guitar revolution that saw this instrument take on many new functions. . . . Many of these developments were due to the impact of rock, for it was the rock musicians who enabled the guitar to surpass the piano as the most played, most purchased instrument in contemporary society."

Wes proved many listeners' introduction to jazz guitar, among them Larry Coryell, who in recent years has worked freely in both rock and jazz settings, as a solo guitarist, and as part of several excellent guitar duos. "At that age, as a teenager," Coryell says, "I would listen to Wes Montgomery and just not have any idea how he did it. Not the technique, but just the mind. His really great solos like 'West Coast Blues' just blew me out, so I learned that very solo myself. Not because I wanted to play like Wes, because that would be like asking a Ford to be like a Rolls Royce, but just to understand how his mind worked to get those ideas."

Another was Steve Khan, in 1964 at the age of seventeen, working as a rock-and-roll drummer, who bought one of Wes's albums because the guitar on it resembled a Gibson he'd seen B. B. King play. Khan has become a fine jazz guitarist and several years ago contributed liner notes for *Groove Brothers*.

I'll never forget sitting on the floor with the volume turned way up and being blown away by Wes's interpretation of Duke Ellington's classic "Caravan." That experience literally changed my whole life by opening me up to the world of improvised instrumental music, otherwise known as jazz. I still owned a set of drums, so hearing Grady Tate on that recording was at the same time both uplifting and the final blow to any hopes of becoming a drummer. From that point on I sought out any record by Wes and anything that had Grady as the drummer, thus starting a chain reaction that led me to an overwhelming number of great jazz names: Miles Davis, John Coltrane, Sonny Rollins, Bill Evans, Jim Hall, Grant Green, Oliver Nelson. . . . It was an incredible period of listening and exploring, and out of all this, at the age of twenty, came the decision to try my hardest to become a jazz guitarist. Wes Montgomery, the man and his music, became the total inspiration for what I was attempting to do.

Not long after, Steve's father, composer Sammy Cahn, took him along to meet Wes Montgomery, and over the next two years Khan spent many hours listening to Wes live and talking with him between sets. Like Coryell, Khan was amazed at the guitarist's ideas, "his ability to sit on a bandstand, apparently totally relaxed and wearing that fantastic smile, playing all those incredible tunes and improvising so melodically for chorus after chorus: from single lines to octaves and finally to chords, *and* that gorgeous warm, dark sound." But the only answer he ever got from Wes when he asked how he did it was, "I don't know, I just do it." Finally, in an effort to understand Wes's music, Khan began transcribing his compositions and many of his solos; most of these transcriptions were released in 1978 as *The Wes Montgomery Guitar Folio.*

A friend of Wes's, studio veteran and teacher Jimmy Stewart, had found out how difficult it was to transcribe Wes's music several years earlier. Stewart told *Guitar Player* in 1970,

> Wes had complete trust in me that I would put it down right. I transcribed everything without Wes ever playing a note in front of me. Prior to the printing, Wes and I went over

the music. I was apprehensive because Wes didn't read music. He had a great ear and knew what he wanted to do with his music. I played "Bumpin' on Sunset" and went over the score along with Wes. I was pointing out the rhythms and the notes and he got very excited. "Is that what my playing looks like?" And I said, "It sure does and it was a tough one. I had to listen to that thing hour after hour to get it right." Wes had so much fun that he said he was going to learn to read. I said, "If you do, I'll have four dozen studio men from New York and L.A. down my neck." He said, "Man, it's sure going to be fun when I learn to read."

Among Wes's own favorite guitarists were Barney Kessel, Tal Farlow, Jimmy Raney and Django Reinhardt. Kessel, he said, had a lot of feeling and a good sense of jazz harmony; he felt that Farlow (like himself a self-taught player and non-reader) had less feeling but amazing drive and speed; and he admired Raney's touch, his finesse. Of Django he remarked, "To me, a lot of guitar players don't go to a particular place, they just sit down and play a whole lot of guitar, and Reinhardt is one of those kind of cats."

His own goal, he said in the early sixties, was to move freely among the guitar's many voices, playing a melody/counterpoint/unison line with another instrument perhaps, dropping out and coming back in with phrases and chords, then playing octaves the next time around. This ideal of continual variation showed in the choruses Wes played hour after hour at live gigs; his inventiveness never flagged and he never seemed to lose overall balance and proportion. Yet he was always concerned, Gleason tells us, that when it came his turn to solo he wouldn't be able to maintain the standards he wanted. Asked to join John Coltrane's group, he told classical/jazz guitarist Bill Harris that there was "too much music there. I just couldn't handle John's music and my own all at the same time."

Khan points out that Wes's remarkable single-note lines

and chordal passages were overshadowed by public attention to his use of octaves, noting as well his tasteful and
buoyant comping behind other instruments. In the notes
for *Groove Brothers,* Khan wrote:

> I have described Wes's comping style, as having a big band
> in his hands: his low-register full chord voicings could punc-
> tuate like trombones; at times he'd riff in octaves in a way
> that resembled unison sax lines; and he could build to three-
> and four-note middle- and upper-register voicings like a
> trumpet section. "Snowfall" is particularly noteworthy for
> what was, for that time, some very sophisticated harmony.
> The use of the major seventh with a sharp-four chord (which
> alludes to the lydian mode) was very adventurous then, and
> later was to be an important harmonic element in the music
> of Miles and Coltrane and of current progressive innovators
> like Weather Report, John McLaughlin and Chick Corea.
> Wes had big ears and an open mind, and it seemed to me that
> he never stopped growing.

Guitar was something Wes (and everybody else, the guitar revolution rolling about them) had reason to think
about a lot in the mid-sixties. Wes was microphone-shy and
most interviews with him are less than satisfactory, but on
the topic of guitars he became almost eloquent, always
stressing the difficulty and waywardness of the instrument.
"It's a very hard instrument to accept," he said at one point,
"because it takes years to start working with it, that's first,
and it looks like everybody else is moving on the instrument
but you. Then when you find a cat that's really playing, you
always find that he's been playing a long time, you can't get
around it." Much of what he had to say about guitar brings
a shock of recognition to those of us who began playing in
prerevolution days, when there were few instruction
materials, fewer teachers and decent guitars were hard to
come by, or to those of us who have ourselves put in time
as teachers.

In an interview with Ralph Gleason published in *Guitar Player* after Wes's death, Wes presents the perfect scenario of the would-be guitarist. Thinking he wants to play guitar, this guy goes out and buys a twelve-dollar special. He can't understand why he's not able to just pick it up and play what he's thinking, it *looks* so easy, man, but he keeps on plugging, then after two or three weeks he still can't get two good notes or anything *like* a line out of it, and his fingers are sore. Maybe he'll quit then, and the guitar will drift toward the closet or a garage sale, or maybe he'll go out and find a teacher, probably expecting that teacher to do everything needing to be done in one thirty-minute session a week. And he won't mess with that guitar between times. So the instrument winds up in the closet anyway.

You've got to put in the *time,* Wes said again and again; you've got to stay with it, and most people just don't have the tenacity or stubbornness to ride it out. "You have melodic lines and chords," he said, "and you have the neck before you can do either one. It takes a long time, and you have to think ahead to your limits before you can do anything." There are always so many decisions and choices how to play a note or a line, he says, that you can get in some pretty deep water before you know it.

> After a period of time the beginning player will hear a little difference in his playing, and that little inspiration is enough to go further, and the first thing you know you won't back out. The biggest problem is getting started. Then later every time you hear guitar players everybody plays more than you. . . . And you'll find more people against you than for you, until you get started. Then you'll find more with you than against you.

Both the controversy and immense popularity surrounding Wes Montgomery, those with him and those against him, center chiefly on recordings he made for Verve and A&M in the mid-sixties.

Orrin Keepnews once told Wes, "A year ago you were unknown and broke; now you're a star and broke, and that's real progress." Keepnews's Riverside label itself was having serious problems and finally collapsed in 1964. Wes went over to Verve under the direction of Creed Taylor and cut two albums, *Movin' Wes* and *Bumpin'*, which were, at least by jazz standards, commercial successes. The next, *Goin' Out of My Head*, won a Grammy.

"Wes Montgomery was probably the best hard bop guitarist," Marc Gridley writes in *Jazz Styles*. "It is ironic, though, that his reputation with non-musicians was earned by recordings for Verve and A&M which did not reflect much of his great talent. He played tastefully on these records, but his work of the late 1950's and early 1960's is a far richer jazz vein."

Ironic perhaps, but not altogether surprising. Until recently straight jazz had little currency among general listeners and thrived primarily as a ghetto art with a small audience of hardcore fans, intellectuals and other artists. What *is* surprising is that Wes Montgomery, this innovative, soft-spoken pure jazz guitarist, became popular at all. No one's really sure how it happened, or why, and controversy circles the fact that it did like many tiny worlds around a single sun.

"It's simple," remarks Dom Cerulli in the liner notes to Verve's posthumous *The Best of Wes Montgomery, Volume 2*. "He took today's better pop tunes and played them with such jazz feeling and power that he caught the ear of the pop listener by *what* he was playing, and the imagination of the jazz listener by *how* he was playing what he was playing."

And that is certainly part of it. But if Wes did retain his power and the emotional content of his work, there was just as surely a diminution in what he played, and as his popularity grew (with, one assumes, mounting pressures from his record company in proportion) his playing became increasingly spare. "You know," Howard Roberts remarks, "he was really a heck of a jazz guitar player, but you wouldn't know it from the last two or three years of his career. You would think that all he could play was the melody and octaves."

Roberts used to drop by and have a drink with Wes when he was playing jazz clubs during this period. Wes would complain, he said, that whenever he tried to play something —anything besides "Goin' Out of My Head" or one of his other hits—people would get up and walk out. He was a victim of his own popularity, or of the trivialization of his talent, depending on how you perceive it, and as a result that talent went largely unheard for the last years of his life. There's a tremendous democratic pull in America to simplify everything, iron out all the wrinkles, reduce it to its lowest denominator, pasteurize, homogenize; and somehow Wes Montgomery went down that disassembly line. Over and over again he would say, "You should have heard me fifteen years ago when I was *really* playing."

Another, more benign viewpoint comes from Joe Pass. "Wes Montgomery became a big seller," he said in a 1972 round-table discussion on jazz guitar for *Guitar Player*, "and he played much more sophisticated guitar than you'd normally hear on the radio. Stan Getz became very big without playing any differently, maybe songs that weren't as long or not as intricate, but I don't think either of these artists sacrificed their integrity. They played what they felt. I think a lot of it was packaged around them afterward. They sold because somebody said, 'Let's do it.' "

Such talk of integrity and artistic conscience, of course, is *de rigueur* to creative artists. It does require a certain high-mindedness, a cautious elitism likely to decay with the bearer's age but just as likely essential to his work. Still, the truth is that the "great beast" of democracy feeds and feeds on its artists yet remains hungry. Through our media we approach a condition suggested by Andy Warhol: in the future, everyone will be world famous for five minutes.

However it happened, Wes seemed aware of his attenuation, in his own gentle way accepting it. "I remember talking to Wes Montgomery when he was playing to a packed club," Barney Kessel says. "He wasn't bitter, just realistic. He said, 'See those people out there? They didn't come to hear me, they came to see me play one, two or three of my hit records, because when I decide to do a tune of mine or Coltrane's "Giant Steps" instead of "Goin' Out of My Head" they get bored and start talking. In fact they get very insulted, because they drove sixty miles to hear "Tequila" so they can sing this one part and show their friends they know what's happening. They're not here to see if I'm better this year than last, they're here to hear me perform like it was a record hop.' "

George Benson, who called Wes "the most modern and hippest guitarist of our time," offers yet another view, though one wonders if Benson is not speaking more for himself than for Montgomery. "People who love jazz musicians, love us when we play what we want to play, and we're starving. But then, as soon as you commercialize your sound, as Wes did, the jazz fans and critics are down on you! Wes told me about this a week before he died. He was very unhappy and disturbed by this attitude. He died a very sad man."

Following Wes's death, Creed Taylor tapped Benson as his successor. The relationship did not last, but for the time it did, it reiterated precisely the course of Wes's own last years. In his excellent book, *Riding on a Blue Note,* Gary Giddins quotes Benson on his final meeting with Wes. They'd been talking, and Wes wasn't happy with the music coming out under his name:

But then when we finished talking, he got into his new car, better dressed than I'd ever seen him. Only a couple of years before, I drove my stepfather two hundred miles to see him, because he wasn't convinced that Montgomery was as good as Charlie Christian. There were three people in the joint; Wes had a raggedy old car and was eating in those funky, jive restaurants that probably took his life.

Benson: "Want to hear me play jazz? Pay me. Give me a million dollars and I'll make the greatest jazz record you ever heard, 'cause that's what I'd lose by playing it."

And: "Why shouldn't a man do what he's capable of?"

But he *should,* and that's the point of all this: it's singularly telling that Benson's "capability" refers not to creative achievement or artistic expression, but to earning power. One imagines Mammon in the back room (smoke-filled of course) with the boys, rubbing his hands and telling them, "We got a hot one here, guys, and he's all ours."

Curiously, I happened across the following excerpts from Beethoven's letters while writing the final draft of this piece, and set them here for contrast:

> I adhere to the sum of fifty ducats, which is in fact nowadays the usual price for a string quartet. I feel positively ashamed when I have to ask a price for a really great work. Still, such is my position that it obliges me to secure every possible advantage. It is very different, however, with the work itself, when I never, thank God, think of profit, but solely of how I write it.
>
> • • • • •
>
> I do not fear for my works. No evil can befall them; and whoever shall understand them, he shall be freed from the misery that burdens mankind.

Giddins includes in his book a self-professed polemic titled "Jazz Musicians, Consider Wes Montgomery." (Both this and the Benson piece appear in a section called "Adventures in the Jazz Trade.") Here he traces the devaluation of Wes on the jazz market, proceeding inexorably, he says, from "Taylor's cost-accountancy approach to producing music." Wes from time to time managed to break through the hack arrangements and unimaginative material, but most of it was dreary stuff. "With each A&M release, Montgomery became more encumbered by pretentious arrangements. It is the highest possible tribute to the man's genius that he managed to inject so much feeling, such unmistakable soul, into situations that clearly displeased him."

Giddins reports that Wes made sure distinction between the two kinds of music he played ("There is a jazz concept to what I'm doing, but I'm playing popular music and it should be regarded as such") and recalls Wes's appearance at the Kansas City Jazz Festival a month or so before he died. Several members of the audience were getting ready to leave by the time Wes came on, he writes, "not wanting to hear a rehash of 'California Dreaming' and 'Goin' Out of My Head.' But the temptation to hear him was irresistible, so we decided to wait. Surrounded by four rhythm players, his regular group, he immediately shot off a single chorus of 'Goin',' and followed it with the most fiery, exquisite set of guitar music I've ever heard. What a feeling there was in that huge auditorium. Clearly, he had compromised only on disc and would eventually be recorded more seriously."

Verve's posthumous release *Willow Weep for Me* in several ways symbolizes Wes's career. Derived from tapes made with the Wynton Kelly Trio at the Half Note in New York in the summer and fall of 1965 (other tapes from the same period earlier yielded *Smokin' at the Half Note*), the album was wrapped in swaddling clothes before it was laid away in the record bins—specifically with brass and woodwind arrangements by Claus Ogerman, who'd done arrangements for the top-selling *Tequila* album. There's considerable evidence that Verve knew it was getting caught with its pants down, the liner notes by Richard Lamb being quite defensive.

Wes himself used to complain that he felt a little constricted with all his arrangements written out. But this record remedies that: Wes's work came first, free as the wind. With Wynton, Paul and Jimmy just playing for all they're worth. Nothing written. Moreover, the horn charts were totally derived from what they're doing. The orchestrations are merely an enlargement of what four guys laid down three years ago in that musty room.

Of course the purists will protest—at least *prior* to listening. We direct their attention to the aforementioned album [Smokin'] and to the three tracks on this album untouched by Gross Gimmickry. On "Surrey With the Fringe on Top," "Four on Six" (a Wes original) and especially on "Impressions" you'll get all of Wes and Wynton winging it that you can take. These are priceless performances that should make any purist proud to own this collection.

There is of course a fair chance that the purist will protest not only prior to, but during and after listening, and at some length. Grinding fine beefsteak into hamburger simply makes little sense. And rarely has Procrustes advertised his bed so freely.

Wes of course remains himself whatever clothes he wears, and nothing can diminish his immense talent as a guitarist or colossal impact on jazz and popular music.

The year Wes Montgomery died of a heart attack, 1968, was something of a watershed in the world of pop music. The Beatles's avant-garde *Sgt. Pepper's Lonely Hearts Club Band* had come out the previous year; 1968 brought their single "Hey Jude," which sold three million copies in two months, and a new album simply called *The Beatles,* filled with allusions to and quotations from old-time rock and roll. (That same year Aaron Copland said, "When people ask to recreate the mood of the sixties, they will play Beatle music.") Bob Dylan's *John Wesley Harding* hit the stores that year, as did *Cruisin' with Ruben and the Jets* by Frank Zappa and the Mothers of Invention, a curious return to the ballad-style rock of the fifties and early sixties. Top artist of the year was Aretha Franklin, whose eleven million records made her the best-selling female vocalist in popular-music's history, and *Melody Maker* named Jimi Hendrix "The World's Number One Musician." The Motown sound reached its peak popularity that year, and blues was surging back into favor with bands such as Paul Butterfield's Blues Band, Cream and Canned Heat. Woodstock would take place the following year.

John Coltrane died in 1967. A classic Bill Evans trio with Eddie Gomez and Marty Morrell was recording and touring widely, and people like Cecil Taylor, Sun Ra and the Art Ensemble of Chicago were beginning to introduce new aspects of jazz sound. In 1968 Miles Davis used guitar for the first time in the cut "Paraphernalia" on *Miles in the Sky;* George Benson was the guitarist. By 1969 John McLaughlin had joined Davis, *In a Silent Way* and *Bitches Brew* both coming out that year. *Brew* sold more copies than any other Davis album and, with other examples of the emerging jazz-rock, helped create what is today the biggest audience jazz has known since the swing era.

CARRYIN' IT ON:

Michael Bloomfield

BY THE LATE FIFTIES something rather strange was seeping up around the cracks in the music business. Rock and roll had come along early in the decade (interestingly, just about the same time as bluegrass settled into its own) and was still plunging on, head lowered, through the charts and airwaves. In 1958 three men known as the Kingston Trio, direct descendants of the Weavers and other folk groups of the forties but with button-down collars instead of union cards, recorded "Tom Dooley," an old mountain song.

It's difficult to say why folk music so completely captured the country's imagination from about 1958 to 1963. Obviously, it was at least in part a reaction against the wantonness of rock and roll spawned by the likes of Bill Haley, Buddy Holly and Elvis. But that supposed wantonness by this time had been largely tamed, yoked into mechanical formula songs little different in kind from their Tin Pan Alley predecessors, suggesting that folk music succeeded simply because it was novel, something radically apart from current trends. Publicity attendant on the payola investigations may have abetted this turn away from slick pop music. To adults, folk music seemed safe (just look at those neat pinstripe shirts and fresh haircuts); to their offspring, accessible (all you had to do was listen, go pick up a guitar and learn three chords, and you had a group going). The young always seem to require a secret language, a shibboleth, and folk music fit that need for some time.

The "urban folk revival" virtually obliterated all else from the media. The Kingston Trio was followed by The Brothers Four, the Chad Mitchell Trio, Peter, Paul and Mary and many others. Folk clubs and schools hosted regular "hootenannies" and TV networks carried their own hyped versions of them. Musicians such as Bob Dylan, Joan Baez and John Hammond made their earliest appearances on the scene, while older performers like Pete Seeger (a member of the Weavers blacklisted from broadcasting for many years for supposed Communist sympathies, another victim of Joe McCarthy's headlong ambition) found their careers suddenly refurbished. The music became rather quickly entangled with social movements and, thereby, with college campuses, where folk-music societies developed and began sponsoring numerous folk festivals.

Contemporary folk music soon yielded, in this context, to more traditional and ethnic forms, bluegrass returning fans to Appalachian music, the blues of Dave Van Ronk introducing them to bluesmen like Mississippi John Hurt, Bukka White and Reverend Gary Davis. The kids with button-down collars had discovered funk, grit, the real thing. And button-down collars, chinos and penny loafers were replaced by chambray work shirts, jeans, boots or work shoes.

It would be difficult to overstate the importance of this period to subsequent music. The folk era paved the way for bluegrass's large following and the near-universal popularity of country music today. It gave rise to poet-songwriters who revolutionized both lyric and song forms. It introduced blues to young musicians who would in turn inject their rock and roll with heavy doses of it (leading to Jimi Hendrix, Cream and Eric Clapton) or create their own blues styles. Perhaps more than anything else, it returned popular music, for a brief time at least, to the people. Yet underlying all this is a more profound and often overlooked influence.

"The folk boom did more than introduce northern college students to traditional southern music," George Gruhn wrote in "Unsung Heroes of Rock and Roll," his *Guitar Player* column for May 1979. "It also introduced them to the guitar. Prior to this, the guitar was not really respectable. It was generally considered to be the instrument of rock and rollers, cowboys, hillbillies and black people (preferably blind ones). . . . All of a sudden, thousands of white, middle-class youngsters were playing guitars, and this has had a profound effect on the course of American music."

Many important popular guitarists got their start in music during this period, Gruhn goes on to point out in his excellent article—people such as Mike Bloomfield, Jerry Garcia, Ry Cooder, Clarence White and David Lindley—and their music continues to be shaped by the various musics they studied when starting out. The guitar itself, Gruhn writes, certainly would never have achieved its current prominence without the folk revival.

By about 1962 the folk movement began to weaken, but at the University of Chicago "folkies" had become aware of the black music thriving in the community that surrounded the school and started inviting local bands to play there. Before long students who'd been idolizing hillbillies and acoustic blues players adopted a new group of idols, bluesmen like Muddy Waters and Buddy Guy. Soon a number of young, white rhythm-and-blues bands appeared on the scene, beginning with the Paul Butterfield Band. These musicians thought of themselves as rhythm-and-blues players and were insulted if their music was mentioned in the same breath as rock and roll, which they associated with the rather tame thumps and hollers, now passé, of Bill Haley. Gruhn goes on:

> The progression of many of the folk musicians of the early sixties into rhythm and blues points up one of the most unusual aspects of the folk boom: During this period everyone learned to play at virtually the same time. Today we see guitar players of all ages at all levels of proficiency. But at that time, nearly everyone started at about the same age and within a year or two of each other. By 1962 or so, some of these people had gotten pretty good. As their technique developed, many had moved up a sort of mythical musical ladder, starting from very basic folk-music accompaniment, to old-timey music, to something more demanding like bluegrass or acoustic blues, and finally into electric rhythm and blues, which they considered to be more sophisticated. In later years the movement continued into things like acid rock and jazz-rock.

It also prepared its own demise as interest in rhythm and blues spread quickly throughout the country and to England, the arrival here of the American-styled Beatles and Rolling Stones finally slamming the door on the folk revival.

What that revival gave us more than anything else was an awareness of possibilities (probably as good a definition of "intelligence" as exists). Music was opened up in ways it never before had been. We began to perceive strains of influence, connections: the bedrock of our music. And for many of us the blues of Robert Johnson, Hawaiian guitar, Gid Tanner and His Skillet Lickers, Sonny Boy Williamson and Charlie Christian became important parts of our daily lives, of what we were. We retrieved, in small part, our history.

So those notes from the Butterfield Blues Band's amps still echo among us, the New Lost City Ramblers are still playing real country music, and gangs of young guitarists still hover (at least figuratively) about Lonnie Johnson and Big Joe Williams. And today's bands often feel quite free to play whatever they wish: thirties' swing tunes, big-city blues, fiddle-banjo duets.

"I am a musicologist by bent," Mike Bloomfield said in his last major interview, published in *Guitar Player*'s April 1979 issue. "I am rooted in American music of all sorts—Cajun, Mexican, all the jazz players up to Django Reinhardt, like Teddy Bunn and Eddie Lang, plus all the blues and folk forms, music you play on all the fretted instruments. . . . I would like to help keep those forms alive, so that people will know: This is how America played."

Bloomfield had effected an uncommon passage from contemporary bluesman to rock-and-roll superstar and junkie, and finally to solo performer of a variety of traditional and popular American musics. His last records reflect that odyssey: a fine all-acoustic album of traditional stylings; a documentary of blues guitar styles through history; several uneven and sometimes shabby electric-oriented albums; one of gospel duets with guitarist Woody Harris.

Mike Bloomfield was a man of strong likes and dislikes, of raging enthusiasms. "Mike Bloomfield . . . just lives and breathes music," Eric Clapton once remarked to *Rolling Stone*. "He's one of those people who don't think about anything else. . . . His way of thinking really shocked me the first time I met him and spoke to him. I never met anyone with so many strong convictions." Nor was Bloomfield reluctant at any time to express those convictions. "MCA is such an incredible merchandiser that the record *sold*," he said of one album he held in contempt. "I swear, they could be selling pig farts, whales copulating—it wouldn't matter. They would sell it successfully."

Away from home, the musical adventurer was a displaced person and hopeless insomniac, touring or traveling with great discomfort and repeatedly abandoning gigs *(Super Session, Live Adventures of Mike Bloomfield and Al Kooper)* after protracted sleeplessness. A visit to the Stanford sleep clinic yielded only fourteen days and nights of wired wakefulness and recommendations from doctors there that he never travel.

On May 15, 1981, Mike Bloomfield slept. He was found dead in his car on a San Francisco street, of an apparent overdose, early that morning. It seemed at first the heroin he'd kicked in the early seventies might have returned to claim him. The coroner's report read: cocaine and methamphetamine poisoning—accident.

Analine came out in 1977. It was mostly acoustic, a photograph on the back depicting a pile of standard, electric and Hawaiian guitars, a five-string banjo, mandolin and tiple gathered around a vintage wheelchair; Mike also played piano, organ, ukulele and bass. He was joined on one cut by drummer Bob Jones and on the final cut by a full rhythm section and his old friend from Chicago days, Nick Gravenites. All the rest is multi-tracked Bloomfield.

"The records I have recorded in the last four years or so are very poorly distributed," Mike told *Guitar Player,* "or if they are well distributed there are no print ads, or the company doesn't have enough money to promote them the way I'd like them to." Actually, despite its general excellence and prominent position in Mike's career, *Analine* was not a particularly commercial album and wound up selling mostly to devoted Bloomfield fans. It appeared on the small Takoma label, one of the many independents that sprang up during the later years of folk music; Mike did three others for the label before his death.

In content the album resembled the solo gigs Mike had begun playing in small northern California clubs: a jumble of hard blues, folk music, old standards, early jazz and rock. Audiences there were not always prepared for his act. He'd come out with his acoustic guitar and get down with some blues, and after a while somebody would yell *"Super Session!"* "I started discovering these old blues records when I was thirteen or fourteen," Mike said, "and I've been playing it that long, though not on record. Audiences don't always know. They think, I don't know—maybe they think I just saw Leon Redbone on *Saturday Night Live* and just got into it or something. . . . People resent it sometimes when we move on and we don't fit their preconceptions."

Analine opens with a paean to voyeurism, "Peepin' an' a-Moanin' Blues," inspired by the immensely popular "hokum" of Tampa Red and Tom Dorsey. The second cut is a tribute to the Lonnie Johnson-Eddie Lang duets ("Mr. Johnson and Mr. Dunn"), the third a traditional "Frankie and Johnny." "At the Cross" is an old Swans Silvertones song of which Mike said, "I was trying to get a sound like the vocals of Claude Jeters. Jeters was one of Ray Charles's greatest influences. I was trying to get as much Claude into my guitar playing as possible." The final cut on this side is "Big C Blues," an original with Mike playing piano, organ, guitar, bass and drums: a one-man jam.

Side two opens with "Hilo Waltz," an attempt to capture the sound of old-time string bands that played semiclassical and brass-band music, rather in the tradition of the banjo and mandolin societies. The second cut, "Effinonna Rag," is a solo guitar piece; the third a fine reading of Duke Ellington's "Mood Indigo." The title piece, a mellow, mournful ballad, rounds off the album, composer Gravenites taking the lead vocal while Bloomfield plays guitar, organ and mandolin behind him.

Analine is an impressive document of Mike's renewed dedication to traditional sounds and styles. It also suggests that he had come under the influence of new traditionally biased musicians such as Taj Mahal and Ry Cooder, and Mike does credit Cooder in the *Guitar Player* interview: "A lot of things influenced my confidence in the worth, the value of all this. Ry Cooder is an example. I thought, here is a man who had his eye on a certain sparrow, making record after record and constantly refining his diamond, so to speak."

It was really not so much a change of cast as casing. Bloomfield had studied and played this sort of material privately for years, and in later albums he did return to the hardass electric blues more commonly associated with him. But from this point on, in almost everything he did there was an unmistakable nod to the encompassing traditions he worked in and, mixed with searing amplified leads, sizable portions of traditional acoustic music—as though Bloomfield strove to integrate himself through his music.

Michael Bloomfield was born in Chicago on July 28, 1943, and began playing guitar at age thirteen. He had a guitar teacher for a little over a year, learning chords and a little theory, some basic lead. "Mostly what I would do," Mike told *Guitar Player* in 1971, "was toward the end of the lessons, I would just learn the chords. He had a 'Fake Book,' with all the famous standards. . . . I would play the chords to tunes from the book and he would play the lead to it and I would like him to improvise. And I learned how to play rhythm guitar."

His own tastes, quite naturally, did not run to old standards, but to fifties' rock and roll: Chuck Berry, Carl Perkins and anybody on the Sun label, the Ventures, Duane Eddy. On his own he discovered Chicago black radio stations hovering up there at the end of the dial and added those to his regular listening. He also had an ear open to the folk music just then making headway, mostly commercial folk music by people like Josh White and Odetta. "But as I got older, I got real interested in more ethnic type folk music. . . . if it were like blues, I would prefer Lightnin' Hopkins

to Brownie McGhee, because he seemed more real. . . .
Now, it's all mixed together, but then it was polarized into
definite categories."

By fourteen he was playing in suburban rock-and-roll
bands, "a regular hot-licks kid." The guys who were really
hot (things haven't changed much) were the ones who
could copy the solos from Duane Eddy and Buddy Holly
records, so Mike learned those. His own early strong influences came from Scotty Moore, who played guitar on
Elvis's early sides; James Burton, who replaced him; and
Cliff Gallop, who was with Gene Vincent.

Bloomfield had started off listening to lots of rockabilly
and blues without really being able to differentiate; he just
knew it had lots of energy, something he was drawn to.
"Yeah, it all has this sort of outlaw quality to it that I was
dying to get into any way I could. . . . I couldn't really tell
which I wanted to be more—a Presleyesque greasy hillbilly
or a jivey blues singer." As he discovered the Chicago stations catering to southern blacks and playing all blues, he
learned the difference and started going down to hear
Muddy Waters, B. B. King, Magic Sam and others in person. Before long he was taking his guitar along, walking on
stage out of nowhere and plugging in as he said, "Hey, *mind*
if I sit in?" The players (people such as Howlin' Wolf, Otis
Rush, Albert King, Little Walter) must have been as-
tounded—here's this fat little Jewish kid playing all this
bluesy rock-and-roll stuff—but they tolerated him. He also
met other young white musicians who were hanging out
with blues, notably Nick Gravenites, Norm Dayron and Paul
Butterfield. And eventually his notes (they'd always been
the right notes, he said) began falling in the right places.

Bruce Cook wrote in *Listen to the Blues,*

> Butterfield, who had been a student at the University of
> Chicago and lived nearby, began making the blues scene with

Nick Gravenites (now a songwriter and man-about-music in San Francisco) as early as 1957. Mike Bloomfield, years younger and a nervy young guitarist in suburban rock-and-roll groups, began on his own sometime later. Mike Bloomfield learned a lot of guitar out there at the wrong end of town and got what no amount of practice or instruction could have given: a real feeling for the blues. It is there in everything he plays today.

Tom Wheeler agrees:

Unlike the music of Jimi Hendrix and Eric Clapton, whose blues roots were one step removed and sometimes obscured by the smoke and sparks of the acid-rock milieu, Bloomfield's blues were unadorned, accessible, assimilable. His guitar technique churned with such soulfulness that he broke a color line of sorts, demonstrating a blues sensibility uncommon among white instrumentalists and earning respect from the sacred heroes of his youth.

By age eighteen Mike was managing the Fickle Pickle Coffeehouse, scouring Chicago for obscure bluesmen who'd made important records in the 1940's and bringing them to the coffeehouse for concerts alongside contemporary bluesmen like Muddy Waters and a guy from Texas, Johnny Winter. Washboard Sam, Jazz Gillum, Little Brother Montgomery, Tommy McClennan, Kokomo Arnold: these were people Mike had only read of. He was as amazed to discover them still living there in Chicago as they were to discover that anyone (especially a young white kid) remembered or cared.

About a year later, in 1964, Mike inherited (or grew) his first band. He'd been playing piano with Big Joe Williams at a club called Big John's and when Joe went on the road, Mike switched to guitar and fronted the band. "I trained Mike Bloomfield there," Williams said years later, "I started Mike there. And give Mike his first job. I had to go to Milwaukee to play a coffeehouse, and I got him to play there, him and Charlie Musselwhite." (Another musician Big Joe took under wing and helped launch was young Bob Dylan.) Musselwhite, who'd hung out with old bluesmen down in Memphis, was on harp. They had a washboard player for a while, then a drummer named Norm Mayall who'd worked with Sopwith Camel; later a bass player joined them. Nick Gravenites played piano, Mike Johnson sang and played guitar. Together a couple of years, the group eventually signed with Columbia and cut an album that was never released. They played "absolutely straight stone city blues"—not well, Mike said, but with great feeling.

Mike had also been concentrating on acoustic playing, learning the ragtime fingerstyles of Blind Blake and Mississippi John Hurt, and in the early sixties he recorded as sideman with several blues and folk performers in the Chicago area. The most important of these are certainly his Delmark recordings with Sleepy John Estes and Yank Rachell. He also continued working and sitting in with other bands at small clubs and lounges such as Pepper's and Magoo's, and at the Limelight Theater.

In 1964 Bloomfield sat in (on electric piano) with John Hammond and the Hawks (soon to be the Band) on Hammond's album *So Many Roads,* cut in New York City for Columbia. "Michael wasn't much of a guitar player back then," Robbie Robertson recalled, "but he was really into it. He played better piano than guitar, so I played guitar, he played piano, Charlie Musselwhite was playing harmonica and Levon played drums." In various ways, this quiet introduction signaled the next major trend in pop music. Hammond brought together the Hawks and Bob Dylan, who had been casting about for something new, and Dylan and Robertson quickly became friends, jamming together frequently. In May of that year Dylan went into the studio to cut his first electric number, "Like a Rolling Stone," a major landmark both in folk and popular music.

Paul Butterfield was working with an all-black blues band on the South Side at the time. He and Bloomfield were not very friendly—he was "too hard a cat" for Mike and probably more than a little skeptical of the young guitarist's sincerity—but Mike soon got a chance to move into a better club and offered Butter the gig at Big John's. "He got a really good band together," Mike said later, "and when they hit they were like dynamite and it was the best band I had ever seen at that time." It included Sammy Lay on drums, Jerome Arnold on bass, Elvin Bishop on guitar and Butter, of course, on vocals and amplified harp.

To some extent, Mike's observations concerning Paul Butterfield are self-revelatory. Butter stands apart from the other white Chicago players, Mike said, because he adapted himself, *changed* himself, to fit the music; he dissolved his past and took to the streets. "If Paul opens his mouth to sing it would have to be the blues, because that's his thing. . . . Everything I dug in and about the blues, Paul was."

Butter called him in to play on his first recording session for Elektra Records in 1965. Elvin Bishop was on guitar, so Mike played mostly piano, but he did add slide-guitar parts to two or three tunes. He used a "rotten" three-quarter-size Fender he'd bought at his uncle's pawnshop for twenty-three dollars, and after the New York sessions returned to Chicago. He hadn't been there long when he got a call from Bob Dylan.

"He had played in this club in Chicago and I had heard his first album and thought it was shit," Bloomfield told *Guitar Player.* "I told him that and he said, 'I'm not a guitar player, man, I'm a poet.' And so we sat and talked and played all day and goofed around and got to be friends. And then he left and I hadn't seen him until he called me up and asked if I would play on a record with him."

The record was "Like a Rolling Stone," and for the session Mike went out and bought a Fender Telecaster, "a
really good guitar for the first time in my life." Later col-
laborator Al Kooper was also at that session and wrote
about it in *Backstage Passes.*

> Suddenly Dylan exploded through the doorway, and in
> tow was this bizarre-looking guy carrying a Fender Tele-
> caster *without* a case. Which was weird, because it was the
> dead of winter and the guitar was all wet from the rain and
> snow. But he just shuffled over into the corner, wiped it off,
> plugged in and commenced to play some of the most incred-
> ible guitar I'd ever heard. That's all the Seven Lick Kid had
> to hear; I was in over my head. I anonymously unplugged,
> packed up and did my best to look like a reporter from *Sing
> Out!* magazine. . . . That's how I made my introduction to
> a man who can still make me smile whenever he picks up a
> guitar.

Kooper wound up bungling his way through an impromptu organ part, creating by pure chance a sound that
became closely associated with "the new Dylan" and
brought Kooper a steady stream of studio session calls.
Anthony Scaduto, in his biography *Bob Dylan,* writes,

> When you heard "Rolling Stone" back then it was like a
> cataclysm, like being taken to the edge of the abyss, drawn
> to some guillotine of experience. The rock band set up an
> enormous tension. Bloomfield on guitar, Al Kooper on
> organ, Bobby Gregg on drums and four other musicians.
> *Wham!* It opened with a quick drum beat, and then organ
> and piano and guitar rolling over the listener, setting up an
> overwhelming sense of immediacy, drawing the nerves taut.
> And then Dylan: "*Once* upon a time . . ." Biting off a word,
> spitting out venom, spreading a virulent emotion, infecting
> the listener. It is still probably the best song Dylan has ever
> done. . . . Back then, it destroyed the Dylan worshipers and
> brought him many new ones. Released in June, it quickly

moved up the charts, hitting number one on some charts in August, the first popular hit by Bob Dylan.

It was also the first eddy in what would become an overwhelming wave of new music loosely designated "folk rock"—the Byrds, Joni Mitchell, Creedence Clearwater Revival, Crosby, Stills and Nash, the Eagles. And for a growing nation of "street people," the disinherited, disenchanted, disconnected, it became a veritable anthem.

Mike had returned to Chicago and was playing guitar in a go-go club at this time. Butter was having second thoughts, came down and listened, offered him a job with the band. Bloomfield said sure, but he'd have to play lead guitar, not piano. So Elvin Bishop started playing rhythm and the band went to work with a vengeance. They bought a minibus and traveled all over the country playing one-nighters. The grind was excruciating, the bus (Mike claimed) "dehuman," and nobody made any money out of it. But they carried the gospel to far lands, and it was heard.

Meanwhile Bloomfield was getting a crash course in jazz from Pete Welding, an early Chicago collector-historian and one-time associate editor at *Down Beat.* "He played me all the jazz I had ever wanted to know in my life," Mike told *Guitar Player* in 1971. "He gave me a chronological history of jazz in a short period of time. I understood how you could get from a Coleman Hawkins to a Ben Webster to a Charlie Parker to a Coltrane to an Ornette Coleman to an Albert Ayler and Archie Shepp. I could understand the musical line, you know, like who was playing like who and how it went." The idea of lineage—of working in a tradition—became very important to Bloomfield; in later years he would continually refer to it.

"Try to understand the whole field of music, the whole genre. And once you understand that, then you will see how everything relates to everything. One of my great fetishes is American music and how everything relates to it," he remarked in that same interview.

The goal of the musician, he told *Rolling Stone,* should be "to understand the whole vernacular, the whole mystique, the whole thing. . . . If someone listens to me, he should listen to what I have listened to to know how I got where I am. A young guitar player won't know anything about what I'm talking about. There's really nothing to say. They can come close, but you've got to understand."

Bloomfield was playing almost constantly with the Butterfield Band—a situation in which one rarely fails to improve—and he began picking up basic theory (modes and relative keys and harmony) from pianist Mark Naftalin. The jazz and theory were, he said, a whole other side to his musical goal, which remained basically to be a good blues player; but they opened up his ear to new possibilities and liberated his playing, and from this point Mike's mature style began to emerge.

In the month between June, when "Like a Rolling Stone" was released, and August, when it hit top place on the charts, both Dylan and Bloomfield attended the Newport Folk Festival. Mike was with the Butterfield Band, well received at the Sunday matinee, and Dylan got together with the band for some jamming. His previous album, *Bringing It All Back Home,* included acoustic numbers on one side, electric accompaniment on the other, so they started off jamming on a song from that album, "Maggie's Farm."

July 25, 1965, was the day of the debacle. Introduced by Peter Yarrow of Peter, Paul and Mary, Dylan emerged. No introductions were really necessary: "Like a Rolling Stone" was on top-forty radio, and the new album was selling thousands of copies each week.

"When he came running out on stage there was little doubt this was a new Dylan," Scaduto writes. "Gone were the boots and the jeans and work shirts. . . . he came out onto the Newport stage in a black leather jacket, black slacks, a dress shirt and pointed black boots with Chelsea heels. Carrying a solidbody electric guitar.

"The audience sat transfixed as someone plugged his guitar into the amps and as a rock combo took its place behind him—the Paul Butterfield Blues Band. . . . The audience was bewildered, upset. . . . When he swung into 'Like a Rolling Stone,' no one clapped, and the boos and hecklers' shouts rang through the Festival site . . . laughter rolled up from the audience and across the stage. Dylan turned and stalked off, driven from the stage."

He returned shortly thereafter with his acoustic guitar and, unaccompanied, did songs from the other side of his album.

This moment at Newport instantly attained the stature of myth, passing in various interpretations throughout the country. It is difficult today to understand the fervor and denunciation that answered Dylan's supposed impudence. One has to realize that the folk musicians were hanging on hard to their (again, largely supposed) purity in the face of mongrel hordes of kids with Silvertones. More importantly, one must try to recognize the ways in which folk music was as much life-style, self-definition, as a body of music. Dylan's "going electric" was perceived as direct betrayal, a very personal kind of betrayal, because listeners had always responded to Dylan in a very personal way.

As with most myths well polished by time, it's difficult to assess what actually went on that year at Newport. Popular legend then more or less credited Dylan with rebuilding Babel there on the stage. Pete Seeger was reported as having tears in his eyes, also as threatening to cut the amplifier cables with an ax. Rick von Schmidt on the other hand believes that it was all a misunderstanding. As he told Scaduto,

That historic '65 thing with the Butterfield Band has been totally misconstrued by everybody, including Dylan. The resulting thing, the attacks on him, would probably have happened anyway, but they happened at Newport in a bizarre fashion. . . .

Nobody knew Butterfield was going to back him up, that Sunday night. They just showed up there on stage. It was remarkable in that Bob, who always seemed to know when to make the moves, this one time he got taken advantage of —the Butterfield Band was so anxious to be on stage and inadvertently they took advantage of him.

What happened was, whoever was controlling the mikes messed it up. You couldn't hear Dylan. It looked like he was singing with the volume off. He got through the first song, with the Butterfield Band pulling out all the stops, Sam Lay beating hell out of the drums, the whole thing sounding like a Butterfield boogie and no Dylan.

People up front started shouting that they couldn't hear Dylan, von Schmidt goes on, and people further back in the press of noise couldn't really make out what was being said and decided Dylan was being put down for playing electric, so they joined in. Before long, as things will in crowds, feeding on themselves and growing, the whole business was out of control.

Al Kooper was up there playing organ, and his recollection of the event is curiously divergent from both von Schmidt's and the popular version.

Our portion of the show opened with "Maggie's Farm" and concluded with "Like a Rolling Stone." In the middle of "Maggie's Farm," somebody fucked up and Sam Lay turned the beat around, which thoroughly confused everyone until the song mercifully stumbled to its conclusion. But "Like a Rolling Stone" was A-one and we really got it across. Dylan came off and appeared to be satisfied, and people were yelling for an encore.

If you've read any accounts of that evening, chances are they centered on how Dylan was booed into submission and then returned for a tearful acoustic rendering of "It's All Over Now Baby Blue." A romantic picture, maybe, but that's not the way I saw it. At the close of the set, Peter Yarrow (of Paul and Mary fame and the emcee for the evening) grabbed Dylan as he was coming offstage.

"Hey," he said, "you just can't leave them like that. They want another one."

"But that's all we know," replied Dylan, motioning toward the band.

"Well go back out there with an acoustic guitar," says Yarrow.

And he did. That's all there was to it. I was there.

Whatever really went on at Newport before legend bore it aloft, Dylan seems to have been confused and hurt by it. But the publicity brought him an ever wider audience among the young, many of them with little exposure to folk music. Album sales accelerated, and "Like a Rolling Stone" bobbed toward the top of the charts.

Highway 61, in Scaduto's words "one of the most brilliant pop albums ever made," was cut the following month. It was all-electric, kicking off with "Like a Rolling Stone," including two other songs almost equal in bitterness and spleen ("Ballad of a Thin Man" and "Queen Jane Approximately"), and ending with two incredibly beautiful, absolutely unique surrealist poems, "Just Like Tom Thumb's Blues" and the eleven-minute "Desolation Row." Bloomfield contributed lead-guitar parts, Al Kooper the organ and piano. The album took only two or three days to record, and Bloomfield later remembered it as a "really weird" session, very disorganized, with Dylan singing these long songs over and over while the musicians fit themselves around him.

By the time the album was finished, Dylan had decided

to take the band on tour, but Bloomfield elected to stay with Butter. "All I want to do is play the blues, man," he told Kooper. "Ah likes tuh play de blues."

East-West by the Paul Butterfield Blues Band was released in August 1966, the first electric act on the folk-based Elektra label. It contained some hard city stylings of traditional blues like "Two Trains Running" and "Walkin' Blues," some more uptown pieces like Allen Toussaint's "Get Out of My Life, Woman," and it concluded with the thirteen-minute title piece, an original by Mike Bloomfield and Nick Gravenites for which Bloomfield was still receiving royalties at the time of his death.

Rich Kienzle wrote in *Guitar World*,

> At that time, the band had one LP of raw blues under their belts, and Bloomfield had his work with Dylan behind him. But this album presents many of the licks that became known as "progressive rock" guitar in their infancy, with Bloomfield bringing jazz and raga overtones (particularly on "East-West") into his standard blues playing. Most of the San Francisco-based rock players, from Jerry Garcia to Jorma Kaukonen to Carlos Santana, sopped this record for all it was worth, and it showed in their playing.

It also affected a whole new generation of guitarists just coming up. Steve Burgh was fourteen or fifteen when he first heard the band, about the same age that Bloomfield started playing seriously, and like Mike he was working in various suburban rock-and-roll bands; he'd later play with David Bromberg, John Prine, Don McLean, Willie Nelson, Billy Joel and many other top musicians. "These guys changed my whole idea about guitar playing," Burgh told *Guitar Player*. "I decided that the blues was it. Here was some music with feeling that I could relate to emotionally. So I started learning some of the things that Bloomfield was doing." All over the country, others joined him. "You guys are going to carry it on for us," Muddy Waters and older bluesmen had told the band. And so they did.

Bloomfield meanwhile was increasingly dissatisfied with just playing Butter's music. There was friction with Elvin Bishop, who was not altogether pleased with his rhythm guitar slot, and Bloomfield had vague notions of starting his own band. Things finally got too close for him and in 1967 he quit.

"You know, for a long time all of us in Paul's band had wanted horns," Mike told *Guitar Player* in 1971. "All of our blues records, or many of them, other than Chicago stuff and stuff that came out of the South and Detroit, had horns. Fats Domino, Ray Charles and B. B. King especially were guys that had horns in their bands. And as a guitar player, I really wanted to hear that sound of the guitar interacting with horns. So when I went out to form the Flag, man, that was still in the back of my mind. I wanted just a good old blues band with horns in it."

Peter Strassa and Nick Gravenites were old associates. Barry Goldberg was another longtime friend (he'd played piano with Butterfield behind Dylan at Newport). Mike knew bassist Harvey Brooks from the Dylan sessions and met drummer Buddy Miles at a rock show where Miles was playing with Wilson Pickett, Mike with Mitch Ryder. One horn player was a friend of Barry's, a second was recommended by guitarist Larry Coryell. And so, like desperadoes coming together one by one from all over the country for the big job, the Electric Flag fell into place.

Mike bought a house in Mill Valley and everyone came down to put the music together. "We all lived here and I lost my ass—a fortune feeding and housing them. We worked and like the millions of ideas that I had never came true. The band sort of fell into the bag of soul band because of Buddy's dominant personality." He said often later on that the Flag was a good band but suffered greatly (and terminally) from its haste to become an instant hit; it never had time or the chance to mature and so fell easy prey to the usual factions and attrition. More than anything else, Bloomfield was troubled by the growing sense—reaffirmed with the Flag's debut at the Monterrey Pop Festival in 1967 —that he and the band were simply *product*.

"Saturday was blues day," Jerry Hopkins writes of Monterrey in *Festival.*

> The first of the bands was a reasonably new one from Los Angeles, Canned Heat, then little known outside its small but enthusiastic southern California following. Followed by the Butterfield Blues Band, probably the first of the young white blues bands to come out of Chicago . . . the Steve Miller Blues Band and the Quicksilver Messenger Service and Moby Grape and the Jefferson Airplane and Country Joe and the Fish and Big Brother and the Holding Company. It was blues, conceived in Chicago and deep Delta booze and run through a lot of California dope.

Others who appeared at Monterrey would go on to become "superstars" in following years—notably Janis Joplin, the Who, Simon and Garfunkel, Otis Redding and Jimi Hendrix. The Flag's debut performance, to Bloomfield's surprise and bewilderment, met with wild approval.

"I felt we played abominably," Mike told *Rolling Stone* a year or so later, "and they loved us. I thought it was flooky. I couldn't understand, man, how could a band play that shitty and have everyone dig them? I said, 'Well, it's festival madness.' "

Al Kooper had been drafted as assistant stage manager for the festival and was backstage checking out the talent with an eye toward putting together a soul-rock-jazz band with horns that eventually became Blood, Sweat and Tears.

His memory of the Flag's debut, related in *Backstage Passes,* is somewhat different.

> This was their first gig, and they were terrified. Buddy Miles had a suit on fer chrissakes; one of those jobbies like James Brown wore, with no lapels, and a shirt and tie! Bloomfield came out and gave one of his great speeches about how we (the audience) were all one and it was all peace, love and incense, and here's some music by the way.
> Heavy drama. But they played great. The crowd went nuts. I was standing backstage with Susie Bloomfield (Michael's wife), and she was crying tears of joy and relief. Buddy Miles came off after playing to his first large, predominantly white audience and he was sweating and crying.

Thus launched, the Flag toured extensively throughout 1967 and 1968, cutting an album for Columbia as well as the soundtrack album for the movie *The Trip,* scored by Mike Bloomfield. In later years scoring movies became an important source of income for Bloomfield; aside from numerous porno movies such as *Sodom and Gomorrah* and the Mitchell brothers' *Ultra-Core* series, he did scores for *Medium Cool, Steelyard Blues* and Andy Warhol's *Bad.* During the same period as the Flag albums, Bloomfield recorded as a sideman for saxophonist-singer Eddie Vinson and produced and orchestrated recordings for James Cotton, both on the Verve label. He also appeared on Columbia's anthology album *Live at the Fillmore.*

Mike met Steve Cropper for the first time at Monterrey. Cropper is one of those legendary guitarists whose playing is part of a whole sound: the Stax rhythm-and-blues sound which in many ways the Flag was emulating.

"I had been digging Mike before then," Cropper told *Rolling Stone.* "I heard several things he had done. My impression of him is that he's one of the best white blues guitar players around and there's several out there in that same kind of bag. I'm not weighing him against any other or vice-versa, I just think he's one of the best. Everything he does is done in good taste with a lot of control. He doesn't play frantic or try to overplay like a lot of people do. Just really well done." The comments must have pleased Bloomfield. Control (of attack, vibrato, dynamics, nuance, precise pitch) was something he insisted on again and again in interviews, often likening it to the absolute breath control a singer or horn player has to master.

The Electric Flag came to an end in 1968, general attrition and instability having run their course. Mike returned to California and worked a few casual gigs, but mostly just sat around and read, depressed and without ambition.

Al Kooper had split with the Blues Project, hadn't yet put Blood, Sweat and Tears together and was just as purposeless. He visited Bloomfield at one point "in an effort to relieve my boredom and anxiety," and they sat around all day with Mark Naftalin listening to records, talking about old bluesmen and smoking joints. Kooper reports in *Backstage Passes,*

> Michael's dog was lying on the kitchen floor crying the whole time we were sitting there. We were real stoned. . . . Maybe that's why I didn't notice right away that the "cookies" Michael was munching on while he talked about Howlin' Wolf, were "Fives," a popular California brand of kibble for dogs and cats. I called this to his attention, secretly hoping his sense of *something* had been dulled temporarily by his stoned state.
> "Oh no, man, I eat this all the time. S'good. Want some?"
> *Sure.*
> When no one was looking, I snuck my handful down to the dog, and he stopped crying.

Kooper precipitated Bloomfield's next project. Recently hired as a producer for Columbia and panicked to deliver, he decided to get together a group of proven players and wing it. Maybe the thing, he thought, would even pay for itself.

"I didn't want to make that record too much," Mike said. "It was just a favor for Al Kooper and he said we'll make a lot of bread out of it and subsequently he was absolutely right."

Kooper rented a house in Los Angeles, decided on ex-Flagman Harvey Brooks for bass player (Mike picked drummer Eddie Hoh from the Mamas and the Papas' band) and flew everyone out.

"That night we hit the studio and got right down to business," Kooper writes. "Barry Goldberg, also late of the Flag, came down and sat in on a few tracks. We recorded a slow shuffle, a Curtis Mayfield song, a Jerry Ragavoy tune, a real slow blues, a three-quarter modal jazz-type tune, and in nine hours had half the album in the can. . . .

"There was a real comfortable feeling to the proceedings, and while listening to one of the playbacks I noted that I had gotten the best recorded Bloomfield ever and, after all, that was the point of the album."

Kooper's assurance was swept away by a phone call the next morning about nine, asking if Bloomfield had made his plane. *What plane?* He rushed into Mike's room to find the note: *Dear Alan. Couldn't sleep well . . . went home . . . sorry.* "I couldn't go to sleep, man, I was so uptight," Bloomfield said years later. "So I snuck out early in the wee hours of the morning with a guitar in my hand. I got a cab and flew home. And when Al went to look for me in the morning I was already back in San Francisco."

The situation would repeat itself not long after when Kooper set up a live session (and attendant album) at the Fillmore West. That time Mike made it through four days of rehearsal and two nights of playing; the third morning his wife called to tell Kooper that Mike was in the hospital being sedated. Steve Stills, at liberty following the collapse of Buffalo Springfield, had bailed Kooper out on *Super Session* ("Stills is playing the wah-wah and I'm playing the straight guitar," Bloomfield said) but was now otherwise committed. Kooper called around, and Elvin Bishop, Steve Miller and Carlos Santana all wound up playing to fill in for Mike, each coming onstage for three or four songs.

Super Session, which cost only thirteen thousand dollars to make, hit the top twenty a few weeks after release and leveled off at number eleven, soon becoming a gold album for sales exceeding four hundred fifty thousand. *Live Adventures of Mike Bloomfield and Al Kooper* was released by Columbia as a double album with a specially commissioned Norman Rockwell portrait of the two musicians and sold well, though not as spectacularly as *Session.*

Bloomfield continued to work the Fillmores East and West, and in 1969 played the Super Cosmic Joy-Scout Jamboree at the Auditorium Theater in Chicago with Muddy Waters. The Chess double album *Fathers and Sons* (with Otis Spann, Butterfield, Stax bassist "Duck" Dunn, Sam Lay and Buddy Miles) was recorded live here and released a couple years later. In the period from about 1969 to 1971 Mike also played solo and pickup gigs at clubs like the Keystone Korner and the Matrix in San Francisco, the Auditorium in Long Beach and Los Angeles's Ash Grove.

Mike next cut an album with Barry Goldberg called *Two Jews' Blues* (for which he was never paid) and a "pretty bad" solo album titled *It's Not Killing Me* ("Columbia was nice enough to release it"), then blew a wad of Columbia money messing around in the studio for six weeks with Mark Naftalin. When the company decided against releasing his next solo album, *Try It Before You Buy It,* even though he thought it was good and would have recouped their losses, Bloomfield understood: "They had lost a lot of money on me, and you can't blame them when you think about it."

That album was cut about 1974. The previous year had

seen Mike's soundtrack album for *Steelyard Blues* and *Triumvirate,* a joining of forces from Bloomfield, Dr. John and bluesman John Hammond. Hammond told *Frets,*

> I made a commercial shot called *Triumvirate,* which was my attempt at making an R&B hit record, but in the middle of its release, Clive Davis was fired, the head of A&R resigned and they froze all the money that was supposed to go into the promotion of the record. It was an expensive record, too. Actually, that was *my* record—I mean, I got everybody together, selected all the material, got Michael Bloomfield and Dr. John to play as sidemen and Columbia went for it. Then Dr. John had a hit, "I Was in the Right Place at the Wrong Time," in the middle of the recording dates, and Columbia decided to exploit his name and make it *Triumvirate*—like *Super Session*.

Neither of Hammond's previous albums (one of them the soundtrack album for *Little Big Man*) had sold well. Though *Triumvirate* proved successful on the market, it was not a direction in which Hammond greatly cared to move, and he departed the label shortly thereafter, returning to his preferred solo country-blues style.

Bloomfield appeared with Muddy Waters on PBS's *Soundstage* in 1974 and participated also in the "debacle of debacles," a resurrection of the Electric Flag contrived by Barry Goldberg, "a genius for all sorts of scam/hustle things." The following year he worked for a time at the Family Light School of Music in Sausalito, scored a film short titled *Hot Nasty* and again followed Goldberg into the moral abyss.

"It was a pure scam," Mike said of his participation in the band called KGB. "It was filthy lucre. It had nothing to do with an affinity for playing with each other. Just a name, a marketable name, like Fruit Loops." Bloomfield's lengthy description of this episode in the 1979 *Guitar Player* interview is a marvelous comedic set piece.

"Barry Goldberg took me to see this manager friend of

his," Mike recalled, "and the guy looked across the table and said, 'Boys, let's put a *supergroup* together!' " The producer set up a showcase in Hollywood for all the record executives.

> It was like *Roots.* We were up on the auction block: "This is a *supergroup,* people! This is *rucka rucka* from *humma humma.*" All these execs who came to see us looked the same: pinky ring, leisure suit, shirt open to the tits, fabulous complexions and blow-dried hair. Also, some real cigar-stub guys: "Hey, Mike! I've been following your career ever since . . . what was that group you were with? You were with *Bloomfield,* weren't you?" One word I heard over and over was "bankable." We were a product, we were hula hoops, we were skateboards.

They were also signed, to MCA.

"MCA's president at the time was a corporate guy who was transferred from some other branch of this big conglomerate, and as far as he was concerned he wasn't buying music. He wasn't into music; he was into *platinum potential.* His company paid huge chunks of money for us."

The band members (Bloomfield, Goldberg, bassist Rick Grech and drummer Carmine Appice) got along well and had a great time when they just messed around together, but the whole band business was so artificial and arbitrary that nothing much came of it. The other members wound up recording the album in Los Angeles and flying the tapes up to Sausalito for Mike to overdub his parts—he "phoned them in, like in *Doonesbury.*" When MCA booked the band for a fifty-city tour Mike called it quits. He'd already blown the whistle on the group by spilling the whole scam to a reporter from the *Los Angeles Times.* But *KGB,* issued in 1975, sold almost half a million records.

One has to question, finally, why Bloomfield repeatedly let himself be sucked into these scams, precipitating as they did such anguish, soul-searching and destructive behavior. We can assume, of course, that he was lured by the same prospect of easy money as others and had subsequent difficulty accommodating his artistic conscience. Mike also seems, for all his strong convictions, rather indeterminate of will; witness the manner in which the Electric Flag was allowed to drift its own way. ("If somebody had taken control of the group, we would be together now. We'd have been even more beautiful," he said in 1971.) Nor is it out of the question to suggest that, like many creative people, Mike perhaps thrived on and required crisis; he certainly would not be the first to create crises for himself when none occurred naturally.

It is particularly interesting that this final grand scam came at the end of a period when Mike had spent considerable time assessing his past, consolidating his own sense of his music and deciding his true direction. The first fruit of this was *If You Love These Blues,* an almost scholarly LP of blues styles issued by *Guitar Player* the following year (1976), which Mike called (with justification) "my best record, me at my hottest." But first we must deal with the darker implications that brought him to that reassessment.

The first couple of years of the 1970's were largely a blank for Mike Bloomfield. Nothing much happened in his career between 1969 and 1972 or 1973, or more properly (he never had a career, actually) in his music. He told *Guitar Player* at the end of the decade,

> There was a period when I didn't play guitar at all, around '70 or '71. I was really down and out, and I lived in this little dive. The Flag had just broken up. I had cut *Super Session,* and then I got really into shooting junk. . . . I put the guitar down, didn't touch it. See, a junkie's life is totally, chronically fucked. You either eat and move and be productive, or else you're a junkie. There's no choice. Or at least there wasn't for me. . . . Some people can do something behind it—they can play, they can go to the gig, they can control their motor functions. I'd just lay there and watch TV and smoke cigarettes and nod off or whatever. I couldn't keep my act to-

gether, couldn't function. Actually, there was no prolonged period like this—it was more of an on-and-off type thing.

One day a delegation, some of the best guitar players in the San Francisco area, people like Terry Haggerty from the Sons of Champlin and Carlos Santana, came to Mike's "little dive." And they said, "You ought to be ashamed to charge people to see you, Bloomfield, because you're a joke, man, a laughingstock." They told him, "We used to learn from you; when Butterfield came to town we all came to see *you;* we *loved* you, man, loved what you did. You're a fraud," they said, "a pitiful relic of what Michael Bloomfield used to be. You can't even *hold* a guitar anymore!"

Mike responded that he wasn't into that anymore; he was into "watching *The Tonight Show* and shooting dope." But these guys wouldn't quit. They sat down and said, "Now you're going to listen to *us* play."

He listened—and what he heard both frightened and inspired him. They were so much better than he was; there was so much *feeling* in what they played. And he decided that was it: no more junk. That got him back into guitar, and the next several years were a period of profound reintegration and creativity for him.

Again, Bloomfield's immolation in heroin and the circumstances surrounding his abnegation of it suggest an essential passivity or ductility of will. Indications are that Mike instinctively realized this about himself and struggled fitfully against it, further complicating the tangle of strange bedfellows and fabricated defaults.

If You Love These Blues, Play 'Em as You Please was a kind of atonement for his participation in the KGB scam; he wanted, he said, to do something with integrity. What he produced was a catalogue of major blues guitar styles, a thoughtful, valuable and beautifully realized album. Its protean essay of our most distinctive American musical form prefigures closely Mike's work both in personal appearances and on albums in the years to come, and he always thought he did some of his best playing ever on that album; it was one he himself liked to listen to again and again.

"I was striving to get the sounds of various old records, and that came through," Mike said later on. "I was trying to look at not just different guitar styles, but also the whole setting, the feel, the persona, the ambience of certain musics—sort of a musicological travelogue."

The idea for the album originated with *Guitar Player* publisher Jim Crockett, who, after discussing it with Mike, turned the project over to Eric Kriss, director of the magazine's newly founded (now defunct) books and records division. The album was distributed through the magazine for about a year, then by Takoma Records. At the time of Mike's death all rights had returned to him, and one hopes the album will soon become available again.

If You Love These Blues opens with the title song, an eight-bar blues patterned after B. B. King's sixties' style, then segues to a white rural blues ("Hey, Foreman!") with the lead taken on Hawaiian guitar. Next comes "WDIA," named after Memphis's groundbreaking black radio station. "This song," Bloomfield pointed out in accompanying notes, "epitomizes the stylistic evolution of electric guitar in the blues. There is a direct line from Lonnie Johnson, who played with Duke Ellington in the twenties, to T-Bone Walker in the thirties, to B. B. King. On his first album, B. B. played a lot like T-Bone." Next comes "Death Cell Rounder Blues," an homage to the piano-guitar duets of people like Scrapper Blackwell-Leroy Carr and Tampa Red-Tom Dorsey. "City Girl" is a tribute to T-Bone, and the final tune on the first side, "Kansas City," a country-blues standard from the twenties played in a modern finger-picking style.

Side two opens with "Mama Lion," a Gravenites piece in the early urban blues style of people like Howlin' Wolf and John Lee Hooker; on this one, the composer plays a drone guitar while Bloomfield plays electric slide leads. Then comes "Thrift Shop Rag" in the highly syncopated style of Blind Blake. "Death in My Family" is dedicated to Eddie "Guitar Slim" Jones, "an electric guitar player who was influenced by T-Bone Walker but was remarkable for his ability to sound completely unique." Another ragtime piece, "East Colorado Blues," is followed by a Lonnie Johnson tune, "Blue Ghost Blues," also played fingerstyle on acoustic "in a way that combines the styles of Blind Lemon Jefferson and Blind Blake." "The Train Is Gone" directly imitates the pioneering single-string work of Lonnie Johnson, Eddie Lang and Teddy Bunn in the thirties. On the final "Altar Song" Mike recites a litany of blues names and influences over an old gospel melody, played on electric slide with Mike supplying his own acoustic guitar, piano, bass, organ and drum accompaniment.

The same year Mike cut *If You Love These Blues,* he worked the Newport Jazz Festival in New York, the San Francisco Blues Festival at McLaren Park, and the Band's farewell concert at Winterland Auditorium in San Francisco (documented on film as *The Last Waltz*). *Analine* came out the following year, 1977; he played that year with Big Joe Turner at the Palms, worked solo at the Old Waldorf in San Francisco and at the University of Oregon, played the New Orleans Jazz and Heritage Festival. The sequence then is this:

Count Talent and the Originals, 1978. "I'm not real *un-* happy, but I sure didn't accomplish what I set out to do. For that album I was influenced by these old New Orleans horn sections of a certain sort, touched with a tinge of the Stax Records horn sound. . . . I especially like 'You Was Wrong,' and I like 'Peach Tree Man,' and I like 'When I Need You.' " Bloomfield junked three weeks of studio time and results and started over on this one, then put it together in a hurry with new session men.

Michael Bloomfield, 1978. "It was exactly planned that way by Norman Dayron—who's my producer—and me. It was to be as raw and sleazy as possible. Two of the cuts were recorded live in a club, and I think those are the best tracks: 'Sloppy Drunk' and 'Women Loving Each Other.'"

Between the Hard Place and the Ground, 1979. All the final electric albums share something of *Michael Bloomfield's* "sleaze," an uneven, homemade quality. (One listener referred to "Mike's garage band albums.") Woody Harris believes this is because Mike had little interest in doing any more of this, wanting instead to recreate the older acoustic blues, but was pushed into recording electric blues by record companies and "friends" using Mike to their own ends. *Hard Place* contains gutsy city blues with a full rhythm section, including songs by such artists as Joe Turner, Dr. John and Sleepy John Estes.

Bloomfield/Harris, 1979. Excellent guitar duets from Mike and classical-style folk player Woody Harris are featured here, using two acoustic guitars or one acoustic and electric slide lead. All are gospel tunes: "Gonna Need Somebody on My Bond," "I Am a Pilgrim," "Farther Along," "Peace in the Valley." This is a haunting, beautiful album, also a great tutor for guitarists wanting to learn how to turn the bare bones of a tune into effective music.

Living in the Fast Lane, 1980. Each side here ends with acoustic fingerpicking, but the rest is patent-leather raunch —electric guitar and rhythm section (with organ) doing things like "Andy's Bad" from a Warhol soundtrack and the "Roots" theme via Motown.

Cruisin' for a Bruisin', 1981. Including a full band with horns, this album is stranger than usual, both in choice of material and presentation: there's little polish or slickness to these versions of Ray Sharpe's "Linda Lu," Jack Dupree's "Junker's Blues," "Mathilda" or "Snowbird."

Mike played a lot of solo gigs at small clubs and music festivals during his last few years. He'd never much liked playing live, but that became the major outlet for his music, allowing him to preach his own particular gospel of blues, tradition and American music.

Those gigs included material as diverse as Hoagy Carmichael tunes, Sophie Tucker's "Some of These Days," an old opium song called "Willie the Weeper," Delta and Chicago blues, "Deep in the Heart of Texas," and George Jones's "Bartender Blues." Some nights Mike would just sit at the piano and play Fats Domino, Little Richard, Jerry Lee Lewis and Ray Charles songs for hours. Or he might do guitar instrumentals on old standards like "Somewhere Over the Rainbow," "Maria Elena," or "Danny Boy." "I'll do *anything,*" he said, "anything that occurs to me right at the time." He never arranged or preplanned his solo sets, preferring to try for ambience, a flow that adjusted to situation.

For most of this solo work he eschewed his trademark Telecaster and Les Paul Custom for an acoustic guitar with DeArmond pickup. "Of course, if I'm playing with the band, I'll play a lot of electric," he told *Guitar Player,* "but I can't get enough out of a solidbody guitar just playing by myself, enough sound, enough tone, like, say, Ted Greene gets out of those modified Telecasters, but I can get it out of an amplified acoustic guitar. I can really get my kind of sound out of it." He also grew to prefer using his fingers instead of a pick when playing electric, finding the funkier sound and wider range of tone more to his taste.

On the later albums Mike also played an assortment of other stringed instruments—ukulele, tiple, mandolin, five- and six-string banjos, even accordion—and occasionally hauled those along to gigs.

> I play everything I can tote onstage. I like to be comfortable. I tote a lamp, and a chair, a couple of guitars, a banjo, maybe an accordion. I prerecord piano parts on a cassette, and I mike the cassette player, so if they want to hear something flashy I can flash out for them and play along with the piano parts. . . . I also take along a nice old Kay arch-top

guitar with one stock pickup—I think I'm Charlie Christian when I play it. And sometimes I'll take a mandolin. It's pretty easy to kill an hour's time with all that stuff.

And so Michael Bloomfield passed his final years.

"In recent years," Jimmy Stewart wrote in *Guitar Player*, "Mike has devoted himself to revitalizing various indigenous American forms of music, most notably blues, and in the evolution of rock guitar, his name ranks among those at the top of the list."

Mike Bloomfield encompasses the dominant forms and fashions of the music of his day in much the same manner as Roy Smeck and Eddie Lang did the music of theirs. Beginning as a rock and roller, he pursued folk music and became a very important part of the blues revival as lead guitarist with the Paul Butterfield Band, itself a landmark in contemporary music. He played on Dylan's extremely influential early rock records and did specialty session work for many others, also becoming a key figure at the rock festivals that in large part defined the 1960's. He introduced horns to rock and roll with the Electric Flag, and in later years prefigured the growing interest in acoustic music, which has led on one side to the popularity of bluegrass and old-time music, on another, to increasing numbers of jazz guitarists working with nonamplified instruments.

Blues purist, rock superstar, traditionalist, innovator, Bloomfield is as responsible as anyone for the eminence of guitar today and the styles in which that guitar is played. He was a voluble spokesman for the history and the unity of American music, both reflected in his own playing, and this may finally prove his greatest legacy. It was not revival but continuation of our musics that he championed. Mike Bloomfield felt that only the linear progression of history, passing through contemporary expression and extension, could produce meaningful music. T. S. Eliot had come to the same conclusion many years before; in a seminal essay he called it "Tradition and Individual Talent."

CURRENTS:

Ry Cooder · Ralph Towner
Lenny Breau

"ONE FRIDAY EVENING, I was playing in a club on Broadway, New York City," Howard Morgen wrote in *Guitar World* recently, "when a guitarist named Ray Tico came in and asked if he could entertain during one of our breaks. Ray got up there all by himself and proceeded to blow me away with something I'd never seen or heard before. He played melody and chords to 'How High the Moon,' accompanying himself with a walking bass line played with his thumb.

"Now, I'd heard classical guitar many times, and also arrangements of popular standards played in a classical style. But I'd never heard anyone apply the thumb-and-finger techniques of the classical guitarist so logically and convincingly to a purely jazz conception. Ray was from South America, where classical techniques had long ago been applied to flamenco and other popular forms—so why not to American jazz?"

Why not indeed, and one of the most liberating aspects of recent guitar has been the overthrow of the plectrum's dominance for fingerstyle playing which embraces the polyphonic nature and potential of the instrument. Jimmy Wyble, who began his career with country bands around Houston and went on to play with Bob Wills, Red Norvo and Benny Goodman, has worked extensively in recent years with polyphonic guitar, developing methods to play widely diverse lines simultaneously—in short, new ways of *thinking* about guitar. Reclusive teacher and author Ted Greene is a direct successor to George Van Eps, his *Solo Guitar* album a fine contemporary example of the chord-melody, self-sufficient playing first developed in Van Eps's "lap piano" style. Solo guitar in fact seems an idea whose time has definitely arrived. Joe Pass, Paul Chasman, Larry Coryell, Guy Van Duser and Alan de Mause (like Greene a teacher, and author of an excellent survey titled *Solo Jazz Guitar*) are but a few of the players exploring new concepts of unaccompanied guitar and turning out fine, original music along the way.

Nor should the emergence of fingerstyle guitar prove too surprising. The background of American guitar is in blues, and early bluesmen, possibly in deference to ancestral African instruments, generally played with their fingers. Much of Lonnie Johnson's ground-breaking solo work was played fingerstyle, and Eddie Lang became increasingly interested in the possibilities of fingerstyle playing in his later years. Van Eps, Laurindo Almeida, Bill Harris and Charlie Byrd established clear precedents in jazz guitar, and with the appearance of bossa nova in the early sixties, the work of Byrd, Almeida and other South American guitarists such as Bola Sete, Baden Powell and Luis Bonfa entered popular music. Chet Atkins and Merle Travis assured the style's persistence in country music.

Another important vector in the guitar's recent development is the legacy left by the sixties' folk revival, which not only popularized the guitar but also a profusion of stylistic possibilities. One arm of this, with John Fahey and Leo Kottke at the fore, worked to forge a new tradition of "American primitive" guitar. Others such as John Hammond and the Red Clay Ramblers elected to recreate or reinvest traditional styles. And many folk players (James

Taylor, David Lindley, Clarence White) eventually passed by natural process into rock and pop music, carrying with them sensibilities and tastes that remain extremely influential. A few—David Grisman, David Bromberg and Duck Baker come first to mind—created their own distinctive idioms from this mulch of synthesis and recapitulation.

One of the most eclectic yet individualistic of younger musicians is Ry Cooder. Blending gospel, rhythm and blues, Hawaiian, Norteno, old vaudeville and jazz tunes, folk and blues sounds ("a crossbreed of endangered musical forms," as one writer put it), Cooder has turned out ten albums of startlingly fresh music unmistakably his own.

"I know a lot of musicians who like all kinds of music," says Chris Strachwitz, whose own label, Arhoolie, specializes in regional and ethnic musics, "but very few of them seem able to incorporate these elements into their own music and make it come out as a kind of personal music." And this is just what Cooder does, again and again, often with the most disparate material: a Tex-Mex version of "Goodnight Irene," a tough rhythm-and-blues ballad with lush vocals in the manner of Gabby Pahinui, an old show tune by way of Bahaman guitarist Joseph Spence.

Much of this Cooder himself attributes to coming up during the folk period. "The styles were all swimming around—nothing was clearly defined," he told Steve Fishell for a 1980 *Guitar Player* interview. "One guy finger-picked; one guy flat-picked. One day you'd be playing some country music, the next day some blues. Then here comes some Turkish cats into town, so you'd go hang with them and see what they were doing. . . . I always took it as it came, and the people that I knew in those days had the same attitude."

Neither does he see his annexation of widely diverse styles as all that unusual in American music. "American music was always a synthesis," he says. "It was always a combination of one guy plus another guy who was different. Like Mexicans playing German polka music, or black people in Louisiana like Clifton Chenier taking Cajun music, and making it syncopated. Sam Phillips is a good example, trying to make blues with Elvis Presley. And that's the stuff that hits me."

He describes his own records as shots in the dark, efforts to "make something like R&B tangible in your own right," intuitively reaching for a sound he hears but has thus far only approximated.

Ryland Cooder was born in 1947 in Santa Monica, where he still lives, and began playing tenor guitar about age three after watching his father and friends strum guitars and sing folk songs; his father presented him with a Martin 000-18 a few years later. He became deeply involved with country blues and learned the finger-picking styles of bluesmen like Blind Blake, Leadbelly and Reverend Gary Davis. Joseph Spence and Blind Willie Johnson were other important early influences, Cooder adopting Spence's eccentric syncopations and open tunings and Johnson's bottleneck style as his own. Many of the older players, such as Jesse Fuller, Sleepy John Estes, Skip James and Mississippi John Hurt, he was able to see live at the Ash Grove, a Los Angeles folk club and musicians' hangout. Cooder also began playing mandolin and banjo about this time. He dropped the latter after a couple of years, but, basing his mandolin playing on Yank Rachell's blues style, went on to record with the instrument on his own albums and other cuts as diverse as those from Columbia's *A Tribute to Woody Guthrie* and the Rolling Stones' "All My Love in Vain." He worked with Taj Mahal briefly in a group called the Rising Sons, with Captain Beefheart on the album *Safe As Milk,* then as a studio sideman for a few years. In 1970 he brought out his first solo album, *Ry Cooder,* in Steve Fishell's words "a largely unnoticed masterpiece."

That first album contains in germ everything Cooder has developed; the unmistakable Cooder sound was strong from the first, and subsequent variations in that sound are really more a matter of refinement than of change. Material includes rhythm and blues and country blues, old-time fiddler Blind Alfred Reed's "How Can a Poor Man Stand Such Times and Live," Randy Newman's mock folk song "Old Kentucky Home." Two bottleneck pieces—an original Cooder instrumental called "Available Space" and Blind Willie Johnson's incredibly beautiful "Dark Was the Night"—bracket traditional blues from Leadbelly, Blind Blake and John Estes on the second side. Cooder's emphasis on rhythm (he still thinks of himself primarily as a rhythm guitarist) is clear on each track, and that rhythm, like the overall sound, is peculiarly his own, a pulsing, energetic stop-time reminiscent of ragtime.

Into the Purple Valley and *Boomer's Story* consolidated the ground Cooder staked out with his first album, adding classics such as "How Can You Keep on Moving," "Teardrops Will Fall," "Taxes on the Farmer Feeds Us All," "Rally 'Round the Flag" and "Maria Elena" to the Cooder canon. With *Paradise and Lunch* in 1974 he initiated use of male gospel singers (led by Bobby King) as a basis for his sound, which he continues today; the album also introduced a brass band on "Jesus on the Mainline," prefiguring the later *Jazz* album, and in the song "Mexican Divorce," Cooder's first use of Spanish rhythms. Another highlight was a duet with pianist Earl "Fatha" Hines on Blind Blake's "Ditty Wa Ditty."

Over the next three years Cooder apprenticed himself to Hawaiian music and to the Norteno sound of bands like Flaco Jiminez's, resulting in the album *Chicken Skin Music,* which added Flaco's button accordion and Atta Isaac's slack-key guitar to the now well-established gospel harmonies. Cooder also contributed tiple and mandolin to Panini

Records' *Gabby Pahinui Band* album. Cooder told Fishell for *Guitar Player,*

> I started with the gospel thing, because that's my main premise for everything—I line up my chord sense and my hearing with gospel; by now I do it by habit. Then I said, "We'll segue the Mexicans here." If you do "Stand By Me" in bolero rhythm with accordion, you've supplemented and simplified that song. "Stand By Me" by Ben E. King has certain New York pop qualities, but if you take those away you've got a church song, and Ben E. King is a church singer, of course. So we made it church again, but with accordion and bajo sexto and a very rich, soothing sound. Then we added background singers . . . and I'm in the middle with what I consider my church guitar playing, and we had a good sounding thing. It's not too easy to do, but once you've done one, you do the next one and the next one, and pretty soon you're into a style.

Cooder's sixth album, *Showtime,* was recorded live during his 1976 tour with the Chicken Skin Revue and reprises several favorites such as "Alimony," "Jesus on the Mainline" and "The Dark End of the Street," with Flaco Jiminez and his band as backup. The next was called *Jazz* and included "pre-thirties vaudeville tunes, hymns and 'slow drag' ragtime." With two exceptions Cooder is accompanied on each cut by bands of various sorts, the exceptions being Bert Williams's "Nobody" (with only Cooder's guitar and a backup gospel quartet) and "The Pearls/Tia Juana" (a beautifully textured piece overdubbed by Cooder on guitars, mandolins, tiple and Mexican harp). Shortly after its release an hour-long segment of PBS's *Soundstage* recapitulated the album's tunes, opening with "Big Bad Bill Is Sweet William Now" and closing with Cooder and David Lindley (musicians of astonishingly like mind and ability) playing an impromptu guitar-mandolin duet on "Coming in on a Wing and a Prayer."

Cooder does not care for *Jazz* now, believing it too academic and self-conscious, and his next album was mostly late fifties' and early sixties' rhythm and blues. Just after its release he told *Rolling Stone,* "Your music should be an exchange with your audience. I've always been aware that my records didn't sell real well, and at one time it didn't matter. But it's hard not to worry about that now. You have to try to get your numbers up." *Bop Till You Drop* ("Rock's First All-Digital Recording") did this for him in 1979; with it, Cooder went public. It sold, he said, over three hundred thousand copies, "which is six times what the rest of 'em sold."

A soundtrack album for *The Long Riders* followed, an excellent folk album attempting to recreate 1870's music. Lindley's fiddle, guitar or banjo-mandolin were featured on many cuts, as was Curt Bouterse's fine hammered dulcimer. *Borderline,* at this writing Cooder's most recent album, returned to *Bop*'s predominant rhythm-and-blues mode and has been similarly successful.

In one twelve-year period, Ry Cooder has put out ten albums, each of great originality and interest. He has virtually rethought the entire concept of bottleneck guitar, widely influenced young musicians in several disciplines and created for himself out of unlikely junctions a specifically American idiom—an identity, or signature, instantly recognizable.

Certainly one of the most eclectic, fascinating and popular developments in recent jazz has been the group Oregon, and it's for his work in this group that guitarist Ralph Towner is, at least at present, best known. Some may question whether Oregon actually plays jazz, but they indisputably play American improvisational music (as good a definition for jazz as any) and their work has expanded general concepts of improvisation. "In an article in Australia," Oregon member Colin Walcott told Mark Humphreys for *Frets,* "someone wrote that we combine the spontaneity of jazz with the completeness of statement of classical music. That rang pretty well with everybody."

Ralph Towner was born in 1940 in Chehalis, Washington. Both parents were musicians and by age three Ralph was "improvising" on piano, going on to formal training on trumpet beginning at age seven. He attended the University of Oregon as a composition major and there began playing classical guitar in his final year. After graduation he traveled to Vienna for a year's study with Karl Scheit. He returned to Oregon for a couple of years of music theory, then supported himself for a time as a jazz piano player in Seattle before returning to Vienna for further study with Scheit. In 1968 he settled in New York and began playing both piano and guitar with various Brazilian and jazz groups. He joined the Paul Winter Consort two years later and soon began writing for the group.

> An interesting thing about the Winter Consort was that they were avoiding any style I was capable of playing in; but it was quite an eclectic mixture that they were into. I really wanted to try and write some music for their format—trying perhaps to weld it into something more unified. Not making it a synthesis group, playing all kinds of music from all over the world with all kinds of instruments, but using those instruments to make *a* music.

He also began playing twelve-string guitar while with Winter and credits that instrument with leading him away from "jazz" as a limiting concept into broader areas. The twelve-string has become something of a trademark for him, an extremely important element in both solo and ensemble work.

In 1972 Towner and three other members of the Paul Winter Consort seceded and regrouped as Oregon.

Paul McCandless (oboe, English horn, bass clarinet, wood flute): "It's exploration—finding out what's *in there,* what's possible. . . . We take some care to improvise in a style that really sounds as if it's a composition."

Glen Moore (bass, piano, violin): "Using the thumb and fingers, in really the most elementary classical guitar technique, puts you miles and miles further than bassists traditionally get. . . . We can change the entire character on stage by someone picking up a different instrument. If I bow a melody with Paul on oboe, there's another whole character in that unison that's not the oboe and not the bass."

Colin Walcott (sitar, tabla, percussion): "Paul's and Glen's and Ralph's roots were in jazz. . . . I was much more interested in the whole Third-World thing—African music, Indian music of course, even American folk music."

With Oregon, Towner plays not only classical guitar and twelve-string, but also piano, trumpet and occasionally French horn or flügelhorn. All members move freely among several instruments and once estimated that they play some eighty instruments among them, everything from dulcimer and tambourine to homemade ones. The first cut of *Oregon in Performance,* for example, running almost eleven minutes, is built around an insecticide can converted by Walcott to a rudimentary thumb piano; the piece is titled "Buzzbox."

Upon hearing Oregon, the immediate impression is of synthesis: jazz and classical and Third-World strains inextricably wound together—swing time on tabla, banjo music on the sitar, a guitarlike bass, pianistic guitar. And this synthesis of musics is certainly one goal, but a goal intermediary (really almost incidental) to the final one, which is to push past all that to a true synthesis of *sound,* a kind of homogenous, poetic musical instant. Texture and color become primary ways of being in this music, their varieties endless, the music as a result boundlessly atmospheric, mysterious, suspenseful.

McCandless told Michael Zipkin for *Down Beat,*

> We're professionals, and we're very good at certain things we do. But we also allow ourselves to become amateurs in the sense of exploring and not knowing exactly how it's going to come out. And what comes out is so much more than you could ever think of, because it just didn't exist until it came together. . . . We'll discover textures in which all the individual instruments disappear, because of the particular sound quality each is making. And they blend with other sounds so that a sound is created that is just *this sound.*

Towner agrees. "My notion of a song, including the improvisation on that song, is that from the first sound you establish a character, a sense of motion, and you are committed to develop a history, a miniature lifetime that is a faithful development of the original atmosphere stated."

The subject here is Ralph Towner, true, yet to understand his contributions one must consider Oregon, for this is the context in which he has chosen most often and engagingly to work, and Oregon's goals are largely his own. And just as Oregon is responsible for much of the new emphasis on acoustic music in jazz, Towner himself has created a new role for guitar in the small ensemble. "Most people are sort of looking hysterically for new material, when they really haven't exhausted what's already available under their hands," he says. For both Oregon and Towner the voyage is not *out* to extensions of instrumental sound, increasingly abstract harmonies and cerebral or virtuoso music, but *in,* to further, unexplored possibilities of their instruments and the inner motions of music.

Towner is perhaps unique among guitarists working in jazz for his rigorously classical background. "I wasn't on the jazz scene until I got a classically oriented technique on the guitar," he told Charles Mitchell. "It's a matter of training, just the way it worked out for me." Still, he regards that training only as access, an opening of channels: "It's the classical technique that allows me to make discriminations in volume, tone and accent for individual notes and groups of notes within the total chord," the final (and only important) result being a greater emotional range in his playing. Similar thoughts have been expressed by McCandless: "The thing about having a classical technique, or having played that music, is that you can bring a different conception of what's possible on the instrument—from the classical tradition—to the style you're addressing."

Towner's guitar style, influenced strongly by piano trios, remains keyboard-oriented, with discrete melody, inner and bass voices. These do not appear simultaneously (though that is often the impression) but in a kind of overlapping approach: he may play a figure on bass, then state a portion of melodic material and leave that suspended while moving down to play (more quietly) an inner voice, then quickly return to the melody and pick it up where he left it. This interweaving of musical motives—along with his jagged, ringing chords and polyrhythms in which agitated strumming works its way in and out of flowing lines—creates a dense, ever-changing and highly emotional texture.

Towner's guitar is best represented on two solo albums, the first from 1974, the second a live album recorded in 1979. Of the first, *Diary,* Towner has said,

> We did every piece immediately; there was no laying down of one track and coming back the next day to overdub. The album took only two days to finish—one session of about four or five hours, another hour the next day, and then the mix. I discovered a really good technique for overdubbing, though. I didn't want a situation where one instrument was accompanying another. I wanted to have more of an improvised interplay between instruments. The music had to flow

without one instrument stuck in a backup position. I would start a piece on one instrument, play it so far in a primary role, and then stop within the piece. Then I'd go back, pick up another instrument, playing it in the secondary role underneath the first instrumental voice. But then I'd go beyond the point where the first track stopped, bringing the secondary voice to a primary role.

Thus even his recording technique for *Diary* echoed Towner's stylistic approach to guitar and to composition (or improvisation) itself. "It sounds, in fact," Charles Mitchell wrote in *Down Beat*, "as if Towner is playing in a mirror much of the time, so sensitively is each voice reflected in the other," a good description, as well, of Oregon at work.

Solo Concert, recorded in October 1979 during concerts in Munich and Zurich, is Towner's most complete statement as a guitarist, but there is truly excellent work on two duo albums with fellow guitarist John Abercrombie, *Sargasso Sea* and *Five Years Later;* on at least a dozen Oregon albums; and on four others issued under Towner's name by ECM.

Of the three guitarists in this chapter, Lenny Breau is the only one working in a clearly defined historical idiom: he is resolutely a jazz guitarist. Yet his approach to the instrument, blending flamenco, classical, country and Indian elements with more typical jazz improvisation, and his style of playing, which features simultaneous bass lines, chords and melody, are anything but traditional.

Breau was born in Maine in 1941 to country musicians Hal Lone Pine and Betty Cote. The family moved to Canada shortly thereafter and Lenny took up guitar at age eight, his first teacher being the guitarist in his father's band, Ray Couture. Breau played Gene Autry or Roy Rogers guitars from Sears for a while but got a Gibson a few years later, about the same time, as it happened, that he first heard Chet Atkins. He was able to work out what Atkins was doing by ear and before long progressed to guitarists such as Tal Farlow, Johnny Smith and Barney Kessel, all of them strong influences. At seventeen he moved to Winnepeg, Manitoba, there meeting a number of serious jazz musicians, among them pianist Bob Eulison, who explained chord theory and jazz harmony to him. Breau's first jazz gig, as a bassist, came shortly after: "I was compelled to learn a whole bunch of tunes pretty fast." At home he labored over the record player, slowing Farlow's records to 16 RPMs to figure his runs out, and soon was working not as a bassist, but as a guitarist with a rapidly growing reputation.

"Basically I was into comping and a single-string approach at the time," he told Brawner Smoot for a piece in *Guitar Player,* "but things changed fast after I heard Bill Evans's piano work on 'Nardis.' I was around twenty-one at the time, and I recall going for a few years after that experience without even listening to guitar. All I wanted to hear was piano because that was giving me ideas I wanted to develop. I'd hear the pianist's left hand first, then I'd listen to his right hand and try to work out the voicings." It's interesting that Breau's guitar concept, like Towner's, should derive from piano, and specifically from Bill Evans; "Nardis," incidentally, is one of only two non-Towner compositions on *Solo Concert.*

Breau also developed strong interests in flamenco and classical guitar, and eventually in sitar, these becoming important parts of his vocabulary. He worked the studios for a while, increasingly frustrated with his role there and wanting just to play his own music.

"Breau evolved a unique piano-guitar style which combined Travis/Atkins country picking and flamenco technique with the musical influences of Bill Evans jazz piano voicings," Howard Morgen wrote. "He could thus 'comp' rhythmically independent, beautifully voiced chords while improvising single-line jazz choruses. His albums also display his command of country, rock, classical and flamenco idioms. His application of Atkins-inspired artificial harmonics to create the aural illusion of rapidly flowing harplike note 'showers' is particularly interesting."

Atkins signed him to RCA in the late sixties, but after producing two albums, *The Guitar Sounds of Lenny Breau* (1968) and *The Velvet Touch of Lenny Breau* (1969), Breau withdrew from public life for almost ten years because of personal problems, teaching and playing only occasionally. In 1977 he appeared with George Benson at the NAMM Convention concert, and two years later brought out *Five O'Clock Bells* on Adelphi. That album opened with a marvelous reworking of "Days of Wine and Roses," something of a Breau classic, and proceeded through five originals to "Funny Valentine" and a fiery version of pianist McCoy Tyner's "Visions." "I cut it just as if I was playing in a club," Breau says. "I didn't really think about which tunes I'd do or anything. I sat down in the studio, and once I got going they just let the tape run. Later we picked the best things off that for the album."

Another album, cut piecemeal in Chet Atkins's home, had come out earlier that year but was distributed only by direct mail. Titled *The Legendary Lenny Breau . . . Now!,* it includes a beautiful reharmonization of Hank Williams's "I Can't Help It (If I'm Still in Love with You)," a version of "Freight Train" which starts off with Atkins-like fingerpicking and evolves slowly into typically Breau styling, another reading of Tyner's "Visions" and the same artist's "Ebony Queen"; on two cuts, Breau overdubbed a second guitar part for improvised duets.

Breau repeated the folk music-to-jazz idea with "Don't Think Twice (It's All Right)" on the direct-to-disk *Lenny Breau,* filling out the first side with a country number ("You

Needed Me") and Coltrane's "Mister Night"; the second side featured two originals. For all the sophistication of his jazz harmony and simultaneous lines, Breau's work retains a sense of its country roots, reminding us (and we do forget) that the foundations of jazz lie in American folk music. In 1981 Breau appeared with Chet Atkins on an album of duets and on the solo Adelphi album *Mo' Breau*. The latter begins with a reprise of "Ebony Queen" and passes on through three standards to a side of originals, one of them "I Remember Hank" (Williams? Garland?), another (presumably for his father) "Lone Pine."

For some time now Breau has divided his attention between classical guitar and a custom-made solidbody electric with classical-width neck; recently he's taken to playing a seven-string classical, placing the additional string as a high A. His work has become less directly concerned with melodic and harmonic material as such, and more engaged in the sort of coloristic, textural pursuits represented by Oregon or Ralph Towner. "When I'm alone," he says, "and all the conditions are right, I try to be like an Impressionist. Instead of just playing, it's almost like I'm painting tonal colors." He would like someday to be able to walk out and completely improvise a thirty-minute piece, to be that spontaneous yet have it sound as though everything were planned. "I think in terms of the colors and the inversions of the chords," he told Brawner Smoot. "When I play chords, I consider the inversions because every inversion has its own color. If one color is blue, another may also be blue—but a different shade. Every time you play a different inversion that shade will change."

On a recent album Lenny Breau is quoted as saying, "I just improvise and keep it going and see what happens. Just one big long tune," a marvelous comment on the consistency of his work. There is to that work a sameness of voice, an identity, that comes not from circumscription or limitation but from personal vision. Much as has America, Breau has taken many seemingly diverse elements (country music, jazz improvisation, Spanish guitar) and reconciled them in a music uniquely and seamlessly his own. Like Towner he forces us to think of (or remember) jazz as *potential;* and like Cooder, to face once again the unity of American music stretching out beneath us like the ground itself, rolling between our cluttered histories, occult horizons.

INDEX

Abbey, Leon, 36
Abercrombie, John, 276
Adams, Gus, 134
Adderley, Cannonball, 217
After the Riot at Newport (album), 208
Aladdin Records, 47
Albertson, Chris, 48
Alexander, Texas, 31, 35–36, 68, 69
Almeida, Laurindo, 266
"Altar Song," 261
American Folk Blues Festival, 171
Analine (album), 236–38, 261
Anthony, Eddie, 36
Appice, Carmine, 257
"Arkansas Blues," 60
Armstrong, Louis, 21, 31, 33, 40, 46, 69, 181
Arnold, Eddy, 195–96, 205
Arnold, Jerome, 242
Arnold, Kokomo, 87
Ashby, Irving, 108–9
Ashley, Clarence, 126
Atkins, Chet, 20, 173, 183, 198–99, 201–6, 208, 266, 277–79
"At the Cross," 237
Avakian, Al, 117

Bacon & Day, 85
Bailey, Blanche, 133
Bailey, Mildred, 72, 106
Baker, Duck, 51, 267
Banjo-guitar, 59
Banjos, 14–17, 56–57, 122, 127
    tenor, 55, 78, 85–86
Barber, Dave, 120
Barker, Danny, 59
Barnes, George, 20, 41, 45, 73, 83, 145, 173–93
Barnes, George, Quartet, 175–76
Barnes, George—Ruby Braff
    Quartet, 191–92
Barrett, Bucky, 209–10
Basie, Count, 97, 98

Beatles, The, 228–29
Bebop, 114–15
Beefheart, Captain, 268
Beethoven, Ludwig van, 226
Beiderbecke, Bix, 62–65
Bell, Eddie, 89
Benjamin, Joe, 209
Benson, George, 110, 210, 225, 229, 278
Bernstein, Artie, 107, 111
Between the Hard Place and the Ground
    (album), 262
"Big Bad Bill Is Sweet William Now," 71
Big Broadcast of 1932, The (film), 73
"Big C Blues," 237
Bigsby, Paul, 146
Biloski, Count, 162
Bishop, Elvin, 242, 244, 250, 255
Bitches Brew (album), 229
"Black and Blue Bottom," 64
Black & White label, 166, 167
Blackwell, Scrapper, 33, 38, 161
Blake, Blind, 37, 241, 261, 268, 269
Bland, Jack, 59
Blanton, Jimmy, 105
Bloom, Rube, 67
Bloomfield/Harris (album), 262
Bloomfield, Michael, 157, 235–64
Bloomfield, Susie, 252
Bluebird Records, 46, 138, 140–41, 180
Blue Devils, 98
"Blue Ghost Blues," 261
Bluegrass, 196
Bluegrass Boys, 196
"Blue Guitars," 70
"Blue Room," 70
Blues Going Up (album), 193
Blues guitar, 156–58
Blues of Lonnie Johnson, The (album), 46, 49
Bolden, Buddy, 14
Bond, Eddie, 207

Bonfa, Luis, 266
Boomer's Story (album), 269
Bop Till You Drop (album), 271
Borderline (album), 271
Boswell Sisters, 73
Bouterse, Curt, 271
Boyd, Bill, 144–45
Bracey, Ishman, 22
Bradley, Harold, 202–8, 211
Bradley, Owen, 198, 204
Braff, Ruby, 191–92
Braff, Ruby—George Barnes Quartet, 191–92
Breau, Larry, 276–80
Bringing It All Back Home (album), 245
Bromberg, David, 267
Brooks, Harvey, 250, 254
Broonzy, Big Bill, 33–36
Brown, Milton, 140
Brown, Ray, 128
Bryan, Mike, 111
Bumpin' (album), 223
Bunn, Teddy, 42–43
Burgh, Steve, 249–50
Burns, Jethro, 183
Burton, Gary, 208, 209
Butterfield, Paul, 239–40, 242, 244, 247, 255
"Buzzbox," 273
Byrd, Billy, 202, 206
Byrd, Charlie, 266
Byrd, Jerry, 204–5
Byrdland guitar, 206

Cahn, Sammy, 219
Calt, Stephan, 22, 67, 175
Capitol Records, 168, 197
Carlisle, Cliff, 87
Carmichael, Hoagy, 68
Carolina Tar Heels, 126
Carr, Leroy, 33
Carson, Fiddlin' John, 123, 131, 132
Carter, Bo (Bo Chatmon), 21–23, 26
Carter, Maybelle, 144, 198, 201
Carter family, 198, 201
Castle Studio, 203
"Cathy's Clown," 207
Celestial Express (album), 118
Cerulli, Dom, 223
Challis, Bill, 62
Charles, Ray, 172, 237
Charlie Christian–Lester Young: Together (album), 118
Charters, Sam, 32, 40, 70, 170–71
Chasman, Paul, 266
Chatmon, Bert, 24
Chatmon, Bo (Bo Carter), 21–23, 26
Chatmon, Edgar, 24
Chatmon, Harry, 24
Chatmon, Henderson, 20–21
Chatmon, Lonnie, 21–24
Chatmon, Sam, 21–27
Chatmon, Willie, 24
Chatmon Brothers, 21, 23–26
Chatmon family, 20–22

"Chattanooga Shoe Shine Boy," 204
Chicago, 177–81
Chicken Skin Music (album), 269
Christian, Charlie, 19, 67, 97–120, 162, 163, 176, 213–15
Christian, Tom, 130
"City Girl," 260
Clapton, Eric, 235
Clark, Roy, 119–20, 174
Clarke, Kenny, 112–14
Clayton, Buck, 97
"Clementine," 63–64
Cline, Patsy, 206
Clouds of Joy, 106
Cohen, Norm, 128, 131, 143
Cohen, Paul, 203, 204
Cohn, Lawrence, 41–42
Cole, Nat King, Trio, 101
Coltrane, John, 216, 220, 279
Columbia Records, 130–34, 162, 198
"Come in My Kitchen," 21
Connors, Eddie, 83
Cooder, Ry, 71, 237–38, 267–71
Cook, Bruce, 29–30, 239
Cook, Josephus, 161
Copas, Cowboy, 203
Copland, Aaron, 228–29
Cordle, Joel, 143
Corn Licker Still in Georgia (comedy skits), 134
Coryell, Larry, 218, 266
Cotton, James, 252
Count Talent and the Originals (album), 261
Country music, 199–200
    See also Bluegrass; Hillbilly music
County Records, 139
Couture, Ray, 276
Covarrubias, Arnold, 111
Cramer, Floyd, 200
Crayton, Pee Wee, 165
Creath, Charlie, 34, 35
Crockett, Jim, 260
Cropper, Steve, 252–53
Crosby, Bing, 27, 73
Crosby, Israel, 118
Cross, Hugh, 136
Cruisin' for a Bruisin' (album), 262

Dallas String Band, 155, 162
Dandridge, Putney, 44
D'Angelico, John, 119
Davis, Clive, 256
Davis, Miles, 229
Davis, Reverend Gary, 59, 268
Dayron, Norman, 239, 262
"Dear Old Pal of Mine," 88
"Death Cell Rounder Blues," 260
"Death in My Family," 261
Decca Records, 46, 141, 177, 180–82, 198, 203
Delmore, Alton, 125
Delmore Brothers, 125
Diary (album), 275–76
Dickens, Jimmy, 207

Diero, Pedro, 83
Disc Records, 47
Dobro, 87
Dodds, Warren "Baby," 44
Dolphy, Eric, 216
Dorsey, Jimmy, 62
Dorsey, Tom, 237
Dorsey brothers, 59, 70, 130
"Down Yonder," 137
Dunn, Blind Willie (pseudonym of Eddie
    Lang), 68
Dunn, Bob, 73, 87
Dunn, "Duck," 255
Dupree, Jack, 262
Durham, Eddie, 97–99, 101, 103
Dvořak, Antonín, 13
Dylan, Bob, 241–49, 264

Eades, Elmer, 138
"East Colorado Blues," 261
East Texas Serenaders, 126
East-West (album), 249
Eddie Lang and Lonnie Johnson: Volume One
    (album), 46
Eddie Lang: Guitar Virtuoso (album), 67
"Eddie's Twister," 64
Edwards, Cliff, 62
"Effinonna Rag," 237
Electric Flag, 250–53, 256, 258, 264
Electric guitar, 87, 88, 90, 104, 145,
    156, 164, 184–85
Eliot, T. S., 264
Ellington, Duke, 31, 41–43, 237
Ellis, Herb, 184–85
Ellison, Ralph, 103
Emery, S. A., 130
Emmett, Daniel Decatur, 130
"Epistrophy," 113–14
Estes, Sleepy John, 241, 262, 268, 269
Eulison, Bob, 277
Evans, Bill, 277
Everly Brothers, 207

Fahey, John, 266
"Farewell Blues," 92
Farlow, Tal, 109, 182, 205, 220, 277
Fathers and Sons (album), 255
Fatool, Nick, 111
Feather, Leonard, 57, 218
"Feelin' My Way," 73
Fender, Leo, 146
Fenton, Nick, 112
Fiddle, 36–37, 122, 123, 127
Fiddling contests, 134–35
Fingerstyle guitar, 18
Fishell, Steve, 267, 268, 270
Five O'Clock Bells (album), 278
Five Pennies, 64
Five Years Later (album), 276
Flanagan, Tommy, 217
Flatt, Lester, 196
"Flying Home," 108
Foley, Red, 204, 207
Folk music, 231–33
Ford, Tennessee Ernie, 196

"For No Reason at All in C," 63
Foster, George "Pops," 34
Franklin, Aretha, 229
Frazier, "Mom," 116
"From Spirituals to Swing" concert
    (1939), 118
Fuller, Jesse, 268
Fulson, Lowell, 38, 158, 163, 165, 167,
    168, 170

Gabby Pahinui Band (album), 270
Galbraith, Barry, 205
Gallop, Cliff, 239
Garland, Hank, 20, 183, 200–211
Garon, Paul, 49
Garroway, Dave, 181
Gatewood, Ruby, 45
Georgia Cotton Pickers, 202
Georgia Wildcats band, 137, 140
"Get a Load of This," 64
Getz, Stan, 224
Gibbons, Billy, 158
Gibson, Don, 208
Gibson, Guitars, and Girls (album), 208
Giddins, Garry, 213, 225–27
Gid Tanner and His Skillet Lickers (album),
    139
*Gid Tanner and His Skillet Lickers: The
    Kickapoo Medicine Show* (album), 139
Gleason, Ralph, 101, 106, 175, 214,
    216–18, 220, 222
Glenn, Charley, 166
"Goin' Out of My Head," 227
Goin' Out of My Head (album), 223
Goldberg, Barry, 250, 254–57
Goldkette, Jean, Orchestra, 62–63
Good Feelin' (album), 172
Goodman, Benny, 66–67, 73, 100, 101,
    106–9, 181
Goodman, Benny, Band, 110, 111
Goodman, Benny, Quintet, 111
Goodman, Benny, Septet, 117, 118
Goodman, Benny, Sextet, 108, 115, 117
Gordon, Robert Winslow, 179
Gorman, Ross, 61, 62
Grand Ole Opry, 145
Grappelli, Stephane, 65
Graupner, 16
Gravenites, Nick, 236, 239, 240, 241,
    249, 250, 260–61
Grech, Rick, 257
Greene, Ted, 65, 263, 266
Gregg, Bobby, 243
Gridley, Mark, 215, 223
Griffin, Rex, 71
Grimes, Tiny, 113
Grisman, David, 183, 267
Grosz, Marty, 68, 74, 191
Gruhn, George, 233, 234
Grunfeld, Frederic V., 13, 18, 100
Guitar, 121–22
    Byrdland, 206
    electric, 87, 88, 90, 104, 145, 156,
        164, 184–85
    Hawaiian, 78, 86–88

Guitar(cont'd.)
   introduction and emergence of, 17–19
   seven-string, 184, 189–90
Guitar Album, The (album), 191
Guitars, Anyone? (album), 189
Guitars Galore (album), 185
Guitars Pure and Honest (album), 191
Guy, Buddy, 49
Guy, Freddy, 55, 57
Guy, Joe, 112

Hadlock, Richard, 40, 61, 73
Haesler, Bill, 49
Haggerty, Terry, 259
Hall, Edmond, 18
Hall, Edmond, Quartet, 118
Hall, Roy, 206
Hammond, John (guitarist), 241, 256, 266
Hammond, John (producer), 98, 106–8, 115, 116, 119
Hampton, Lionel, 101, 111, 214
Handy, W. C., 91
Harmon, Buddy, 200
Harmony Company, 89–90
Harris, Bill, 220, 266
Harris, Woody, 235, 262
Havenga, Clarence, 206
Hawaiian guitar, 78, 86–88
Hawkins, Ted, 129, 132, 134, 138, 141
Heath, Albert, 217
Heath, Percy, 217
Helm, Levon, 241
Helms, Bill, 134–35
Hemphill, Sid, 15
Henderson, Fletcher, 64, 111, 167
Hendrix, Jimi, 229
Hentoff, Nat, 160
Highway 61 Revisited (album), 248
Hill, Eddie, 204
Hill, Teddy, 105, 112, 116, 120
Hillbilly music, 124–27
"Hilo Waltz," 237
Hines, Earl "Fatha," 269
Hite, Les, Orchestra, 165–66
Hoh, Eddie, 254
Hometown Boys, 129
Hoopii, Sol, 86–88
Hopkins, Jerry, 251
Hopkins, Lightnin', 238–39
Hornsby, Dan, 124, 134
"Hot Guitar, The," 204–5
Howard, Paul, 202
Howe, Steve, 206
Howell, Peg Leg, 36
Humphrey, Mark, 55, 272
Hunter, Lloyd, 105
Hurt, Mississippi John, 241, 268
Husky, Ferlin, 208
Hutchison, Frank, 87

"I Fall to Pieces," 206
If You Love These Blues (album), 157–58, 258–61
"I'll Never Be the Same," 67

"I'm Coming, Virginia," 63
"I'm Not Rough," 40
Incredible Jazz Guitar of Wes Montgomery, The (album), 217
Inman, Autry, 203
Into the Purple Valley (album), 269
Isaac, Atta, 269
It's Not Killing Me (album), 255

"Jack O'Diamond Blues," 87
Jackson, Papa Charlie, 32
Jackson Blue Boys, 25
James, Duncan, 193
James, Skip, 268
Jazz (album), 269–71
Jazz Winds from a New Direction (album), 209, 210
Jefferson, Blind Lemon, 32, 33, 87, 156, 161, 261
Jefferson, Thomas, 14
Jenkins, Carl, 197
Jernigan, Doug, 190
Jeter-Pillars band, 106
Jeters, Claude, 237
Jiminez, Flaco, 269, 270
John, Dr., 256, 262
Johnson, Blind Willie, 268, 269
Johnson, James (Buddy), 34–35
Johnson, Lonnie, 19, 29–51, 68–70, 100, 145, 161, 173, 175, 237, 261
Johnson, Mike, 241
Johnson, Robert, 21, 33, 37–38, 87, 175
Johnson, Tommy, 22
Johnson, Will, 55
Jolly Jugglers, 103
Jolson, Al, 62
Jones, Bob, 236
Jones, Coley, 155, 162
Jones, Eddie "Guitar Slim," 261
Jones, Jo, 97
Jones, Red, 141
Joplin, Scott, 91

Kaai, Bob, 86–87
Kahn, Roger Wolfe, 65, 66
Kahn, Roger Wolfe, Band, 65, 66
Kaminsky, Max, 63–65
"Kansas City," 260
Katz, Dick, 105
Keepnews, Orrin, 217, 223
Kelly, Wynton, 228
Kelly, Wynton, Trio, 227
Kerr, Charlie, 59
Kessel, Barney, 102, 110–11, 220, 225, 277
KGB (band), 256–57
Khan, Steve, 218–21
Kienzle, Rich, 57, 157, 201, 203–5, 207–10, 249
Killian, Al, Quartet, 167
King, B. B., 38, 69, 117, 156, 157, 168, 260
King, Ben E., 270
King, Bobby, 269
King, Eddie, 62

King, Freddie, 156
King, Pee Wee, 197
King, Riley B., 167
King, Sid, 199–200
King of Jazz, The (film), 72
King Records, 47–48
King Sisters, 90
Kingston Trio, 231
Kirk, Andy, 36, 98, 101, 106
"Knockin' a Jug," 69
Kolodin, Irving, 66
Kooper, Al, 243, 247, 248, 251–55
Kottke, Leo, 266
Kress, Carl, 57, 72, 73, 187–89
Kriss, Eric, 260

Lacy, Rubin, 22
Lamb, Richard, 228
Lang, Eddie, 31, 32, 40–42, 46, 51,
    53–75, 83, 91, 100, 130, 175, 187,
    237
Lang, Kitty, 72
Lange, Arthur, Orchestra, 65
Lanin, Sam, 56
Larkins, Milt, 162
"Laughing Rag," 88
Law, Don, 209
Lawson Brooks Band, 162
Lay, Sammy, 242, 247, 255
Layne, Bert, 134, 141
Leadbelly, 268, 269
Lee, Jerry, 207
Legendary Lenny Breau, The (album), 278
Lenny Breau (album), 278–79
Lewis, Meade Lux, 118
Library of Congress, 179
Lieberson, Richard, 69, 187, 189
"Like a Rolling Stone," 242, 243,
    245–48
Lindley, David, 267, 270
Lion, Alfred, 118
Lipscomb, Mance, 16
"Little Old Log Cabin in the Lane," 131
*Live Adventures of Mike Bloomfield and Al
    Kooper* (album), 255
Living in the Fast Lane (album), 262
Lomax, Alan, 179
Lomax, John, 179
Long Riders, The (soundtrack album), 71
Lonnie Johnson (album), 46
*Lonnie Johnson: The Originator of Modern
    Guitar Blues* (album), 46, 49
Louis, Joe, 166
Love, "Daddy" John, 141
"Lover," 192
"Lovesick Blues," 70–71, 130
Lowe, Mundell, 119
Lucas, Nick, 55–56, 91
Lunceford, Jimmie, 98

McBurney, Al, 90
McCandless, Paul, 273–75
McCoy, Charlie, 22
McDonough, Dick, 73, 187
McGee, Sam, 18, 59, 122, 145

McGhee, Brownie, 37
McKenzie, Bill, 59–61
McKinney, Sam, 116
McLaughlin, John, 229
McMichen, Clayton, 125, 126, 128, 131,
    133–40, 142, 143
McMichen's, Clayton, Hometown Band,
    128
Macon, Uncle Dave, 125–26
McShann, Jay, 36
McTell, Blind Willie, 37
McVea's, Jack, All-Stars, 167
"Maggie's Farm," 245, 247
Magic Ukulele, The (album), 83
Magic Ukulele of Roy Smeck, The (album),
    83
Malone, Bill, 123, 179, 200
"Mama Lion," 260
Mandolin, 55
Maphis, Joe, 145
Martin, C. F., 19
Martin, Grady, 200, 203, 207–8
Marvin, Johnny, 83
"Mary Johnson Blues," 39
Mastersounds, The, 216
Mause, Alan de, 266
Mayall, Norm, 241
MCA, 257
Meadmore, Clement, 192
"Melody Man's Dream," 70
Melrose, Lester, 180
Memphis Minnie, 37
Memphis Slim, 45–46
Mercury, 197
Michael Bloomfield (album), 262
"Midnight Call," 70
Miles, Buddy, 250–52, 255
Miller, Emmett, 70–71, 130
Miller, Joe, 137, 142, 144
Miller, Steve, 157, 255
Mills, Irving, 71
Minton, Henry, 112
Minton's Playhouse, 111–14
Mississippi Blacksnakes, 25
Mississippi Mudsteppers, 25
Mississippi Sheiks, 21–22, 25, 26, 33, 36
Mr. Johnson's Blues (album), 46
Mitchell, Charles, 275, 276
Mo'Breau (album), 279
Mole, Miff, 62
Mongan, Norman, 43
Monk, Thelonious, 112–14, 119
Monroe, Bill, 139, 196
Monroe, Charlie, 145, 196
Montgomery, Buddy, 216–17
Montgomery, Monk, 216–17
Montgomery, Wes, 109, 209, 213–29
Montgomery Ward, 91
"Mood Indigo," 237
Moore, Alex, 162–63
Moore, Bob, 200, 203
Moore, Glen, 273
Moore, Mike, 191
Moore, Oscar, 101–2
Moore, Sam, 88

Moore, Scotty, 239
Morello, Joe, 209
Morgan, Russ, 59
Morgen, Howard, 265, 277–78
Morton, Jelly Roll, 36
Moten, Bennie, 98
Mottola, Tony, 73, 83, 188
Mound City Blue Blowers, 59–60, 66
Movin' Wes (album), 223
Musselwhite, Charlie, 241

Naftalin, Mark, 245, 253, 255
"Nardis," 277
Nashville, Tennessee, 197–200, 203–4, 207
"Nashville Sound," 198–200, 207
National Barn Dance (radio program), 178–79
Newman, Jerry, 118
Newman, Randy, 269
New York Times, 197
Nichols, Red, 59, 62, 64
Noone, Jimmie, 45, 181
Norris, Fate, 133, 134
Notini, Per, 49
Novelty Jazz Trio, 59
Nugent, Ted, 206
Nye, Russel, 72–73, 84, 177

Oakley, Giles, 31, 38, 48, 50
Obrecht, Jas, 23, 99
Octachorda, 88–89
Ogerman, Claus, 227
Okeh Records, 32, 33, 35, 44, 60, 123
Oliver, Joe "King," 68, 69
Oliver, Paul, 25, 26, 34, 35, 39, 44, 45, 48–49
O'Neal, Amy, 159, 162, 163, 167, 169
O'Neal, Jim, 159, 162, 163, 167, 169
Oregon, 271–76
Oregon in Performance (album), 273
Osborne, Mary, 104
Otis, Johnny, Revue, 172

Page, Oran "Hot Lips," 98
Page, Patti, 197, 207
Page, Walter, 97, 98
Painter, Shorty, 201
Palmer, Robert, 15, 17
Panassie, Hugh, 175
Paradise and Lunch (album), 269
Parker, Leroy, 36
Parker, Paul, 217
Pass, Joe, 213, 224, 266
Pastor, Tony, 83–84
Patton, Charley, 21, 36
Paul Butterfield Blues Band, 233, 242, 246, 247, 249
Paul, Les, 145, 146, 175
Peer, Ralph, 32, 33, 60, 123, 129, 133
"Perfect," 70
Perls, Nick, 93
Pettiford, Oscar, 105
Phillips, Sam, 268
"Pickin' My Way," 73

Pierce, Webb, 208
Pioneers of the Jazz Guitar (album), 188
Pizzarelli, Bucky, 183–84, 189–90
Pizzarelli, John, 190
Plays So Good (album), 193
Plotka, Dick, 83
Poole, Charlie, 126–27
Porterfield, Nolan, 130
Powell, Baden, 266
Prairie Ramblers, 179
Prelude in C# minor, 83
Presley, Elvis, 208
Prince, Bob, 117
Puckett, Riley, 121–46
Puma, Joe, 83

Quinn, Snoozer, 43

Rachell, Yank, 241, 268
"Rainbow Dreams," 67, 72
Rainey, Ma, 162
Randolph, Boots, 209
Raney, Jimmy, 220
Rank, Bill, 63
"Rattlesnake Blues," 39
RCA Victor, 197, 203, 208
Redbone, Leon, 71
Red Clay Ramblers, 266
Reed, Blind Alfred, 269
Reeve, Jim, 208
Reinhardt, Django, 65, 101, 104, 105, 176, 203, 220
Reser, Harry, 82–83
Reuss, Allan, 101, 176
Rey, Alvino, 90
Reynolds, George, 197
Rhumboogie label, 166
Rhyne, Melvin, 217
Rice, Hoke, 134
Riley Puckett (album), 139
"Riot-Chous," 209
Rising Sons, 268
Riskin, Irving, 63
Riverside label, 223
Robbins, Robert, 36
Roberts, Howard, 224
Roberts, Joe, 82
Robertson, Robbie, 241
Robinson, Bill, 163
"Rock All Our Babies to Sleep," 129
Rock and roll, 183–84, 206–7, 231, 233–34
Rodgers, Jimmie, 122, 129–31, 135, 139, 144
Rollini, Adrian, 59
"Rose Room," 108
Rounder Records, 139
Royal Hawaiians, 86, 87
Roy Smeck in His Pastime (film), 89
Roy Smeck Plays the Hawaiian Guitar, Banjo, Ukulele, and Guitar (album), 93
Roy Smeck, Wizard of the Strings (album), 77
Rushing, Jimmy, 98
Russell, Ross, 115

Ry Cooder (album), 268–69
Ryerson, Art, 190

"Sail on Boogie," 166
St. Cyr, Johnny, 40, 55, 59
Salute to Rodgers and Hart (album), 192
Salvador, Sal, 119, 120
"San," 60
Santana, Carlos, 255, 259
Sargasso Sea (album), 276
Scaduto, Anthony, 243–48
Scheit, Karl, 272
Schuller, Gunther, 217
Schutt, Arthur, 65, 66, 91
Scott, Bud, 55
Scranton Sirens, 59
Scruggs, Earl, 196
Searcy, DeLouise, 35
Seeger, Pete, 232, 246
Senegambia region, 14
Sete, Bola, 266
Shamblin, Eldon, 145
Shapiro, Nat, 160
Sharpe, Ray, 262
Sheffield, Leslie, 106
Shelton, Aaron, 197
Shines, Johnny, 38
Sholes, Steve, 173, 197, 199, 203
Short, Jimmie, 145
Showtime (album), 270
Siegel, Joel, 99
Signorelli, Frank, 67, 68, 91
Simon, Bill, 37, 118
Sims, Henry, 36
"Singin' the Blues," 63, 65
"Sitting on Top of the World," 21
"Sixteen Tons," 196
Skillet Lickers Band, 124, 126, 127, 133–43
"Sleep, Baby, Sleep," 129, 130
"Sleepy Time Gal," 62
Slevin, Dick, 59
"Slippery Fingers," 91
Smart, "Professor" Alec, 129
Smeck, Roy, 57, 77–96
Smith, Arthur, 201
Smith, Bessie, 36, 41, 68, 69
Smith, Buster, 98, 163
Smith, Clara, 35, 36
Smith, Floyd, 101, 106, 176
Smith, Johnny, 208, 277
Smith, Mamie, 36
Smith, Stuff, 37
Smith, William J., 90–91
Smokey and Intimate (album), 189
Smokin' at the Half Note (album), 227
Smoot, Brawner, 277, 279
"Snowfall," 221
Solo Concert (album), 276, 277
Solo Flight (album), 118
Solo Guitar (album), 266
So Many Roads (album), 241
Something Tender (album), 189
South, Eddie, 37
Spann, Otis, 255

Speck, Paul, 81
Speck, Paul, Orchestra, 81
Spence, Joseph, 268
"Steamboat Stomp," 205
Stevens, Mike, 96
Stewart, Jimmy, 215–16, 219–20, 264
Stewart, Redd, 197
Stills, Steve, 254–55
Stokes, Lowe, 129, 134, 136, 142, 144
Stone Mountain Boys, The, 142
"Stormy Monday," 158, 167–69
Strachwitz, Chris, 26, 267
Strassa, Peter, 250
"Strawberries," 129, 131
"Stringin' the Blues," 64
"Sugarfoot Rag," 204
Sullivan, Joe, 69
Super Session (album), 255
Sweeney, Joe, 16

Taj Mahal, 268
Takoma label, 236
Tampa Red (Hudson Whittaker), 33, 237
Tanner, Arthur, 134
Tanner, Gid, 126, 131–39, 142
Tanner, Gordon, 136, 138, 143–44
Tarlton, Jimmy, 87
Tate, Grady, 219
Taylor, Creed, 223, 225
Taylor, James, 266–67
T-Bones, 171
Teagarden, Jack, 69, 73, 101
Ten Duets for Two Guitars (album), 189
"Tennessee Waltz," 197
"There'll Be Some Changes Made," 68
Thomas, Ramblin', 87
Three Suns, 182
"Thrift Shop Rag," 261
Tico, Ray, 265
Tirro, Frank, 71
Tony Rizzi's Five Guitars Play Charlie Christian (album), 119
Tosches, Nick, 36, 71, 130
Toussaint, Allen, 249
Towles, Nat, 105–6
Towner, Ralph, 271–76
Town Hall Concert (album), 189
Travis, Merle, 145–46, 184, 266
Trent, Alphonso, 103, 104
Tristano, Lennie, 103
Triumvirate (album), 256
Trumbauer, Frank, 60, 62–64, 72
Try It Before You Buy It (album), 255
Tuba, 55–56
Tubb, Ernest, 145
Turner, Big Joe, 261, 262
Two Jews' Blues (album), 255
2 × 7 = Pizzarelli (album), 190
Tyner, McCoy, 278

Ukulele, 55, 78–79, 86, 90
Ulmer, James "Blood," 206
Unforgettable Guitar of Hank Garland, The (album), 208

Vance, Joel, 31, 54, 74–75
Van Duser, Guy, 266
Van Eps, George, 64–66, 185, 189, 190, 266
Vaudeville, 83–84
Velvet Guitar (album), 209
Venuti, Joe, 58–59, 61, 62, 64, 66, 67, 72, 73, 193
Venuti-Lang All-Star Orchestra, 73
Verve Records, 227–28
Victor records, 138, 177
Vinson, Eddie, 252
Vinson, Walter, 21–24, 26
Violin, *see* Fiddle
von Schmidt, Rick, 246–47

Waitin' for the Evening Mail (album), 139
Walcott, Colin, 272, 273
Walker, Frank, 124, 131–34, 136, 141
Walker, Ruby, 41
Walker, T-Bone, 38, 155–72, 260
Waller, Fats, 64
Ward, W. E., 18
Warner, Harry, 89
Waters, Muddy, 21, 255
Watson, Doc, 122
Watson, George P., 130
WBAP, 178
"WDIA," 260
Weavers, The, 146
Wein, George, 191, 192
Welding, Pete, 118, 169, 244
Wells, Kitty, 208
Wes Montgomery: Groove Brothers (album), 217
Wes Montgomery Guitar Folio, The (album), 219
West, Irene, 86
Wheeler, Tom, 240
White, Bukka, 87
White, Clarence, 267

White, Hy, 56
Whiteman, Paul, 71–72
Whiteman, Paul, Orchestra, 71, 72
Whittaker, Hudson (Tampa Red), 33, 237
Whitten, Mike, 134
"Whole Lotta Shakin' Goin' On," 206
Williams, Bert, 270
Williams, Clarence, 68
Williams, Claude, 36
Williams, Hank, 71, 130, 195, 278
Williams, Martin, 115
Williams, Mary, 36, 38–40
Williams, Mary Lou, 106
Williams, Spencer, 33
Willow Weep for Me (album), 227
Wills, Bob, 71, 140, 202
Wilmer, Valerie, 31
Winburn, Anna Mae, Orchestra, 104
Winston, Neil, 22
Winter, Paul, Consort, 272
Wise, Chubby, 196
Witherspoon, Jimmy, 165, 168, 170
WLS, 178–79
Wolfe, Charles, 122, 125, 129, 132, 136, 138–40, 143, 195
Wright, Wayne, 191
"Wringin' and Twistin'," 64
WSB, 122–23, 126, 129
WSM, 195, 197
Wyble, Jimmy, 202, 265–66

Yarrow, Peter, 245, 248
Yellin, Robert, 89
Yodeling, 129–31
Yoder, Roselyn, 84–85
Young, Lester, 97, 103
Young, Marl, Orchestra, 166

Zappa, Frank, 229
Zipkin, Michael, 274